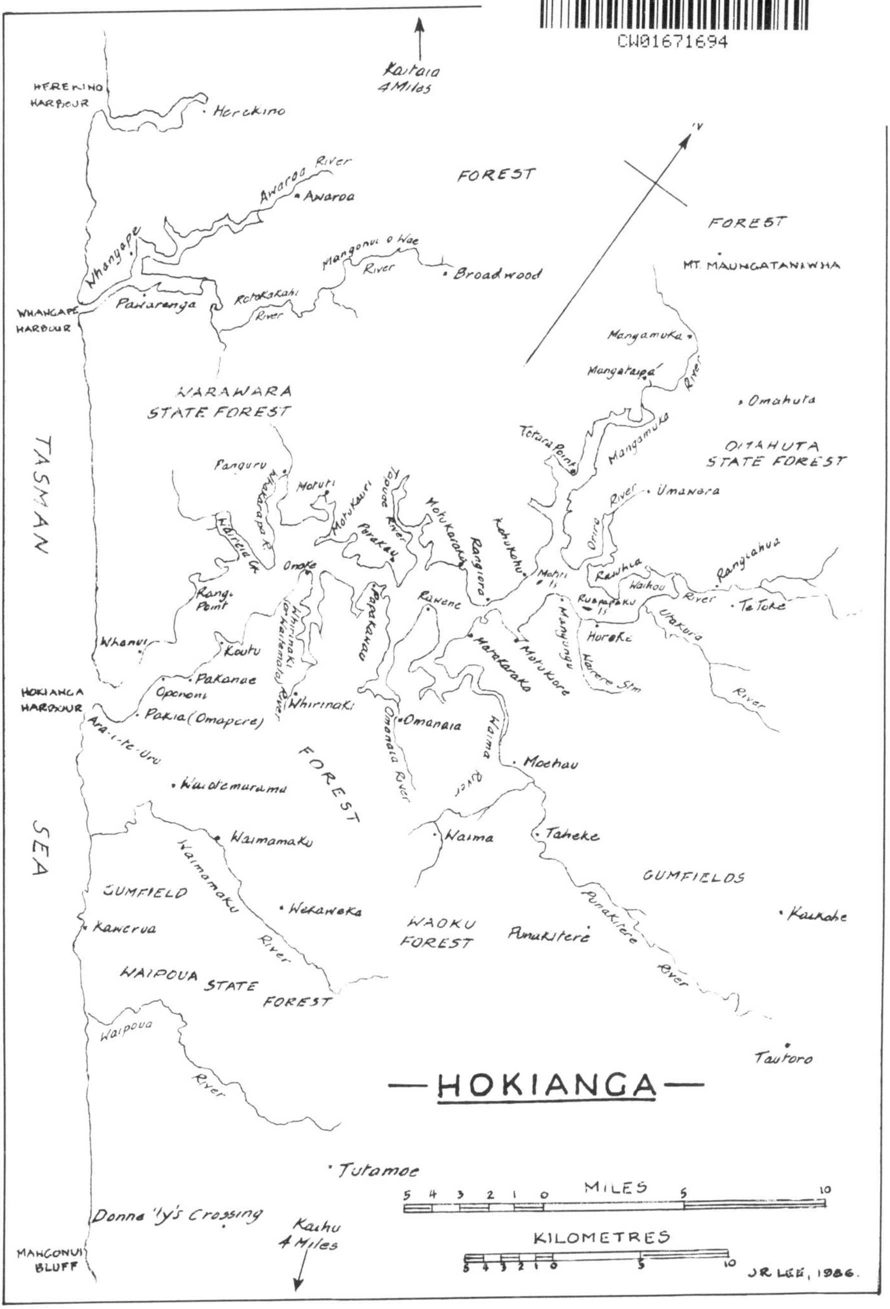

Kaitaia
4 Miles
HEREKINO HARBOUR
Herekino
Awaroa River
Awaroa
FOREST
FOREST
MT. MAUNGATANIWHA
Whangape
Mangonui o Wae River
Broadwood
WHANGAPE HARBOUR
Pawarenga
River
Mangamuka
Mangataipa
River
WARAWARA STATE FOREST
Omahuta
Mangamuka
OMAHUTA STATE FOREST
TASMAN
Panguru
Motuti
Motukauri
Umawera
River
Orira
Motukaraka
Rangiora
Kohukohu
Rawhia
Rangiahua
Omake
Rangi Point
Rawene
Waihou
River
Te Tuhe
Horeke
Whanui
Koutu
Pakanae
Opononi
HOKIANGA HARBOUR
Pakia (Omapere)
Whirinaki
Omanaia
River
Moetau
Waimamaku
FOREST
Waima
Taheke
GUMFIELDS
SEA
GUMFIELD
Wekaweka
Kawerua
WAOKU FOREST
Punakitere
Kaikohe
WAIPOUA STATE FOREST
Waipoua
River
Tautoro
— HOKIANGA —
Tutamoe
MILES
5 4 3 2 1 0 5 10
KILOMETRES
5 4 3 2 1 0 5 10
Donnelly's Crossing
Kaihu
4 Miles
MAUNGANUI BLUFF
J.R. LEE, 1986.

HOKIANGA

Jack Lee spent his early life in Auckland, but has been living in the Bay of Islands since the 1930s, where he served as Chief Surveyor for the former Auckland Regional Authority, eventually retiring from the position of Property Officer.

His impressive knowledge of the Bay of Islands, Whangaroa and Hokianga has been gained over some 50 years and his association with the Maori people is reflected in his treatment of this work.

More recently he has written a book on land claims, specifically, purchases of Maori land prior to the Treaty of Waitangi. He continues to write about aspects of the history of Hokianga and the Bay of Islands.

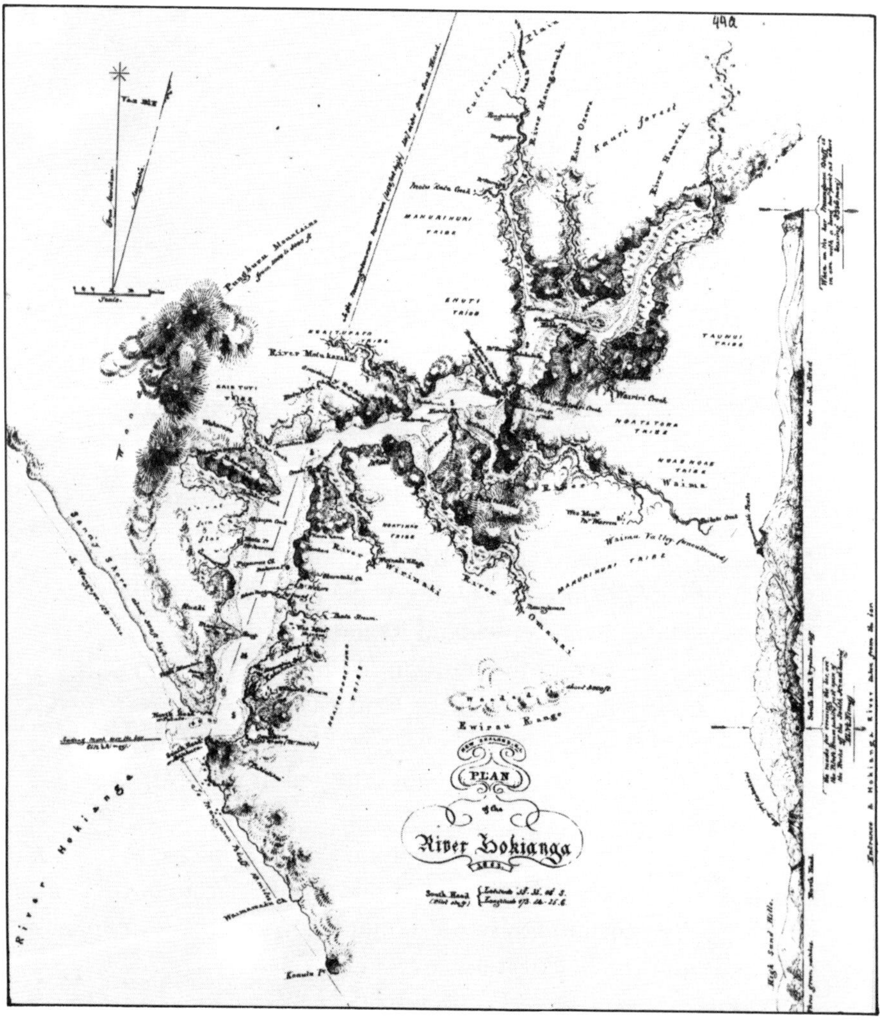

The *Pandora*'s chart of the River Hokianga, 1853.

HOKIANGA

Jack Lee

REED

By the same author

The Bay of Islands
(First published as 'I have named it the Bay of Islands...')

Published by Reed Books, a division of Reed Publishing (NZ) Ltd, 39 Rawene Rd, Birkenhead, Auckland. Associated companies, branches and representatives throughout the world.

ISBN 0 7900 0522 0

First published by Hodder and Stoughton 1987
Reprinted 1996

Printed in Hong Kong

Contents

For

CUSHLA
without whose insistence *Hokianga*
would have remained unattempted,

For

NOELEEN
whose generous help
made its beginning possible,

and for

CATHY
whose encouragement and devoted work
on the text
ensured its conclusion.

Preface

Several excellent histories of specific localities in and around the Hokianga have been produced, and there is scope for more of these. But in the present work it is intended to follow the broad trail of events there, so far as they are known, from prehistoric times until the twentieth century. Thus it is hoped to show how and why the social and industrial conditions now prevailing at Hokianga came to be as they are. Social change and events are dictated by individuals, severally or collectively, or by Government decree. But here in isolated Hokianga individuals probably exerted the greater influence, at least in early times, and there were a wealth of them — people of widely differing temperament, purpose and achievement. And more so than elsewhere, perhaps, their descendants are not submerged in the nonentity of a city population; by name they can still be found, and in a sparse population they remain as their ancestors were — identifiable individuals.

I had the assistance of many kind people in the course of this work, but the three women to whom it is dedicated made contributions to it for which I can never thank them enough. The book is theirs as much as mine. My friend Jocelyn Chisholm, of Wellington, who also worked on my history of the Bay of Islands, was another devoted helper to whom I owe a debt of gratitude. Although there are others too numerous to name who have also contributed, special mention must be made of the librarian, Ian Thwaites, and the staff of the Auckland Institute Library, for their special interest and the help that so lightened my task. The people of the Auckland Public Library, the Turnbull Library and Archives in Wellington, have been most helpful, together with others in Government Departments, the Historic Places Trust and the Hokianga County Council. And, of course, my local people, who both assisted and encouraged me. To all of these, my thanks are due, and gladly given.

Introduction

A great deal has been written about the character and potential of the Bay of Islands and about the activities of its early settlers. A considerable amount of this emanated from the Anglican missionaries and their supporters, the most vocal and literate group among our early European informants, and the material available is often well-organised, eminently usable, and can be readily consulted by the student or author. But those whose research involves Hokianga have rather more dispersed and fragmentary sources to draw from. This is due to some extent to the greater interest of wealthy and influential people in early business and politics at the Bay, and the resultant interest of Government, both in New South Wales and England. The Reverend Samuel Marsden himself was very much alive to the business potential of the Bay of Islands relative to the whale trade.

A factor that emphasised the essential difference in the character and development of the two places was the greater influence, in the political sense, of the Hokianga chiefs over Europeans there. This was due to the relative permanence of these settlers, and their reliance on the goodwill of the Maori people, who controlled the resources of the country on which they depended for their livelihood. The Europeans living there were thus unlike the crews of the whalers, the dominant group at the Bay who at times numbered many hundreds, but who had no stake in the land. Only a relatively small group who serviced the whale industry lived permanently at the Bay.

At Hokianga, Europeans were not generally sponsored by such powerful British and New South Wales business interests as those who financed whaling and sealing ventures. But at the Bay, the Maoris were aware of these interests, and knew also that the Anglican missionaries had influential support abroad. All these things tended to diminish the dominance of the chiefs over European adventurers there. The greater Maori dominance at Hokianga, and the high incidence of intermarriage, would also certainly have contributed to a great extent to harmonious race relations.

Briefly, then, the pre-1840 Pakeha population at the Bay of Islands was a considerably more organised one than that at Hokianga, because of the capital-intensive nature of the whale trade there. At Hokianga, Europeans relied for their living almost exclusively on local resources — felling, sawing and transporting kauri timber for export — and in the early years of settlement this was undertaken predominantly by independent individuals and small groups. The ship-building industry that developed at Horeke was, of course, also based on timber resources.

Those who may be more familiar with the post-European history of the Bay of Islands must bear these essential differences in mind. The story of Hokianga is quite as absorbing as that of the Bay of Islands, although, as we shall see, they are quite apart in character. But the early commercial activities at both places rank highly in the story of early New Zealand. And although what we know of the pre-European history both of Hokianga and the Bay makes fascinating reading, perhaps that of Hokianga is more so, if only because its very early oral records have been better preserved. This may be due to the advance of Ngapuhi, over some centuries, from Hokianga into the Bay of Islands, and the consequent partial or total loss of local traditional history by the people who were absorbed or subdued during this process.

The early part of this narrative, dealing with the Polynesian colonisation of Hokianga, does not purport to be a definitive work on that matter, but it is an attempt to rationalise a great deal of conflicting evidence on the events. Here an account is presented to the reader which has been drawn selectively from the available traditional evidence, and it must be appreciated that Hokianga has been populated by Polynesians for at least 600 and perhaps 1000 years longer than by Europeans.

1. Hokianga

The Hokianga, deep and narrow, framed by mountains and fed by tidal rivers reaching far inland, has an air of brooding grandeur not shared with any other North Island harbour. Seaward and to the east, a girdle of mountains rises at the South Head, and from there to Waima the great ridges of Te Ramaroa, Whakatere and the Waoku rear their shaggy heads to the sky. Here, the Waima, Utakura and Waihou river valleys intervene, but in the north-east and north-west, in a great semi-circle, the Puketi, Omahuta and Maungataniwha ranges guard the head of the harbour, rugged and bush-clad. Broken then only by the subdued farmlands of the Broadwood district, the mountain chain continues westward, where Panguru, Moumoukai and Te Reinga tower above their neighbours and merge into the ridges of the Warawara. These, topped with a frieze of kauri, drift away towards Mitimiti on the coast and the mouth of the Whangape Harbour to the north. Truly Hokianga is mountain country, and its forested beauty must stir the most hardened observer.

The home of the kauri and a place of countless legends, Hokianga is the cradle of Ngapuhi, the tribe whose aggressive expansion and appetite for vengeance made it master of most of the land from Hokianga to the Waitemata. Indeed, in early European times many of the Maori people south of Auckland also trembled at the name of Ngapuhi, and reeled under the impact of its musket attacks.

Whereabouts in New Zealand the early Polynesian groups settled is a matter for conjecture, but wherever they first landed, it is very probable that, having come from tropical climates, they would not have willingly tolerated a southern winter. A reasonable assumption, therefore, is that those who did not land in the North soon migrated there, or attempted to. It is certain, however, that within the last three or four centuries increasing population in this mild and most desirable place, with its sheltered harbours and bays, and its readily available food supplies, led to territorial disputes and the eviction of the weaker groups, and their migration to the south. Traditional accounts from Smith[1] and Yarborough[2] describe the departure from the North under pressure of Ngatiawa people, who may well have been among the original inhabitants there.

It is also true that the kumara could have survived the winter in the ground only in the Far North. And since the technique of pitting them in autumn for future use, and for seed, is a New Zealand one, their survival relied initially on their cultivation in the North.

Testimony of the bitter disputes that were generated, and which led to displacements and migrations, is to be found in the incredible number of pa, or defensive works here. Many hundreds of these are to be found in Hokianga, Whangaroa, Mangonui and the Bay of Islands alone — perhaps more than in the whole of New Zealand south of Auckland.

Submerged as they are in the silent depths of time, the facts of the populating of the North and the movements of the people in and out, may never be fully known. Nevertheless, the overwhelming advantages it offered to a tropical people are obvious, and it is clear, from the evidence of the pa, that here we have the most fought-over territory in this land.

The earliest known Hokianga traditions focus on Kupe, and some of these credit him with the discovery of New Zealand — or at least the first visit to 'The Fish of Maui' since it was pulled up from the sea. The Hawaiki home of the Hokianga Kupe is said to have been Motutapu, at the mouth of the river Awanuiarangi, in Hawaikirangi, and he left this place as a result of his attempted murder of one Hotu, in order to have his wife.[3] After leaving from Wawauateanui, suffering at the hands of various named sea-demons, and being rescued by others of his own, he and his companions finally arrived at Maui's Fish. Maui had not quite killed this fish after he had hauled it up from the ocean, so Kupe and his men sailed round it, killing it gradually as they went. With this accomplished, he called Maui's fish 'Te Ao Marama'. This is now referred to in many traditions as 'Te Ika a Maui', the name of the North Island of New Zealand.

However, Simmons,[4] with persuasive arguments, gives no credence to this discovery, and demonstrates that Kupe's arrival here was some 400 years later than the earliest settlers. But this question is complicated by the existence of conflicting traditions concerning Kupe,[5] found in different parts of New Zealand.

There may even have been two Kupe separated in time, who have become confused. But a consensus seems to establish that the name Hokianga refers to the departure of an adventurer named Kupe from there to return to his homeland, wherever that may have been — *hokianga,* a returning place. It is possible that he was from Polynesia, rather than some other part of New Zealand, and probable that he initiated a Polynesian colonisation of Hokianga.

In some accounts Kupe is said to have left pets *(mokaikai)* to live at Hokianga Heads, called Araiteuru and Niua, or Niniwa, which later traditions describe as taniwha, and the South and North Heads are so named. These were supposed to protect his interests in the place, and to guide later travellers to Hokianga — 'to the spring at Te Ao Marama'. Before he left, however, a quarrel occurred when some of his people opened a hangi before the food was cooked — always a very bad omen — and Kupe, in his anger, cursed those responsible. The place where this occurred is called Kohukohu to this day (*kohu* — a curse). Other traditional reminders of Kupe are said to be petrified in or near Hokianga. There are the posts for his net, his food-oven near Kerikeri, his footmarks and those of his dog on the coast north of the Heads, the baler of his canoe at Kohukohu, and his dog, which is near the mouth of the Whirinaki River. The anchor of his canoe is said to be on the point at Rangiora, near the Narrows,[6] while of the canoe itself, which returned here with Nukutawhiti, some say it lies petrified and upturned at the mouth of the Waima River. Another tradition has the canoe dragged into an unidentified stone cave, where it now reposes, petrified. Rangi Point, too, is often named as its resting-place.

According to the northern tradition, Kupe was contemporary with Nukutawhiti, an undisputed Ngapuhi ancestor, although he was older than Nuku by a couple or so generations. Nuku, it is said, was told of Hokianga by Kupe, either at sea or at their Polynesian home, Wawauatea, and because of a disastrous war at home, he made use of Kupe's canoe *Matawhaorua* on its return, to emigrate to the new land. The canoe was re-adzed to increase its capacity, and re-fitted, and was therefore called *Ngatokimatawhaorua.* In it, Nukutawhiti sailed to New Zealand.

This venture was undertaken with Nuku's brother-in-law, Ruanui, in the canoe *Mamari,* in accordance with sailing directions given by Kupe. Ruanui was guided by Araiteuru and Nuia, and landed at Ripiro, near Kaipara. And at the place called Omamari, about ten miles south of Maunganui Bluff, *Mamari* was driven ashore, wrecked and abandoned.

In one version of the Kupe tradition, he is said to have left his child, Tuputupuwhenua, at Hokianga, and one of Nuku's tasks was to search for him. In others, Tupu was an indigenous inhabitant. All seem to agree that on Nuku's arrival he was at Hokianga, but at once changed into an insect called Kui, disappeared into the ground, and emerged at Kerikeri (*keri* — to dig). But in some traditions, the *tangata whenua* — the original people — are called the people of Kui. Tuputupuwhenua, to confuse matters further, is the name of a Ngatiwhatua ancestor, but he bears a marked resemblance to a person with the same name and preoccupation with burrowing, in very ancient legends throughout the Pacific, some referring to a great flood. Be that as it may, Nukutawhiti got to Hokianga, guided by the sea-demons. Rangiuruhinga, Te Hikooterangi, Maheretuukiterangi and Puhimoanaariki. This Puhi, also called Puhiteaewa (the wanderer) may account for the early name of the Rarawa tribe — Aewa — and Puhimoanaariki was the name given some generations later to the grandfather of Rahiri, the ancestor of modern Ngapuhi. But of him more in its proper place.[7]

The above account is essentially an amalgam of a number of versions, which unfortunately do not agree with one another, although the marvels it recounts undoubtedly have their origin in events now long beyond recall. But historically it seems certain that Ruanui and Nukutawhiti are true ancestors, and early settlers in Hokianga. It is said that Nuku built his *wharekura,* or house of learning, called Pouahi, at Whanui, on the north Hokianga head, and Ruanui's, called Araiteuru, was on the South Head. He became the progenitor of the Rarawa tribe, and Nukutawhiti of Ngapuhi. Although, judging from the later disposition of these people, it might appear that the locations of the *wharekura* may have been reversed. Certainly one of them is so in Aperahama Taonui's version of Ngapuhi history. There, Ruanui's house is called Pouahi, and Nuku's Te Whatupungapunga.[8] The village Whanui disappeared under drifting sand within the author's lifetime.

It seems, however, that the taniwha, Araiteuru, who, with Niua, had been left by Kupe at Hokianga to look after his interests, had young taniwha called Waihou, Waima, Orira, Mangamuka, Ohopa and Wairere, whom she appointed the powerful guardians of the Hokianga rivers that now bear their names, while their mother and her companion kept guard on the mouth of the harbour itself.[9] Hokianga has many such wonder-stories, one associated with the Heads relating to two special rocks there. Akiha shows at low water, but over the other, Porihere, there appears, even at the lowest tides, only swirling water. He represents the quiet person, who considers all matters carefully before taking action, whereas Akiha is the noisy and boastful one, full of promises unfulfilled. With the nearby places named for Araiteuru and Niua, and for the *marae* Pouahi, they were, as Smith says, '... a power and inspiration to the people'.[10] If, in war, the tide of battle turned against them, their tohunga, pointing, would recite this incantation:

Kotahi ki reira,	One (thought) to there,
Kotahi ki Pouahi,	One to Pouahi,
Kotahi ki Niua,	One to Niua,
Kotahi ki Araiteuru.	One to Araiteuru.

The gods of these places were invoked generally for warlike purposes with this incantation. It would be recited by war-parties assembled on the beach at Omapere, so that the spirits of the dead in the cave at Araiteuru would assist them in battle. When the name Pouahi was uttered, that is, the name of the *marae* on the North Head, the priest would throw a lock of his hair toward that place to ensure the sanctity of his plea — his hair, from his tapu head, being a potent offering. But the profound significance of these places did not long survive European times, since when Martin, the signalman, purchased the land at Araiteuru in 1832, the bones in the cave there were removed to another place, and it is no longer tapu.

So, Hokianga lay waiting for colonisation by Nukutawhiti and Ruanui, but having seen them established there, we find the Kupe problem recurring — two men named Nukutawhiti appear in Northern genealogies twelve to fifteen generations apart. They were referred to by Mohi Tawhai in his account given to Smith,[11] as Nos 1 and 2, and Simmons also has something to say about this.[12] However, it may be accepted that the Nukutawhiti who generally appears in these genealogies twenty-five generations from the present — say 1350 — is an historical ancestor of Ngapuhi. It is he, therefore, who figures in the following narrative. But this dispels the notion that our Kupe was the discoverer of New Zealand, since here we see him as a contemporary of Nuku, whereas archaeology tells us that this land has been inhabited for 1000 years. However, we cannot entirely dismiss the possibility that an early Kupe and Nuku were involved in a much older migration, and that time has confused their identities. One of these Nuku has been referred to in tradition by a fuller version of his name, Nukumaiitawhiti, which certainly suggests an origin in Tahiti.

We proceed, then, on the basis that Nukutawhiti No. 2 is the ancestor involved hereafter in this narrative. That there were Polynesians (Maori) in New Zealand before him is beyond dispute on the archaeological evidence alone. It has been said earlier that it is possible Kupe was from Polynesia but it is also conceivable that both he and Nuku may have migrated to the Hokianga from some other part of New Zealand. An internal migration receives some support from a Hokianga account by Ngakura Pene Haare[13] in which he says that Nukutawhiti's voyage to Hokianga took three days. Little can be gained, however, from pursuing the matter further, because of the disagreement between various traditions.

But the names of Hokianga, Araiteuru, Niua, Whanui, Pouahi and Te Ramaroa, the majestic ridge extending from Waima to the south Hokianga head, all evoke the magic of a dimly remembered past. So, too, do placenames such as Moehau, Waimatuhirangi and others, transported from some distant Hawaiki and applied to places here. It is interesting also, that Niua was the name of Ruanui's mother.

There are several different stories that purport to explain the origin of the name 'Hokianga', one being simply 'Hokianga a Kupe', that is, the returning-place of Kupe — the place from where he returned to Hawaiki. Another, which is considerably more evocative, is 'Hokianga whakapau karakia', and unfortunately more than one explanation of this is current. It could mean Hokianga, where prayers were exhausted fruitlessly, and seems to refer generally to ineffective prayers of interloping taniwha, who, after Kupe's departure, tried repeatedly to enter the harbour by overcoming the powers exerted by his taniwha, Araiteuru and Niua.

2. The Emerging Ngapuhi

All tradition agrees that disputes between Nukutawhiti and Ruanui led to Nuku and his people leaving Whanui. Crossing the harbour to the Omapere side, some then made their way inland, ultimately establishing themselves at Taiamai, or Ohaeawai, near Kaikohe. Ruanui, on the other hand, favoured the north-west side of the harbour, and there founded the Aewa tribe, now called Rarawa, and later the Aupouri or Ngatiruanui tribe. Rarawa and Aewa have much the same meaning. Nukutawhiti, at Ohaeawai, had a pa, which is said to be that called Puketapu, above the old Ngawha school.[1] But he soon became involved in problems within his family over his land, which he resolved by the division of his domains between his sons and grandsons.

In due course Nuku died, but not before his youngest daughter, Moerewarewa, had married a Kaipara chief against her father's wishes, and in Mohi Tawhai's narrative explaining the significance of the ancient *pihe,* or lament, for Nukutawhiti,[2] he tells us of the outcome of this. Angry at his daughter's disobedience, Nuku instructed his eldest son and daughter, Ranginui and Papatuanuku, to cut off his head when he died, and replace it with the head of his slave. Moerewarewa would thus be deceived into weeping over the body of her father, but not his head. A chief's head was tapu, of course, therefore the most revered and sacred part of him, and with this gone, the mana of his whole body was destroyed.

It seems that having divided his land, Nuku had returned to Hokianga, where he died by drowning, being drawn into the whirlpool Pipiraueru, in the harbour. Twice his body was carried back and forth across the harbour, before it was finally cast ashore at his old home, Whanui, where, with the slave's head substituted, it was laid on the *marae* of Pouahi. Moerewarewa, approaching Hokianga from Kaipara in her canoe for her father's tangi, had been apprised by her guardian spirit of the interference with his body, but seeing her approach, her brother and sister conjured up a storm, so that she might perish. But Moerewarewa, now in mortal danger, offered up a powerful incantation of her own, and when, as a result, the wind and thunder ceased, she delivered the *pihe* for her father that has come down to us (see Appendix 5). Portions of this were still chanted at funerals until quite recently.

Ngapuhi, probably the most politically and militarily successful tribe among the Maori of New Zealand, have a rather enigmatic name, which could derive from a number of people named Puhi, since 'nga' is the plural form of 'the'. But, as is more likely, it came from the one ancestor who had three Puhi names. Such a man did exist, back in the homeland, wherever that may have been. According to Himiona Kamira,[3] Tamakitera was his father and Arikitapu was his mother. She, when pregnant, craved the heart of a man to eat, and in order to oblige her, Tama killed Rangiuruhinga, an ariki, or high chief. So Arikitapu got her heart's desire, and when her child was born, she called him Puhikaiariki — Puhi the ariki-eater. But when his own ariki birth-rites were performed at Moanarua, he was given the additional and sacred name of Puhimoanaariki, as befitted his status. Being an ariki, and therefore invested with the necessary supernatural powers, he appeared later, as we have seen, as the taniwha, or sea-demon, Puhitaniwharau, that is, Puhi of the hundred taniwha, who guided Nukutawhiti to Hokianga. Thus we have the trinity of Puhi in the one person — *ngapuhi* — from which the tribe undoubtedly got its name, some seven to eight generations later. At that stage another chief named Puhimoanaariki appears, and he was the grandfather of Rahiri, from whom all Ngapuhi of consequence descend.

Perhaps 200 years now elapse, during which we have few traditional accounts. This may well be because little of note occurred in the intervening period until tribal warfare erupted in the North, arising from competition for the best living areas, and accumulating rivalries resulting from affronts by one group to another. Smith[4] tells us that during this time the North was 'invaded' by Ngatiawa people from the central North Island. This could be so, but on the other hand they could have been the *tangata whenua* — the people of the land, or the descendants of the original settlers — asserting their authority over the comparative newcomers, the Nuku groups of Hokianga and the Ngatiwhatua, the *Mahuhu* canoe people further north.

Sporadic skirmishing occurred between these, resulting firstly in the Ngatiwhatua making their way south. Their homeland had been at Muriwhenua, in the Far North, the Kaitaia district and parts of Hokianga and from these places they retired to Waipoua and Kaipara. In Waipoua and Kaihu they are known as Roroa, and there and at Kaipara they now belong. It must again be emphasised that the population in all these areas under discussion was probably not very large, and the events of the period were no doubt a shaking down and sorting out of these people, which allowed the great tribes to develop, undisturbed to a large extent, in their own chosen localities, although passive elements of Ngatiwhatua no doubt remained in the Far North. The tribal name Ngatiwhatua derives from the ancestress, Te Whatuakaimarie, whose mother, Whatutahae (stolen weaving) was so named because her mother, Takarita, Te Whatua's grandmother, acquired the art of weaving by stealth from the ancient people of Kui (see Chapter 1) among whom she lived. For this sin Takarita died giving birth to Whatutahae. Whatuakaimarie was later famed for her hospitality and general benevolence.[5]

The exodus of the main body of this tribe appears to have left three major contending parties in and around Hokianga and north of it. These were Ngatiawa, the Rarawa and Aupouri group — the Ruanui people — and the Nukutawhiti descendants. Apparently Ngatiawa were distributed through the whole area, but they were possibly strongest on the east coast, from Kaitaia to Whangarei. However, from there, some voluntary migration was taking place down the coast to the Bay of Plenty.[6] These events could bring us to about 1550-1650 which might be described as the formative period of the Ngapuhi tribe, when the Nukutawhiti line, which we have dealt with, is joined to that of Puhimoanaariki, and from this union Ngapuhi derived its corporate status.

Puhi first appears in tradition at Whakatane, and is said to have been one of the principal men of the *Mataatua* canoe, which, according to the now largely discredited theories of S. Percy Smith,[7] had arrived there from a distant Pacific Hawaiki. Much dispute has raged, and still does, around the origin and movements of this canoe. Smith's informant told him that *Mataatua* came down to Whakatane from Muriwhenua, the northernmost part of New Zealand, and apparently gave Smith the impression that from Hawaiki it made its landfall there. However, this conflicts with this vessel's tradition of circumnavigation of the North Island — an exploration voyage — before this. Throughout the Pacific, Hawaiki is fairly consistently the previous place that any group lived at, and *Mataatua*'s Hawaiki was very likely Northland. It is interesting that some Rarawa people claim descent from one Mirupokaiape, and associate him with this canoe. Yet this man does not figure in the Whakatane occupation at all. So he was no doubt involved in the exploratory voyage, but stayed at home when the canoe went south.[8] His descendants, Ngatimiru, appear to be essentially Ngatiawa, and he was the progenitor of the Ngatikuri people of Whangape. Ngatimiru were once a widely dispersed group, but owing to Ngapuhi expansion they are now extinct.

Mataatua's return to the North arose, according to Smith, from a quarrel involving Toroa, a former captain of the canoe, and, among others, our Puhimoanaariki. At this point, the story may be taken up by Morore Piripi,[9] a chief of Ngatiwai, near the Bay of Islands, who, in a rather disjointed account, describes the return of the canoe. Puhi, he says, arrived at the Bay seeking a good place at which to settle himself and his people. From there he went to Whangaroa, which was then named, after features at the entrance to the harbour, Te Pokopoko-o-Hine-nui-i-te-Po and Te Ure-nui-o-Maui, that is the genitals of Hine and Maui. The anchor of *Mataatua* was left there, and the place was renamed Whaingaroa, perhaps owing to the lengthy anchorage there. The voyage ended with a return down the coast to Takou, and Piripi says, 'Puhi stayed there, and went into this territory known as Ngapuhi'. Conflicting accounts say that the canoe still lies fossilised in the Takou River, or that it is buried in an adjacent swamp. A Hokianga tradition that *Mataatua* had been transported by land from Hokianga to Takou may well refer to a previous event in its career.

Puhi probably went straight to Hokianga from Takou. He may well have known exactly where he was going, since the easiest route from that part of the coast to Hokianga is from Takou. Perhaps he was returning to join his relatives there, but whether this was the case or not, he certainly married there, before or after these events, and the woman Hauaangiangi, his daughter, married Tauramoko, a descendant of Nukutawhiti. And at Whiria, the pa at Pakanae, near Opononi, their son Rahiri was born, so it is said, and from him all Ngapuhi of importance trace their descent. But the sequence of the events is not clear, although all of them have led us to this point, and Hokianga now truly becomes the focus of this narrative. Here is the cradle of Ngapuhi.

Rahiri seems to have been named after one of the Whakatane community, or was himself in fact the Whakatane man, returning north to his birth-place with his grandfather, Puhimoanaariki. But he appears little in tradition until his marriage to Ahuaiti, a Ngaitahuhu woman of Pouerua, near Pakaraka, some seven miles north-east of Kaikohe.[10] It was at Kaikohe that the couple lived for a short time, until their marriage ended when Ahuaiti, in Rahiri's absence, fed his brothers on choice fern-root he had reserved for himself. For this misdemeanour he deserted Ahuaiti, then pregnant, and in due course she gave birth to her son, Uenuku, called Kuare, The Ignorant One, because he had no father to teach him the wisdom and mysteries of his tribe. In later years, however, Rahiri acknowledged his son, and attended to his education at his pa at Whiria.

Thus the inland component of Ngapuhi was founded. Upon his desertion of Ahuaiti, Rahiri went to Hokianga, and there, at Rawene, married Whakaruru, described by Smith as Ngatiawa.[11] Some tradition says that he then took Whiria, which since his possible birth there, could have been taken and occupied by enemies. Be that as it may, Whiria now became the citadel of Ngapuhi, from where the inexorable advance of the tribe inland and to the Bay of Islands was initiated. Here, Whakaruru gave birth to Kaharau, the man who, with his sons, is credited with the early expansion of his tribe. Soon a move into the interior arose from an incident involving the marriage of Kaharau to Houtaringa, at a place called Puketaka, some two miles south-west of Kaikohe.

A strange story relates the circumstances leading to this marriage. One day Kaharau made a kite and released it from Whiria. It first came down at Whirinaki, but he flew it again, letting it go free, and he followed it. It is a long way from there to Kaikohe, some eighteen miles over bush and mountains as the kite flies. But Kaharau was apparently not dismayed by this, and eventually came upon the kite where it had come to earth at Puketaka. And alongside it stood the woman Houtaringa, whom Kaharau, making the most of this opportunity, promptly married.[12] It was then not long before the Hokianga and Kaikohe branches of Ngapuhi were united, when Uenuku's daughter, Ruakiwhiria, married Kaharau's son, Taurapoho.[13]

Houtaringa appears to have been the daughter of Reipai, a woman, who with her sister, Reitu, is credited with flying up from the Waikato on the back of a huge bird. Both were to marry a Hokianga chief called Ueoneone. However, the bird made a comfort stop at a place which various versions of the story locate in different areas, but the upshot was that Reipai lingered too long at her toilet, and the impatient bird took off with only Reitu, who in due course arrived at Hokianga, and she only married Ueoneone. Reipai seems to have wandered around until a local chief named Korowhau came upon her, married her, and between them they produced Houtaringa. As a sequel to this, Kauae, daughter of Ueoneone, later married Tupoto, Kaharau's grandson.[14] Whangarei is the locale of most versions of the Reipai tradition, and the name of this place is believed to be an abbreviation of *whangaarei* — Rei's harbour.

After this adventure Kaharau returned to Hokianga and occupied his own pa Kokoparitehe, at Pakanae. He defended this successfully against attacking Rarawa (Ngatiawa?)[15] but only after he had killed his son and roasted his heart, so that the smoke from it settled on the enemy, ensuring their destruction. He then initiated a campaign which resulted, apparently in his lifetime and that of his son, Taurapoho, in the eviction of most of the Ngatiawa from Hokianga.

But before we turn to the account of the Ngapuhi advance into the interior of the Bay of Islands and to the coast, we should notice an instance of the rapport that then existed between the Ahuaiti and Whakaruru people — the descendants of Rahiri's two wives. This occurred shortly after Kaharau's desperate stand at Kokoparitehe, and it arose from the marriage of Torongare, of Pouerua, near Kaikohe, great-grandson of Rahiri, to his aunt, Hauhaua, of Pakanae, on the Hokianga. After the marriage, the couple went first to live at Waimamaku, on the north side of the Waipoua forest, but after a disagreement with the Ngaitamatea, Hauhaua's people, they went to Waiwhatawhata, just south of Hokianga Heads. From there they drifted up the eastern shore of Hokianga and around the great Whakatere range at Waima (*whakatere* — to drift), past Puhanga Tohura and into the Mangakahia valley by way of Awarua. All this took a good deal of time, but eventually the two, now with a family, turned back towards Torongare's old home, going around the south of the great Taraiorahiri range and through Kaikou to Waiomio, now the home-place of the Ngatihine people. Hauhaua may well have died before they reached Waiomio, but this sub-tribe of Ngapuhi is named for her first-born daughter, Hineamaru. Her other children, born on this protracted journey, were Tamangana, Kotata, Torukao, Rongopatutaonga and Aongaua. Both Tamangana and Aongaua later married their cousin Rangiheketini — an indication of either a very sparse population or a mistrust of other tribal groups.[16]

3. Ngapuhi Expansion

Kaharau's defence of his pa was perhaps the event which launched Ngapuhi on its aggressive progress into the fertile interior of the Bay of Islands, and to the Bay itself, and it preceded an unremitting assault on Ngatiawa. This is summarised and described by A.C. Yarborough, who also gives interesting figures on the population of Hokianga in 1810, some 200 years after Kaharau's time.[1] These indicate that in the whole Hokianga watershed there were about 2000 fighting men, which suggests the presence of a relatively small population eight generations beforehand. Of Ngatiawa Yarborough says, 'About ten generations ago Rahiri expelled them from South Hokianga and captured their pas. He drove them back through Whirinaki until their power on the south side of the river was broken, although it was not until the time of Taurapoto [sic], his son, or grandson probably, when he himself was getting old, that they were finally expelled or left. On the north side of the Hokianga river they seem to have lingered on longer, in a part of the country densely wooded and not so thickly populated. On the Mangamuka and Waihou rivers, but along the coast and at Whangape they had already begun to retreat shortly after Rahiri's first capture of the only pa existing at that time at Pakanae, called Whiria. At Horeke, on the Waihou, are three pas, one of which was occupied by Ngatiawa, who were not driven out until six generations ago by Rahiri's great grandsons, Tauratumano [sic] and Toma. The migration of Ngatiawa from Whangape, or a small part of it, came down the Mangamuka to the island of Motuiti, where they took refuge, were surrounded and massacred. With the capture of the pas at Horeke and Wairere the Ngatiawa seem to have finally cleared out from the valley of the Hokianga and retreated eastwards, making their way south by the sea coast.' Yarborough wrote in about 1905, but others before him told of Ngatiawa retreating also down the west coast, where remnants of the tribe were still to be found in recent times. But most of these people are now located in the Bay of Plenty, and, as Atiawa, in Taranaki.

Kaharau flourished about fifteen generations ago, say 1600, that is, at approximately the time of Abel Tasman's visit to New Zealand. Perhaps archaeology may yet establish that the great pa-building period in the North was the century or so before this, when Ngatiwhatua, Ngatiawa and the early Rarawa and Ngapuhi groups were disputing one another's title to territory. In this period Ngapuhi was struggling toward the supremacy it finally achieved in the North in the nineteenth century. Although the retreat of Ngatiawa is disposed of in most sources in a few sentences, it is likely that it extended over a considerable time, during which its people would have taken many stands and constructed many pa. Ngapuhi, some of the old people say, built few of the pa we now see, since as a tribe they were seldom seriously threatened. On the other hand, embattled Ngatiawa, in their slow retreat, built many pa, and left them abandoned. Only later, when internecine squabbling erupted within Ngapuhi, did they have a serious need for defensive works.

From the Hokianga another incursion was made into the interior in Kaharau's time, by Ueoneone, accompanied by Tauraitepo, who built Whakaruangangana, an ancient pa.[2] They came, it is said, from Ponahi (Pouahi?) at the Hokianga Heads, and their hapu is Uetaora. In evidence before the Land Court it was stated that Ueoneone was buried at Araiteuru and his children at Tuitahi. Taonui[3] says that Ueoneone belonged to Whangape, the harbour north of Hokianga, and was therefore likely to have been Ngatimiru. Whakaruangangana is close to where Kaharau's kite came down at Puketaka, where for centuries the spot has been marked by a ***kohatu*** (rock).

So Ngapuhi expansion continued. The thrust into the Utakura valley early reached as far up as Whakarongorua, so named because the sound of two seas, on the east and west coasts could be heard there. From the north and north-west of the harbour, Rarawa pushed its way north towards Muriwhenua, the northernmost part of the North Island, and from these Ruanui people came the Aupouri tribe. In time, a deadly feud arose between them and a group later known as Ngatikuri. The chief Papatahuri's younger brother, Pakewa, was murdered by Aupouri, who inflicted a terrible defeat on Ngatikuri in the battles following this. Ngatikuri, then part of the Ngatiawa people, having lost most of its fighting men, retreated to the Whangape River, where their remnant settled under the Panguru mountains, along the Rotokakahi river flats.[4]

In time, by the attraction of the young men of Hokianga to their handsome women, Ngatikuri recovered its fighting strength, by *whakatupu tangata* — the growing of men — and they were then ready to take their revenge on Aupouri. This tribe had a strong pa called Whangatauatea at Ahipara, or, as another version states, between Herekino and Ahipara. But since the Ngatikuri chief, Papatahuri, planning revenge, knew his people had no chance of taking the pa by storm, he resorted to guile. One asset that the tribe did possess, as its name implies, was a multiplicity of dogs, and these were the basis of the ruse he devised. To use these dogs was a sacrifice in itself, since they were commonly eaten, and their skins were used for clothing. But they were all killed, and their skins were taken north to a bay close to Ahipara. Here they were sewn together and stuffed with fern to form the shape of a whale, and this was launched into the sea before dawn below the pa of Aupouri. And a whale it certainly appeared to them to be — a gift from the gods of food, oil and bone. Almost to a man they deserted their pa to exploit this incredible piece of luck. But too late they realised they had been deceived, and caught outside their pa virtually weaponless, were slaughtered like cattle. Thus, did the victors become Ngatikuri, the People of the Dogs. Aupouri, in earlier times, had lived in a pa called Makora, on the south side of the Whangape Harbour, but following the death in battle of their chief, Te Aranui, at Hokianga, they had abandoned their pa, burned it, and had retreated to Ahipara, where the dog-skin calamity later occurred. From the 'dark smoke' arising from the burning pa, the tribe had derived its name.

The retreat of Ngatiawa and the taking of their various pa in Hokianga apparently left the Ngapuhi people based on Pakanae, and probably with Ueoneone as an ally, in a very strong position on the east, or south-east side of the upper harbour. Advances to Waima, Taheke and to Kaikohe had been made and consolidated, and similar expansion inland from the southern side at the head of the harbour had also occurred. Perhaps before the end of the seventeenth century, then, an early inland Ngapuhi hero, Mahiapoake, appeared, well established, with his father, Taurapoho, at the pa Pakinga. This, a couple of miles south-west of Kaikohe, is close to Tauraitepo's pa Whakaruangangana, which we have noted. To Mahia's father, and his grandfather, Kaharau, much of the credit for these advances appears to be due. Mahia himself seems to have been responsible for establishing some order out of the chaos among the squabbling inland groups, Ngatimiru, Ngatiawa and others. Subsequent inter-marriage also consolidated the Ngapuhi position there.

Several stories of Mahia survive, one telling of his encounter with the 'Cannibal of the Swamp', a lone predatory savage called Hihiotote, whose pleasure it was to devour travellers passing his lair between the Kaikohe district and Awarua, to the south. With fair words he would lure them to his hut, and there kill and make a meal of them. Mahia intended to put a stop to this. So, taking the track to this grisly place, he and his son came near to Hihi's hut, where Mahia gave his weapons to his son and went on to the hut unarmed. There Hihi met him with soft and deceitful words, but when he was about to strike Mahia down, the son appeared and felled Hihi. Hihi's words as he lay there stricken are still quoted: *na te tokorua i mate ai a Hihiotote* — 'it took two to kill Hihiotote.' Now the way between the two places was safe, and for this service Mahia was given the mana and chieftainship of Awarua. Until recently, the *wharehui* or meeting-house there was still named Ngatimahia.[5]

By the time of Mahia's grandson, Te Wairua, Kaikohe and the territory drained by the Hokianga rivers Waima and Punakitere, were firmly in Ngapuhi hands, and Rahiri's two families, from Ahuaiti inland and by Whakaruru at Hokianga, had been united territorially and by intermarriage. From the pa Pakinga, then, the inexorable advance of these people from Hokianga to the Bay of Islands proceeded. Ngatimiru, Wahineiti and other Ngatipou or Ngatiawa people were thrust relentlessly aside, until, by the time of the advent of Europeans, the whole of the Bay of Islands, apart from small areas under the Ngatimanu and Kapotai tribes, was dominated by Ngapuhi. Then, in post-European times, Hongi Hika, Te Wairua's great grandson, ousted Ngatipou from Whangaroa.

Another sortie was made into the Bay of Islands, perhaps early in the eighteenth century, through the upper Hokianga, by way of the Waihou River valley, and thence across to the Bay. This was undertaken by a Whirinaki war-party from the south side of the harbour to avenge the death, at Kopemanawa, of Tauratumaru, a chief of Whirinaki.[6] At the Kopemanawa battle, between the Hikutu hapu of Whirinaki and Bay of Islands people, Taura was killed and his eyes plucked out and taken to the Bay to tapu a pipi bank. The resultant attack launched by Hokianga on those responsible for this indignity was successful, and a permanent Hikutu colony from the Whirinaki district was established in the Mangonui Inlet, in the Bay of Islands, at a place called Kaihiki.

Between Te Rarawa on the western side of the lower Hokianga and Ngapuhi on the opposite shore and on both sides of the upper reaches of the harbour, there appears to have been sporadic enmity. However, neither tribe seems to have threatened the other unduly, no doubt owing to the close relationship between them. Both have their special regulating tapu. For instance, Rarawa do not eat the araara, or trevalli, because when their chief Rongomai was drowned, and his body discovered, these fish were found to have been feeding on it. On the other side of the harbour, the majestic ridge, Te Ramaroa, which runs from Waima almost to the South Head, was especially tapu to Ngapuhi, since the bones of many of their great chiefs are in caves in the ridge behind Whirinaki, and elsewhere.

In pre-European times, Ngapuhi expansion was confined to land on the shores of the harbour, and in the direction of the Bay of Islands to the east, and Mangakahia to the south. Little progress was made into the fertile valley of the Waimamaku, which was settled in early times by Ngatiwhatua people. Incursions of this tribe into the territory were made during its migration,[7] apparently to seek utu, or revenge, for the murder of Taureka, one of its ancestors, by the inhabitants of the valley at that time. These would be Ngatiawa or Ngatikahu. This composite people are now called Roroa, and are liberally infused with Ngatiwhatua blood, as well as with Ngapuhi. Kaharau, Rahiri's son, married one of its women, Kaiawhi. The resultant ambivalence appears to have protected Roroa to some extent from Ngapuhi attacks.

A rather generalised boundary between Ngapuhi and Ngatiwhatua was the 1500-foot bluff about twenty miles down the coast from the south Hokianga head, on both sides of which this mixed people lived. But Ngatiwhatua say of this, the Maunganui Bluff, *Ka titiro a Maunganui, ka titiro ki Kaipara; ka titiro a Kaipara, ka titiro ki Maunganui.* That is, Maunganui looks towards Kaipara, and Kaipara looks towards Maunganui, so that Maunganui, as an outpost of Ngatiwhatua, may warn

Kaipara by smoke-signals from the Bluff, or other means, of any approaching danger. This we know did occur when Ngapuhi passed down the coast about the beginning of the nineteenth century, on its way to an attack on Kaipara. On this occasion, smoke from the Bluff warned the Ngatiwhatua chiefs, Murupaenga and Taoho, and at Moremonui, just north of Bayley's Beach, they fell on Ngapuhi from ambush and defeated them with great slaughter. The Ngapuhi war-chief Hongi Hika, then a young man, lost his brother Moka there, and his sister, Waitapu, was barbarously murdered. This event, it is said, was the catalyst for Hongi's subsequent career of conquest, and was merely a prelude to his ultimate crushing defeat of Ngatiwhatua at Te Ikaaranganui, on the Kaipara, near Kaiwaka. A musket he obtained in England during his visit there in 1820 he named *Teketanumia,* so that he would never forget the indignities inflicted on his sister at Moremonui.

At this distance in time, Ngatikahu, Ngatiawa and Ngatipou appear to be almost indistinguishable one from the other. The Ngatimiru and Wahineiti, who inhabited Waimate, later the Anglican mission station inland from the Bay of Islands, were undoubtedly related to these people, and were probably hapu of Ngatipou. So that when Ngapuhi, under Hongi Hika's grandfather, Auha, evicted them from Waimate about the mid-eighteenth century, many fled to Hokianga and settled at Omapere, near the South Head, close to their Roroa relatives.

A remarkable feature of early Maori life in New Zealand was the mobility of the people. It is plain that much intercourse took place throughout the country for trading. A great number of *pounamu,* or greenstone, artifacts occur in North Auckland, and this stone is found naturally only on the west coast of the South Island. Ngapuhi were canoe-builders, and Bay of Plenty people were known for their carving, and trade on the basis of these skills occurred, together with trade in garments requiring local expertise and materials. Warfare similarly resulted in travel over very long distances on foot or by canoe. Patuone, a Hokianga chief, and Te Rauparaha, of Kawhia, joined in an expedition, about 1820, which raided as far south as Wellington, with much slaughter. A portion of the party attempted to cross Cook Strait to continue the action in the South Island, but were drowned when a storm overtook them. Apart from this incident, most of the campaign was undertaken on foot.[8]

A resourceful people, Ngapuhi were known on occasion to have selected a suitable tree inland, for the purpose of building a canoe for an attack on a coastal or river-based enemy. This was a work of immense effort and organisation, since the felling of the tree alone could occupy weeks. The Ngapuhi chief Kauteawha is believed to have built canoes inland, near Waimate, and hauled them to the coast to assist in an attack on Ngatimiru at the Bay of Islands.[9] And earlier, Huatakaroa built a canoe near Kaikohe, and laboriously had it dragged overland some eight miles to Taheke, at Hokianga, to assist the people there in a feud with Ngatimanu. These Ngatimanu people were penetrating into the North at that time, but in European times their power was greatly reduced. They were descendants of Manuhiri, the son of Maki, a Waiohua chief of Waitemata.[10]

In later times, a Ngapuhi raiding party is recorded as having gone by sea from Hokianga down to a point on the Ripiro coast south of Maunganui Bluff.[11] From there they dragged their canoes up one of the numerous sandy gorges, and over very rough country to the Kaihu River, about one and a half miles. Then, paddling downstream, they attacked and took a Ngatiwhatua pa, Motuwhitiki. A canoe in which this raid was undertaken belonged to the chief Te Waha, and was called *Haotu*. It was built from a tree felled in the Hokianga, near Okopako at Whirinaki, some three miles from navigable water, and in very steep country. The whole exercise, then, was one involving tremendous labour.

The pre-European Hokianga and inland Ngapuhi had many contacts throughout the Auckland isthmus and southward. These were both friendly and hostile, and involved social visits, victories and defeats, and although they do not concern us here, our account must be read with this in mind. The northern tribes that were affected by this intercourse were Aupouri, Rarawa, Ngatiwhatua, Ngatimanu, Ngatimaru, Ngatipaoa, Waiohua and others. But we are now entering the era of European contact, and it is inappropriate to do so without reference to interesting traditions concerning the advent and departure of the shadowy figure Rahiri, whose association with Puhimoanaariki and the *Mataatua* canoe has been noted. This man is generally given credit for the initiation of the events which launched Ngapuhi on its way to military pre-eminence at Hokianga and Peiwhairangi, or the Bay of Islands, and ultimately in a good deal of the North Island.

In *Mataatua* canoe tradition, a Rahiri is said to have come north in the canoe with Puhimoanaariki, who, it is generally agreed, is the Ngapuhi Rahiri's grandfather. Now, assuming that Rahiri of the canoe was, say, eighteen to twenty years old, his grandfather need not have been much over fifty, since early marriages appear to have been normal in Maori society. Therefore the Rahiri of the canoe could well have been the Ngapuhi progenitor. But Hokianga tradition says that Rahiri was born at Whiria, the pa near Pakanae, on the Hokianga, as we have already noted. And this event may well have taken place, since it is fairly widely agreed that *Mataatua* had gone south to Whakatane from the North not long before it returned there. As we observed, Puhi seemed well aware of where he was going when he left his canoe at Takou, so he may have been returning to Whiria, where his grandson had been born. Be that as it may, Rahiri is without doubt the Ngapuhi ancestor, wherever he came from.

Ngapuhi tradition does not ascribe to Rahiri any notable military talent, as it does to his sons and grandsons, but descent from him is an essential requirement in any Ngapuhi of distinction. Perhaps his aggressive genes and those of his wives were their contribution to the events which followed, since little can be found concerning his exploits, other than his marriages to Ahuaiti, the Ngaitahuhu woman, at Kaikohe, and the Ngatiawa, Whakaruru, at Hokianga. From these most Ngapuhi are descended, and Whiria was without doubt Rahiri's pa. Strangely, Hokianga tradition has little of any consequence to say about his later life, or his possible departure from the North, or even his death. But Takaanui Tarakawa of the Ngaariki tribe does.[12] He says that ultimately Rahiri, among others, returned from the North by way of the west coast, and settled down at Kawhia — 'his descendants are known to me'. Does this explain the odd silence in Ngapuhi tradition about Rahiri's last years? And it is perhaps equally worth mentioning that in Taranaki there is a Ngatirahiri hapu.

However, before the advent of European adventurers, settlers and missionaries, cracks had appeared in the great Ngapuhi tribal structure which had its genesis with Rahiri, and which the aggressive stance of his descendants over the ensuing half-dozen or so generations had consolidated. Perhaps the most notable event that marked this trend was the attack by Hongi

Hika, the warrior chief of Kaikohe, on the ancient Ngapuhi pa, Whiria, then occupied by Moetara, of the Ngatikorokoro hapu of Ngapuhi. This appears to have occurred in about 1812, and was due to some Ngatipou, who were related to the Ngatikorokoro, having assisted in devouring some of Hongi's relations at the battle of Moremonui. But Hongi's attack on Whiria was repulsed, and his siege was unsuccessful. In the meantime, Tuoho, a Roroa chief, created a diversion by going inland and attacking Hongi's pa, Pakinga, at Kaikohe, with the loss of many women and children, who were practically its sole occupants. In retaliation, Hongi, abandoning Whiria, attacked the pa of Te Tihi, on the west side of the harbour at the Lower Waihou. Te Tihi was killed, and Hongi ate his eyes — a provocative incident that later, during Heke's War, split Ngapuhi over the issue of loyalty to the Crown.

Te Roroa and Ngatikorokoro were ambivalent groups, owing allegiance through relationships to Ngapuhi, Ngatipou and Ngatiwhatua.[13] Incidentally, the tribal name Ngatipou itself is also not without its peculiarity. A dispersed people in the North, the group was, in fact, part of the Ngatikahu tribe, which in turn had its origin with the old northern Ngatiawa, some of whom migrated to the Bay of Plenty and other parts of the East Coast, as we have noted. Here a marriage was contracted between a woman of the migrant group and Pourangahua, a prominent local man, and the northern people to whom she had belonged perpetuated this link by adopting the name Ngatipou.[14]

4. European Contact

There had been direct contact between Europeans and Bay of Islands Maori since the end of the eighteenth century, and with Maori at Whangaroa since 1807. This was due to the initiation and expansion of the whale trade in the Pacific, and the suitability of the Bay both as a strategically placed harbour and a resort for supply and recreation. The earliest whalers were often convict ships, converted for the purpose on their arrival at Port Jackson (Sydney), and they had no occasion to visit bar-bound Hokianga. The whale trade, and the good relationships which had developed between the whalers and the Bay Maori, was interrupted for a year or two by the taking of the *Boyd* in 1809 by the Ngatiuru Maori at Whangaroa. But the furore over this soon subsided, and the previous contacts were renewed. This encouraged the Reverend Samuel Marsden, Chaplain of the convict settlement at New South Wales, to establish a mission at the Bay,[1] and this did occur in 1814. Five years later, two members of the personnel of this mission were the first Europeans to visit Hokianga.

Thomas Kendall and John King set out in June 1819 from their station at Oihi, in the Bay of Islands, and went up the Kerikeri River in the chief Hongi Hika's canoe to the cascade where the stone store now is. From there it seems that they passed over the undulating fern-country between Kerikeri and the Puketi forest and down the Waihoanga Creek into the Waihou Valley. Thence they travelled along the south-east side of the harbour to Pakanae, and returned to Oihi on 16 July.[2] It was perhaps at Tarawaua, in the Waihou Valley, near the present settlement of Rahiri, or at Te Toke, that they met the very prestigious Hokianga chief Muriwai, and others.

There is no doubt at all that the Hokianga people had been very well informed on events on the east coast since the earliest contacts, but out of fear of the displeasure of the formidable Bay of Islands fighting chief, Hongi Hika, they were reluctant to intrude unduly on his territory. However, from comments made in 1821 by the Reverend J. Butler, in charge of the Anglican mission station at Kerikeri, in the Bay, the missionaries were unable to compete with the whalers in procuring food from the Maori people there. This led them to resort to trading at Hokianga for pigs, since they could be obtained there for the trade goods available to the missionaries. At the Bay, few trade articles other than muskets were acceptable, and musket trading was forbidden to mission personnel, although it was carried on clandestinely.[3]

The chiefs in authority in Hokianga at that time who met the missionaries were Muriwai, Moena, whom Elder identifies, probably erroneously, as Te Morenga, and Patuone. And no doubt others, whom King in his meagre account failed to mention. Of the places visited, only Pakanae and Whirinaki are identifiable in King's descriptions. Naiti and 'Oraka, Moodinai's place' are mentioned, but these are obscure. We do know, however, that notable chiefs at Hokianga at that time were Patuone at Tarawaua, or Rahiri; Nene (later Tamati Waaka) at the mouth of the Utakura River; Matangi and Taonui, or Makoare as he came to be known, at Horeke. Wharepapa, Raumati, Pangari and Tarewarewa were chiefs on the Kohukohu side, but since there were few easily accessible settlements on that coast of the harbour, it never captured the attention that the opposite side enjoyed. There, downstream from Horeke, were Tawhai and Pi on the Waima River, and Rangatira and Moetara were prominent at Whirinaki and Pakanae, and from there to the South Head. There were many other chiefs, of course, but these are mentioned because of their influence on subsequent events. Kohukohu gained prominence only after its occupation by Europeans.

Samuel Marsden, who arrived at the Bay on the American brig *General Gates* in August 1819, on his second visit to New Zealand,[4] was eager to examine Hokianga for himself, both as a potential field for mission work, and as a harbour for shipping. And this he did at the end of September, with a retinue of missionaries and assorted chiefs, one of these, Rora, being a Hokianga man.

Their route was apparently from Kerikeri to the headwaters of the Utakura River and thence down into the valley to a settlement which Marsden called Koraka (Okaka?). Here they were greeted by the chiefs Wharemaru and Matangi and by Taonui, who impressed as 'a very well-informed man'. Down the valley from there, at Utakura, they met Muriwai, and after much ritual posturing and haka, a difference between the Matangi and Muriwai factions, relating to unauthorised pig-killing, was more or less amicably resolved. So, on down the river to the upper part of the harbour by canoe, to Motiti island, near Kohukohu, now merely a deserted, barren sand-bank. But then, according to Marsden, although its area was little more than half an acre, it supported 'a little village full of inhabitants'. Having passed through the Narrows the party observed another populous pa on the south side, but continued downstream to Whiria, Rahiri's ancient pa, and were there greeted by the local tohunga Te Manene, who attended them from there onwards. They remained there for two days, not, however, without much cross-examination by chiefs, including Mowenna (Mauwhena?) of Pakanae, and the tohunga, regarding their intentions, particularly as to the investigation of the harbour for shipping. They were clearly terrified of the Bay of Islands war-chief Hongi, and feared that he might be displeased, and regard any intercourse with shipping as poaching his interests. But having consulted Hongi on this, Marsden was able to allay local fears.

So Mr Puckey, one of the missionaries, went off in a canoe with a Maori crew, and sounded in the channel at the Heads, and on the bar. Te Manene was apparently already well-informed on these navigational matters, but more particularly on the tapu nature of the rocks at the Heads, which as we know, were associated with the advent of the Ngapuhi ancestors, Nukutawhiti and Ruanui. He also kindly advised Marsden not to worry about the rising wind and sea, since control over these elements was his, Te Manene's, particular area of authority. This authority he proceeded to exert in loud, commanding tones. But this had no visible effect, according to Marsden, who listened with amused tolerance, confident that his own god had a monopoly of such wonders.

Mr Puckey having obtained the information required, the entourage, now swollen to about one hundred persons of all descriptions, proceeded back up the river to Whirinaki. 'This village is situated in a very rich and extensive valley ...' wrote Marsden. 'Here we found a greater population than in any other part we had visited ....' Also, 'The chiefs were in general very sensible men, and wish for information on all subjects.'

Paddling back up-river, the next stop appears to have been

Rawene, described incomprehensibly as Wetewhahetee, whose chief was, in Mr Marsden's terms, Tarawheka. The village, in any case, was clearly at the mouth of the river now called the Waima, into which, some ten miles up-stream, the Punakitere flows. At this time, however, the Punakitere was apparently considered to be the main stream, and the Waima, at their junction, the tributary. So, on 8 October, a party of fifty, in two canoes, set off up the river, visiting villages called Otaheiti (Tahiti?) and Rangiwakkatakka (Rangiwhakataka?), situated close to each other on the south bank of the river. 'These villages stand at the head of a most beautiful valley, into which a small creek, navigable for canoes, runs from the river.' This was no doubt the Waima. Here, an old chief asked for an axe, and offered his head — his most sacred possession — for it. When asked who would get the axe after he had lost his head, he suggested his son. Then on sober reflection the immediate loss of his head appeared unnecessary, and as a compromise he suggested, 'Perhaps you will trust me a little time, and when I die you shall have my head.' Marsden, having no use for the old gentleman's head, then or in the future, settled for two mats. They then returned down the Punakitere to their host, Tarawheka, who recounted to them some of the Maui legends, in which, with his characteristic disdain for 'savage superstitions', Marsden appeared little interested.

With a much-increased retinue, the expedition now continued up the harbour to Te Papa, at the mouth of the Waihou River. Here they were entertained by Patuone — '... one of the most pleasant chiefs I had met with', in Marsden's opinion. Muriwai was also there, urgently requesting a red flannel night-shirt, a night-cap and a pair of spectacles, which he was confident would bolster his prestige enormously. Patuone, consistent with his later behaviour, was at the time attempting to heal a further breach between Muriwai and Matangi, this time involving interference with a relative's bones. Clearly an incompatible pair, these. But leaving Patuone to deal with this, the party took leave of some of their friends, including Mowenna (Mauwhena?) of Pakanae, whom Marsden describes, with dubious accuracy, as 'the head man of the river'. Apparently not all were happy to venture into Hongi's territory. And so up the Waihou, the Whakanekeneke, and the Waihoanga streams, and on to Kerikeri, still in a group about fifty or sixty strong.

With commendable professional solicitude for his colleague in divinity, Te Manene never left Marsden's side, and to an enquiry about the control of the wind and waves during his absence, he assured Marsden that by prayer he had this matter in hand. But the visit, which occupied a fortnight, did little but satisfy Marsden's curiosity, since nothing of importance arose from it. He judged Utakura and Whirinaki to be excellent sites for mission stations, but the Methodists got the first by common consent, and the Catholics Whirinaki merely by default, in an area where the people had hitherto rejected the blandishments of the Protestants much to their chagrin. Marsden, whose place-naming talent was severely limited, even horrifying, imposed the name River Gambier on Hokianga, but this mercifully died at birth.

Three months later, Marsden was back in the Bay of Islands again with HM Storeship *Dromedary*. The Royal Navy, fifty years after Captain Cook — a little slow to react, perhaps — sent this expedition to investigate the availability of the good quality timber for masts and spars that Cook and others had reported here. These were of vital importance to a naval power in those times — no masts and spars: no warships — and a reliable supply was essential to the retention of power. This expedition, although it did not obtain spars at Hokianga, certainly directed attention to the tremendous amount of kauri available there, and commercial interests very soon exploited this.

So on Sunday, 27 February 1820, the *Dromedary* anchored in Kororareka Bay, just as the missionary Kendall and his friend the formidable Hongi Hika were about to embark on a South Sea whaler for England. Marsden's pretext for undertaking this New Zealand voyage so soon after his last was 'to promote the object of her *[Dromedary]* voyage to these islands'.[5] In other words, to use such influence as he had with the Maori people to establish good relations. But one suspects that his missionaries could have been equally capable of this, and that Marsden's enthusiasm for exploratory jaunts was his more likely incentive. But the *Dromedary*'s people having without much success examined the Bay of Islands for mast and spar timber, Captain Skinner sent a party over to Hokianga by land to assess the position there. Marsden, who went on this journey, left little information concerning it, but the deficiency was supplied by Alexander McCrae, an ensign of the 84th Regiment, who was attached to the ship's military complement.[6]

The party left from Kerikeri on 10 March, and, having met Muriwai on the way, apparently took the route down the Utakura Valley that Marsden had used previously on his outward journey, stopping at Muriwai's village. Here a petty-officer reported that his trousers had been stolen, but since the circumstances of the loss are not revealed, one can only speculate on this strange occurrence. Proceeding then into the main river by canoe, an examination was made in what seems to have been the Wairere River, where there was 'a very fine forest of Koude [kauri]'. Then on to the island Motiti — very populous, as Marsden had found it — and past the entrance to Punakitere. 'Here we saw a very large Pah on a point of land which jutted out into the river forming one of the Heads to its entrance. The Rawene pa Tahere, without doubt. And so, on to Mewenna's (Mauwhena?) village' — Pakanae. It soon became clear that the Hokianga Maori, deprived of the bonanza enjoyed by the Bay people for twenty years, owing to the suitability of their harbour for whalers, could perhaps have similar success here with their kauri timber.

Our ubiquitous priest, Te Manene, who commanded the wind and waves, accompanied the *Dromedary*'s people on their examination of the harbour entrance and bar. He was obviously very knowledgeable on this, and on his information the opinion was formed that the *Dromedary* could enter. That evening, Mauwhena produced an old man, then unable to walk, who remembered Cook's being at the Bay of Islands fifty years earlier, in 1769, although McCrae gives the wrong date, 1777. '... he had walked over to see the Ship but was afraid to go near as Captain Cook had quarrelled with the people at Paroa.' McCrae was impressed with the superiority of these people over those at the Bay. 'These were a remarkably fine race of people and had abundance of food which is not the case at the Bay of Islands and which accounts for their superiority.' But on hearing Marsden's explanation of the creation of the world, they politely advised him that he was quite mistaken, since their god Maui had fished New Zealand up from the sea-bottom. The tohunga Te Manene then described his responsibilities, explaining that he had the winds and waves confined in a great cave on the shore, which he afterwards showed them. At this stage the people were certainly not prepared to exchange their superstitions for

Mr Marsden's.

On 14 March the expedition returned up-stream to Motukaraka, 'one of Moodywy's [Muriwai] Pahs', and examined the river there, probably the Tapuae, to look at some very fine timber. Here McCrae makes an interesting comment, noting that 'A Ship was seen off Shooke Hanga' [Hokianga], which, from later information turned out to be the *Cumberland,* South Sea whaler, driven on to that coast by bad weather, where no whaler ever ventured, given a choice. But at Motukaraka the investigation was abandoned, and, accompanied by Hokianga Maori, the party returned to the Bay, where the search for suitable and accessible spars was not prospering.

Encouraged then by the reports on Hokianga and by the attitude of the people who came to the Bay with McCrae's party, Captain Skinner decided to take the *Dromedary* around. This he did, arriving off the Heads on 30 March, prepared, with the bullock-team he had aboard, to start work there. But having buoyed and sounded the channel, Skinner considered it too dangerous for a ship the size of his to attempt an entry. This decision, which was not supported by subsequent events, was, however, conveyed to Captain Kent, of the *Dromedary*'s tender, the *Prince Regent* schooner, which had arrived in the harbour on 29 March. The schooner, then, was thought to be the first European vessel to enter the Hokianga, but a very old man told an interesting story, related to him, he said, by his father — '... that a boat full of white people, armed with muskets without locks, came into the river a very long time ago. He also told one of the gentlemen, that a ship had been lost off this part of the coast at a much later period; and that a boat's crew having gone on shore to trade for provisions were cut off by the natives; but we did not hear of anyone who had been able to discover a vestige of the wreck'.[7]

On 1 April both vessels left to return to the Bay, leaving very disappointed Maori people at Hokianga. The timber was there for the asking and taking, and to supply the vessels 'they had already collected their hogs and potatoes from a considerable distance ...'. Cruise remarked 'The people here seemed to be of industrious habits, of milder manners, and far more under control of their chiefs, than those at the Bay of Islands.' But they were clearly as eager for trade. Apprehension concerning Maori boarding the *Prince Regent* had soon been dispelled by Muriwai, who went on deck and tapued the vessel to any one boarding it without permission. Both vessels were generously supplied with potatoes while there. And who should be present to deal with any problems arising from the action of the wind and waves but the reliable Te Manene? However, on request he was unable to soothe the angry sea from the deck of the *Dromedary,* but stoutly maintained that had he been in his own canoe, 'at his word, the storm would instantly abate'. Perhaps to console himself for this frustration he stole a jacket from the ship, but this was unfortunately discovered.

And so back to the Bay of Islands, where shortly proceedings were enlivened by the arrest of the American sealer *General Gates.* Captain Abilemech Riggs was found to have 'seduced several convicts from Port Jackson' — a serious offence.[8] Eight were then on board, one on shore and two had been put ashore, with others, on a seal island, to collect skins. On 17 April the *General Gates* and her captain left for Sydney for trial, with a British crew. This was indeed a stroke of bad luck for Riggs, since owing to the shortage of labour in this corner of the world, the shipping of convicts, with no questions asked, was common practice. But his ship was unfortunate to be in the Bay of Islands in the very rare event of a visit by a Royal naval ship. *General Gates* was the same vessel that had brought Marsden to New Zealand only nine months previously, and now, as a result of the ensuing inquiry, was to be detained at Sydney until December.

The *Dromedary* finally obtained its cargo of spars at Whangaroa, assisted by the villainous-looking Te Aara, or George, whose ill-treatment by Captain Thompson of the *Boyd* had led to its destruction at Whangaroa in 1809, with most of its complement. George, with the fate of the *Boyd* in mind, was understandably apprehensive at the presence of a British warship, and remained so to some extent throughout its stay. But without taking any action against him, the *Dromedary* obtained its spars near Kaeo, where a road was built for the bullocks to bring the timber out. During its activities there, several further visits were made to Hokianga by the *Dromedary*'s and *General Gates'* people.

McCrae, in a brief comment in his journal[9] states, 'told by Timoranga's people that the Schooner had gone up to Shuke Hanga, that one of her men had killed a boy, the

Grandson of Mowwhawha ...', an enigmatic statement that may refer to an early confrontation at Hokianga. Certainly, some later relations with the people there were not as euphoric as those enjoyed by the *Dromedary* expedition. In a fragmentary note, McCrae also refers to the 'Western branch of the Shuke Hanga of which I was the first European who ever went up it is Manga Mooka'. This journey had to be into the Mangamuka from Whangaroa, since he certainly did not travel this way on his only other visit to Hokianga. He was also, then, the first European to make this journey. Incidentally, he had a strange way of consistently describing a journey *down* a stream, as *up* it.

Mr Clark, the sealing master of the *General Gates,* now bereft of employment and with time on his hands, made the next Hokianga contact.[10] On 31 August he set off from the *Prince Regent,* then at Waitemata, to walk to Kerikeri, where he arrived on 24 September. Marsden had previously walked from the Waitemata to the Bay of Islands, but at Kaipara he had passed up the Wairoa River, and thence to the east coast. Clark, however, 'had gone up the river Wydematta in a canoe, as far as it was navigable, and crossing over to the western side of the island, proceeded along its shores to Shukehanga'. The route he took must have involved a crossing of the Kaipara by canoe near the Heads, and taking the route along the Ripiro Beach all the way up the coast and over the Maunganui Bluff to Hokianga — the normal Maori way. From the South Head, then, he would no doubt have followed in Marsden and McCrae's tracks along the south-east side of the harbour.

Apparently inspired by Clark, Marsden, accompanied by Shepherd, one of his missionaries, went down to the Waitemata in a whale-boat on 30 October, and having climbed Mt Albert (Owairaka) and visited the Manukau, followed Clark's route up the Ripiro Beach, pausing on the way to examine the place at Moremonui where, about fifteen years before, Ngapuhi had suffered its disastrous defeat at the hands of Ngatiwhatua. Arriving at Pakanae, they met survivors of the great Ngapuhi raid down the west coast to Wellington, already described. At Kawhia Ngapuhi had been joined by Te Rauparaha and Te Rangihaeata in what can only be described as a predatory expedition. All the great chiefs of Hokianga — Patuone, Nene, Te Wharepapa, Moetara, Te Kekeao, Tawhai and others — had departed on this wide-ranging campaign, about a year before

Marsden's arrival at Pakanae. And there, the women were now mourning the loss of their men in the savage fighting at Taranaki when the expedition was on its way home.[11]

So, quite unknown to Europeans, except by hearsay, during the twenty or so years that whalers had frequented the Bay of Islands, Hokianga suddenly emerged as a place of some interest. Commerce at New Zealand had until then focussed on whale-oil, but now a profit could be seen in timber, and seemingly inexhaustible amounts of this lay ready for exploitation at Hokianga.

At Kerikeri, where in 1819 Marsden had established the Mission headquarters in New Zealand, the Reverend J. Butler was now lamenting the shortage of food at the Bay — 'The shipping are still gleaning up all the hogs in these parts.' On the same day that officers of the whalers *Saracen* and *Cumberland* passed through on their way to Hokianga to trade muskets for pigs, the missionary King had gone there on the same errand, and Butler plainly suspected that he too might have been in the musket deal. Later he reported his son Samuel and another missionary, Fairburn, returning from Hokianga with ten pigs. The Bay of Islands, as Butler truly said, was 'becoming very thin of pork'. Young Butler and Fairburn had been away twelve days, and Butler complained, 'Meat is very scarce indeed, and the pigs that remain among the natives they will not part from without powder and guns'.[12] But at Hokianga, where the people were at this stage still willing to accept less lethal trade, a commerce in food was developing.

At about the same time, on 19 May 1822, the ship *Providence* entered the harbour. It was the first trading vessel to do so. Captain Herd was hoping to procure a cargo of the kauri spars that the *Dromedary* and *Prince Regent* had reported two years earlier.[13] He was successful: on 28 June he wrote, 'We have taken on board a quantity of fine spars ... . We have obtained five to six hundred loads of timber, the greater part excellent spars for general purposes, and a great many masts for vessels of 400 tons burthen.' The officers and crew of the *Providence* enjoyed excellent relationships with the Maori people and no unpleasant incidents occurred. 'The New Zealanders cut down and brought to the side of the vessel all the spars. There were no thefts committed, nor did the ship sustain any accident or get aground either in sailing in or out of the river.' In the two months or so at Hokianga, Herd made an accurate chart of the river and the bar at the Heads, and left a copy with the Bay missionaries Kendall and Cowell, to whom he attributed the amicable relations with the Maori people. Kendall, it may be mentioned, then enmeshed in an affair with Tungaroa, a teen-age Maori girl at the Bay, was using this time to do some soul-searching on his predicament.

Herd, certainly the European pioneer in trade at Hokianga, retained his interest in New Zealand for some years to come. He is reported on the coast from Stewart's Island to the North Cape, in 1822, 1825, 1826 and 1827, in the *Providence* and *Rosanna.* After he left the harbour in August 1822, however, his successful venture behind him, no further visit of a vessel appears to have occurred until the disastrous incident of the American schooner *Cossack,* which was wrecked at the Heads in 1823.[14] The vessel had entered the harbour on 27 April, looking for provisions to enable it to continue its voyage. Having accomplished this, Captain Dix attempted to take the bar near low water in a high sea; but there was insufficient wind and when the tide turned the schooner went ashore stern first, with all sail set. She broke up in two hours, and the crew, much distressed, turned up at Butler's place at Kerikeri five days later.

Most of the crew got passages on the *Brampton,* then in the Bay, but when she sailed four months later she made only a few miles, and was wrecked in her turn on the reef near Waitangi which now bears her name. All this bad luck was well-deserved according to Hokianga Maori people, since sailors on the *Cossack* had ignored advice about the sacred nature of the two rocks at the South Head — Araiteuru — and struck them with hammers.[15] So Te Manene's god of the wind and waves, who lived in his cave there, got under the vessel's bottom, threw her up and down and cast her ashore. The potency of this god was undoubtedly due to his association with the ancestors Kupe, Nukutawhiti and Ruanui, and their ancient dwelling-places at the Heads. Despite this affront to their god, the Maori people treated the shipwrecked crew very kindly when they got ashore, and no lives were lost.

5. Early European Enterprise

As we have seen, Captain Herd visited Hokianga on a number of occasions in the five years following his 1822 venture. But during that time there was little further activity by European adventurers there until Herd was given command of an expedition, organised in London in 1825 by the first New Zealand Company, to acquire land in this country. The intention was to form settlements here with sawyers and other tradesmen to procure spars and manufacture flax, and it was for this purpose that the *Rosanna,* under Herd, with the *Lambton* under Captain Barnett, entered the harbour towards the end of 1826. A tentative attempt to settle the tradesmen at the Hauraki Gulf had been discouraged by the ferocious aspect and menacing behaviour of the Maori there. And later, at the Bay of Islands, the Anglican missionaries suggested pointedly that Hokianga would be more suitable for their needs, hoping, vainly as it turned out, that a settlement there might draw shipping away from the Bay.[1] The contemporary consensus is that the mission there wanted no such company in their little sphere of influence. So it happened that on arrival at Hokianga with his two vessels, Herd betook himself to Rawene, where, on 26 January 1827, he purchased the land there for the Company from the chief Muriwai and others. Kendall was among the witnesses to the deed. The settlers, however, scarcely ventured ashore because they were discouraged by the demeanour of the Maori, who had apparently discovered that the *Rosanna* had ten tons of gunpowder on board — an irresistible temptation even to the most docile of them. Upon learning from mission sources that an attempt to seize the ship was to be made, Herd abandoned the venture and the expedition departed, arriving at Sydney on 11 February 1827. But three of the bolder of the settlers later returned to Hokianga to join one who had remained there. Herd is frequently described as a timid old man, bluffed by the mission people, but with what truth we shall never know.[2]

The New Zealand Company of 1839, the successor to this

Company, never took possession of Rawene. Colonel Wakefield inspected it in 1839 for settlement, and remarked that the point 'contains good land, and is a good situation; but its size, of course, offers no inducement to form a township on it. Neither does the opposite land, when examined, present a much more flattering prospect.'[3] The 'opposite land' was apparently Motukaraka, which the Company had purchased in 1839 in London, from Thomas McDonnell, a Lieutenant in the Royal Navy who settled at Horeke in 1831. He purchased much land in the River, as the Hokianga Harbour was familiarly known, but the validity of some of his purchases was so much in question that the Company did not get possession of Motukaraka either. [4]

Herd's venture, then, came to nought, but as recently as fifty years ago, Rawene was still known to older settlers as Herd's Point, and what appears to have been its original name, Okura, is never heard.

John Rodolphus Kent, contemporary with Herd, was a rival for the title of Pioneer of the River, and him we have already met as captain of the *Prince Regent* — the first European vessel known to have entered the harbour. Since this occasion, Kent had commanded several Colonial ships in New Zealand waters, notably the *Mermaid* in 1823, and the *Elizabeth Henrietta,* which was wrecked at Goulbourn Island, Ruapuke, in 1824. In 1827, in the brig *Governor Macquarie,* he appears to have been at Hokianga at about the same time, or perhaps later than Herd, and he met with the same hostile reception, as Polack records with his customary florid style.[5] Stripped of his trimmings and facetious comment, the incident as he recorded it involved our friend Te Manene, in this context appearing as Te Waenga, one of his many names. Maori had crowded the deck of the *Macquarie* when she anchored, without apparent hostility. However, Kent and his first mate, John Martin, were alarmed enough to set up two cannons on the poop, loaded with grape-shot. The Maori, unaware of the effect of such guns, at a signal initiated hostilities with a haka, and it was clear that they meant to take the ship. But Te Waenga, *alias* Te Manene, who was involved in all this, had a daughter, later known as Kate, with whom Martin had 'formed an intimacy' as Polack archly puts it, and she, knowing of the destruction that these guns could wreak on her massed people, shouted to them that their intention was discovered, and warned that death would overtake them all unless they fled. Instantly convinced, without further ado they quickly, prudently and *en masse* went over the side. A few years later, Martin, then the River pilot, put his 'intimacy' with the lady on a somewhat more formal basis, but later still he struck a sour note in his will, being ungracious enough to refer to his 'three illegitimate children (by my late housekeeper Kate)'.[6]

The gun incident appears to have had a chastening effect on the Hokianga people, for a time at least, since European activity proliferated at this point. John (Jacky) Marmon, an adventurer of dubious veracity and repute, now emerges as possibly the first European settler at Hokianga, but he himself offers a number of conflicting dates and recounts equally conflicting incidents relative to the event.[7]

Marmon's first acquisition of land at Hokianga was dated 1827 in his submissions made to the Old Land Claim Commissioners in 1844, but he had possibly resided on the River from time to time before that date. This purchase was at Pukeaitanga, now known as Rangiahua owing to the coyness of later missionary-influenced Maori about place-names with sexual overtones. Certainly unaffected by any such scruples, Marmon regales us with vainglorious accounts of his career, in ancient newspaper articles.[8] He appears quite proud of his dubious activities, and particularly about the havoc he claims to have wrought among countless numbers of Maori women. These articles should therefore be read with caution. He even claimed (by implication — a favourite recourse of his) to have had, among so many others, an affair with Tangiwhare, one of Hongi's wives. If he did in fact, this would establish him firmly as the cheekiest of compulsive fornicators of his time, since in so doing he would as surely have been flirting with death as with Tangiwhare. Marmon's acquaintance with New Zealand and its people was certainly an early one, apparently commencing in 1817, when he deserted from the schooner *Sally* at the Bay of Islands. He joined the Hokianga colonist settlement of Hikutu people there, in the Mangonui Inlet, and embarked on a career devoted to polygamy. Bored with this after a time, he sailed off to Tasmania but returned to the Bay, apparently during the visit of the *Dromedary,* in 1820, although he appears then to have discreetly kept out of sight, since no one seems to mention him at that time. Anyway, he convinced his former Maori friends, so he says, that he had returned from the dead, and for this unusual achievement he was duly appointed a tohunga, in which capacity he took part in Hongi Hika's murderous raid on Mauinaina, at Waitemata, and also in the battle at Te Ika a Ranganui, near Kaiwaka, where in 1825, Hongi and Whareumu finally defeated the Ngatiwhatua. Hongi, Marmon claims, was his protector at the Bay, but when the chief died in 1828 the protection was gone, and he decided to settle at Hokianga. Here confusion of dates arises.

With engaging modesty Marmon confesses casually to having been coveted by Muriwai, our Hokianga chief, 'whose highest ambition had been to secure me as a pakeha. For a long time this has been denied him, but now when I arrived at his settlement I received a most flattering and cordial reception. So overjoyed was he that without any difficulty I obtained a large grant of valuable land for the price of my residence amongst them.' Having graciously accepted Muriwai's offer, and with it his usual quantum of wives and concubines, at that point his permanent residence at Hokianga began. But accounts of the time this event occurred are many, various and contradictory. He was, however, certainly living at Pukeaitanga in 1826, since he stated this as a witness to the purchase of land at Horeke by Captains Deloitte and Stewart (he of Stewart's Island) in that year. But regardless of dates, he assures his readers that he 'took the upper hand with Muriwai from the first, accordingly I never had any trouble with him'. A bold fellow indeed, but this relationship was short-lived, since Muriwai died in 1828. Marmon was also a cannibal if his own assurances (by implication again) are to be believed, and he earned additional distinction as an ally of Nene (Tamati Waaka), the so-called 'friendly' chief, at the battles at the Bay in 1845-6, between Hone Heke and British troops.[9] However, one thing that is certain about Marmon is that in 1835 he purchased his land at Rawhia from the chiefs Pangari and Ngau, and this was his home from then, or indeed before that, until his death.

Marmon is as good a starting-point as any in an account of European settlement in the River, despite the uncertainty as to dates. Others better documented could have preceded him, notably one Gordon Browne. In 1826 at Horeke he either bought land for himself or for Messrs Raine and Ramsay, of Sydney, from the chiefs Taonui, Raumati, Kaitoke, Wharepapa and others. The deed relative to this purchase, and also that for the 2200 acres purchased in the same locality, by Deloitte and Stewart, was burned when Thomas McDonnell's house was destroyed by fire in July 1842, an event that has left some uncertainties in its wake. Browne's and Deloitte's Horeke claims overlapped to a small extent, involving this house-site, but in 1836 a meeting of the vendor chiefs resolved this.[10] Without doubt Raine and Ramsay occupied the land in 1826, since in May 1827 this notice appeared in the *Sydney Gazette:* 'A branch of commerce has been entered into by Messrs Raine and Ramsay. The speculation consists of an extension of the trade with New Zealand. A cargo of produce was brought up the other day in the barque *Faith,* probably consisting of spars, fine deal planks, and forty tons of flax.' About three weeks later, the same journal stated: 'About fifty Englishmen from this port are at Hokianga, sawing deals and instructing the natives in shipbuilding.'[11] In October 1827, when Earle, the artist and author, visited the Horeke settlement with Kent in the *Governor Macquarie,*[12] he was surprised to find that, 'Here were store-houses, dwelling-houses, and various offices for the mechanics; and every department seemed as well filled as it could have been in a civilised country.' This place had been given the name 'Deptford', and already the schooner *Enterprise* had been built there,[13] launched, had gone to sea, and was at Sydney with two chiefs aboard, when Earle visited Horeke. Captain David Clark took her over on her maiden voyage. He was probably with Browne when he purchased Horeke for Raine and Ramsay, since the chiefs Nene and Patuone testified that he was the first European resident at Horeke.[14] He was superintendent of the shipyard from its commencement until shortly before his death by drowning in 1831. His schooner also had a short life, ending on 3 May 1828 when it was wrecked at night with the loss of all its complement, a few miles north of the Heads, when running for the River.[15] Strangely, within the next few days the Anglican mission vessel *Herald,* built in 1825 at Paihia, Bay of Islands, was wrecked in much the same locality, but without loss of life. This is a perilous coast indeed, and many ships have been lost here — some, it seems, owing to masters mistaking the Whangape heads for Hokianga.

Earle has left us with a comprehensive view of the Hokianga of earliest European times. On his progress up to Horeke he visited and described the great, heavily-fortified pa Whiria, behind which, he says, was a swamp covered at high water, 'which adds greatly to its security'. At Pakanae, the nearby Maori village, there were about 200 acres cultivated — 'not slightly turned up, but well worked and cleared', which convinced him of the 'frugality and industry of these savages'. Pakanae was the main settlement of the Ngatikorokoro chief Moetara, an amiable gentleman already familiar with the society of Europeans, and trading regularly with them with flax, timber and pork. Pakanae could perhaps have been described then as the Maori capital of Hokianga. By this time Samuel Butler, son of the Reverend John Butler at Kerikeri, had capitalised on his trading talents, which we have already seen demonstrated, and was living with his wife at Pakanae, operating as a business agent.[16] But his career was short, as he was drowned there in 1836.[17] Demise in this way was almost normal in early Hokianga.

The now bare, eroded and lonely island of Motiti, off Kohukohu, had already been noted as a populous place by both Marsden and McCrae, but its importance is emphasised by Earle. The *Governor Macquarie* went ashore for the space of a tide near the island, which he described as 'a small island, or rather sand-bank entirely covered with storehouses for provisions and ammunition. The centre was so contrived that all assailants might be cut off before they could effect a landing' — a curious statement, later derided by Markham. His sketch of the place confirms his general description, however. As he continued on his leisurely way to the Bay of Islands, he also came upon 'a party of men who had come out in the *Rosanna,* the vessel employed by the New Zealand Company'. They were cutting timber, sawing planks and making oars for the Sydney market. This activity seems to have been taking place at Pukeaitanga, now known as Rangiahua, in the Waihou valley.[18]

In New Zealand, this startling irruption of European enterprise was probably a phenomenon peculiar to Hokianga. It all occurred in 1826 and 1827, and was perhaps due to rising prosperity and building activity at Sydney, where opportunities for quick returns on invested capital were limited. And, as ever, missionaries now appeared in the River.

6. Kauri, Ships and Missionaries

With Earle, when the *Governor Macquarie* entered the harbour in October 1827, were the Reverend John Hobbs, one Luke Wade and his wife, and a Miss Bedford. These, with the Reverend James Stack, who had travelled to Hokianga from the Bay of Islands, were the pioneer Wesleyan missionaries to Hokianga. A mission had been established earlier at Kaeo, Whangaroa, in Ngatiuru territory, but there being no element of trading or business there by which the Maori could profit, their interest was minimal, and the mission made no progress. The personnel did, however, survive four years of privation and uncertainty until they were forced to abandon the station when Hongi Hika attacked and drove the dominant local Ngatipou tribe out and into Hokianga. Now at Hokianga themselves, these newly-arrived mission people sought out the chief Patuone, and in November, at Tarawaua in the Waihou Valley, he gave them seventy-seven acres of land at Te Toke.[1] This is at the junction of the Horeke road and State Highway No. 1, near Rangiahua.[2] Although a house was built there the place was abandoned about two months later, and the new station was established on a 483 acre block at Mangungu, which had good access by water to the rest of the harbour, and deep water close-to.[3] Here the site, and an early mission-house, are preserved by the New Zealand Historic Places Trust. Among other missionaries who followed and made their mark at Hokianga were William White, Nathaniel Turner, John Whitely, James Buller, William Woon and J.H. Bumby. Mangungu is only a mile or two down the harbour from Horeke.

The Wesleyan people were forbidden to speculate in land, and this relieved them from much of the adverse criticism that was later levelled at their Anglican brethren at the Bay of Islands. However, William White, one who did fall by the wayside and engaged in commercial and other proscribed activities, attracted considerable opprobrium all by himself, and he figures largely in subsequent events. From this point and for some years, the Wesleyans, with Lieutenant McDonnell at Horeke, and G.F.

Russell at Kohukohu, exerted a strong influence in the upper harbour for good or bad, both on the Maori people and on events involving both races. Little progress was made by the mission for some years, other than in building and in promoting a relationship with the Maori people, until 1834, when the Reverend W. White arrived to take charge. By that time two houses had been built, one 45 by 15 feet and another 31 by 12, for White and Hobbs, and three other substantial buildings. 'Maori domestics' made do with a rush house 24 by 12, and a store for their provisions, and a boat-house and saw-pit coped with communications and building. Considerable advances in teaching and in religious instruction were made from the mid-thirties onwards.

The mission was fortunate in having the support of the solid upper-harbour chiefs Taonui, Patuone and Nene (later Tamati Waaka). On the other hand they were embarrassed by the Whangaroa chiefs of Ngatiuru, the brothers Te Puhi and Ngahuruhuru, in whose settlement at Kaeo, Whangaroa, the abortive Wesleyan mission had earlier been founded. At Whangaroa in 1809, Te Puhi had initiated the attack on the *Boyd,* which apparently arose from the ill-treatment by Thompson, the captain of the ship, of another brother, Te Aara.[4] For this, all except four of the complement died at the hands of Te Puhi's people. Always in a weak position at Kaeo, the mission did not survive the disruptive Ngapuhi attack on the Ngatipou in the upper harbour. But since Hongi's mother was Ngatiuru, he did not harm those people, although Te Puhi and Ngahuruhuru were apprehensive enough of the outcome to flee to Hokianga. There, when the mission was established at Mangungu, they settled close to it in the Waihou Valley, where, Laurenson states, Te Puhi in particular proved troublesome, and 'was ever a sly and subtle trouble maker'.

As we have seen, the Horeke shipyard was already in existence and operating when the Mangungu mission station was established. Its owners, Messrs Raine, Ramsay and Browne, were concerned that their employees should keep the sabbath, set a good example to the Maori and support the mission, and they wrote from Sydney to the Superintendent, David Clark, accordingly. Certainly some of the activities of the staff among the Maori girls could have raised doubts as to the effectiveness of this homily, but little else could hardly have been anticipated.[5]

The shipyard built and launched in succession after the schooner *Enterprise* the brigantine *New Zealander,* 200 tons, at the end of 1827, and the *Sir George Murray,* 400 tons, in 1830 — both substantial projects even in a more civilised environment. But these and three smaller vessels built there had short lives. A curious place-name on the Waima River may be associated with the *New Zealander.* This is at Moehau, which, until not very many years ago, was commonly called 'New Zealand', for a reason no-one has been able to explain satisfactorily to the author. Similarly the creek originating in the river there was called New Zealand Creek, and it seems at least possible that these names are in some way associated with the vessel. But whatever the reason, the *New Zealander,* regarded as one of the fastest sailors out of Sydney, initiated an administrative furore at Sydney.

Ships built in New Zealand were not permitted to register under the British Registry Act, since they were not built in a territory 'subject to His Majesty or to any European power or state'. Registration protected ships from piracy and legalised their entry into, stay in and departure from the ports of the world. However, the Governor of New South Wales had been authorised to issue licences for the New Zealand vessels to trade between Sydney and this country, but the *New Zealander* had apparently breached the conditions of this licence, and was seized by Customs at Sydney. She was later released, but the incident influenced the chiefs who were involved to adopt a New Zealand flag, and to establish a shipping register under their authority. This action was initiated some years later by James Busby, then the British Resident at the Bay of Islands, when on 20 March 1834 the flag was chosen by the chiefs at a ceremony at Waitangi. A vote was taken by thirty Hokianga and Bay chiefs on three designs, and that chosen was a very close approximation to the present house-flag of the Shaw, Savill and Albion shipping line.[6]

But before these events came to pass, European settlement at Hokianga by adventurous individuals had occurred, and the four survivors of the abortive *Rosanna* expedition were sorting themselves out. Earle had found them on the banks of the Waihou, on his way to the Bay, but on his return to Hokianga they had moved down the River to Koutumongero, near Opononi, now known simply as Koutu. Their names were McLean, Nimmo, Gillies and Nesbitt (variously spelt), and in spite of Marmon's comings and goings, they may have been among the first of the independent permanent settlers on the River, although Nesbitt subsequently went to the Bay. In 1828 Captain Kent purchased Koutumongero for Captain Young,[7] and the four moved out. In 1831, three of them, Nimmo, McLean and Nesbitt, purchased 200 acres for £80-5-0 at Motukauri, on the north side of the River, at the mouth of the Motuti Creek.[8] This partnership did not survive very long, due to events following the grounding of the *Fortitude* there, in 1833, of which more later. Captain Young, who in 1831 took possession of Koutu, or One Tree Point, as it was called, also became embroiled in this affair. However, in the meantime, Nimmo and his friends established a timber business at Motukauri. Nimmo, it is said — clearly a man of some forethought — at all times had a coffin ready for his demise, but twice this was appropriated for one of his friends. Many years later he personally occupied the third.

In 1829, only two years after it opened for business, the shipyard and trading establishment at Horeke failed, and at the end of 1830 the whole enterprise, including Raine, Ramsay and Browne's land, purported to be 5120 acres, was bought by Thomas McDonnell at an auction at Sydney.[9]

McDonnell purchased the *Sir George Murray* with the dockyard,[10] presumably at the same time as the land purchase. From that time the original owners do not appear here again. Even Captain David Clark, the superintendent, was gone by 1831, drowned in the harbour. And now, for a time, European activity in the upper harbour is centred on McDonnell's establishment at Horeke, and the mission station at Mangungu.

Names associated with the early timber trade were now to be found throughout the length of the River — the *Rosanna* people, G.F. Russell, then McDonnell's factotum at Horeke, Maning at Kohukohu, Poynton in the Mangamuka with Cassidy, Cochrane and Pearson. The Jew Polack, too, was there for a year or two. Christopher Harris purchased land in the Orira Creek in 1830-1, but the family finally settled at Motukaraka, although he was in Hokianga in 1826, and may have been a contender for first place among the early settlers. Marmon's and Clark's activities we know about, and Captain Young, of Koutu, who also had land on the Waihou and later at Opononi. Fishwick, Captain Clark's partner, bought land up the Waima River in 1831, at Matakaraka, near Moehau, but no purchases appear to have been made in the Omanaia River until 1835. Although Butler was trading at Pakanae, he owned no land there that we know of. Among the settlers of the early Thirties there remains one of note near the mouth of the harbour — that is, John Martin, he of the romantic incident involving Te Manene's daughter. He bought land in 1832, from Moetara and others.

By the end of 1831, then, it could fairly be said that a lively trade in kauri timber with the Europeans had been initiated between Hokianga and Sydney; and in garden provisions and pork as well as timber, with the Maori people. It was at Pakanae — Moetara's settlement — that all this began, but Kohukohu, ultimately the most successful of the timber settlements, soon became the main base for the timber gatherers upstream from the Narrows. In 1831 G.F. Russell had arrived at Horeke from Sydney, at McDonnell's request, to take possession of Raine and Ramsay's property, apparently superseding Captain Clark, who then had his Horeke house shifted over to Kohukohu. There, in partnership with Fishwick, he engaged in the timber trade until his death in 1831.[11] Clark, then, was not only the pioneer settler at Horeke, but also at Kohukohu. He occupied land there, having married two daughters of Wharepapa, one of the owners, and he seems to have been in the process of acquiring it when his untimely death occurred. Fishwick then appears to have sold the house to Maning, the author of *Old New Zealand,* who, in 1834 negotiated the purchase of the land from Wharepapa, Tarewarewa and others. He then sold to Dr Ross, the doctor attached to the Church Missionary Society at the Bay of Islands, who in turn sold to the Reverend N. Turner, and in 1837 G.F. Russell purchased the property from Turner.[12] At one stage in 1834 the land was occupied on lease by one Oakes, but he was unable to finance a purchase. Kohukohu is interesting in that, unlike Horeke and Mangungu, it was founded by industrious individuals, and achieved its success in the same way.

In contrast to Kohukohu, Horeke was a creature of finance — foreign capital at that — and perhaps it was for that reason that it failed. It was taken over by McDonnell, who, when he took up residence there, assumed the role of a tycoon, dabbled in land speculation among his other activities, and leased out much of this land. He had been a Naval Commander, and had served in the American War of Independence. Later he joined the East India Company, commanding a Company ship, and then with his own vessel engaged in the opium trade, after which he gravitated to Australia, and finally to New Zealand. It was at this stage, when about forty years of age, that he purchased Horeke. Of independent means, he came from County Antrim, in Ulster, and he clearly had influential connections. Not an admirable character, he appears capricious, unstable and devious.[13] His advent coincided with intensified activity at Hokianga, and with that came a great deal of trouble.

While McDonnell's behaviour was often provocative and high-handed his excesses were more than matched by the antics of the Reverend William White, and these two dominated events in Hokianga for some years. White was a man of very strong, even arrogant and violent nature, but his very positive attitudes had been a considerable asset to the Wesleyan mission at Whangaroa. He left there for England in 1825 and did not return until 1830, when, as a married man, he was appointed to take charge of the station at Mangungu. There is no doubt that in the six years he was Superintendent there he worked with immense energy and vitality as an organiser and preacher. But he had a predilection for trade which was demonstrated in his personal activities and in those on the mission's behalf. Later, he was also charged with a predilection for Maori women, and this proved to be his downfall. He and McDonnell collaborated in various matters, and a pair less likely to succeed without creating stressful situations can scarcely be imagined. Some of White's escapades have an almost Wild West flavour, and ultimately and inevitably, McDonnell, equally rash, became his deadliest enemy.

Two further Pakeha characters now emerge — two very different people who later had in common many descendants in Hokianga. Although Dennis Browne Cochrane apparently arrived at Hokianga in the 1820s, we hear little of him until 1831, when he acquired land, reputed to be 1000 acres, on the west side of the Mangamuka River. This he purchased from McDonnell and G.F. Russell, who by that time were already into land speculation in the harbour. The price was £68-15-6, but upon the assumption of government by the British Crown, the Old Land Claim Commissioners reduced the grant to 200 acres, and Cochrane took £800 in Government Land Scrip for the balance. The man who was later his son-in-law, James Reddy Clendon, was the first United States Consular Agent in the Bay of Islands, and in 1840 disposed of his property there, at Okiato, to Governor Hobson, for the site of a Government town to be called Russell. This name was later applied to Kororareka. But in 1856, following the death of his wife, Clendon married Jane Cochrane, Dennis' daughter by his Maori wife Takatowi te Whata.[14] They lived at Rawene, having acquired land there, apparently from the Crown, which had resumed ownership of the New Zealand Company's purchase, and their house is now owned by the New Zealand Historic Places Trust. Jane was a very talented lady, and her father a very big man, and both characteristics are distributed among their descendants.

In 1832, Clendon, a merchant and ship-owner, had purchased the schooner *Fortitude,* 132 tons, at London, and sailed for New Zealand in April. Clendon's first mate was Thomas Wing, later a well-known personality in the North, whose daughter, Fanny, was accidentally killed during Hone Heke's attack on Kororareka. The *Fortitude* arrived at the Bay in August, where Clendon and Samuel Stephenson entered into partnership as merchants at Kororareka, sending the vessel trading on the coast and to Australia. It was on one of these errands, towards the end of April in 1833, that she entered the Hokianga Harbour to load timber at Motukauri, the establishment of our acquaintances Nimmo, McLean and Nesbitt. Here the *Fortitude* went aground on the falling tide, with disastrous results to their timber business, and to the accompaniment of the general uproar of a minor tribal war.[15]

Both the Whirinaki people, and the Rarawa on the Motuti River, claimed the Motukauri land and foreshore as their territory, and upon the stranding of the *Fortitude* the law of *muru* (plunder) was deemed by them to operate. This involved the legal plunder by those having the mana of the land, of anything or anybody upon which or whom such a calamity descended in territory under their jurisdiction. Both these groups therefore promptly boarded the stranded vessel, took possession, and helped themselves to whatever they fancied, including the ship's papers. C.O. Davis remarks with some asperity, 'I have no hesitancy in saying, that, if prudent steps had been taken, the purloined articles would have been restored to the owners, and the difficulty amicably settled. Moral suasion, however, was not the mode often resorted to in those days, but the spirit of retaliation was preferred, by both settlers and Maoris.' He then tells of the result of this logic.[16]

Without delay, the Pakeha-oriented chiefs Moetara, his brother Rangatira, Te Kakahi and others, whose territory ranged from Pakanae in the harbour, to Maunganui Bluff on the coast, raised an army and paddled up the River to Motukauri. One suspects that this reaction may not have been due so much to a devotion to law and order as the occurrence of an opportunity to settle old scores. But whatever the motive, this force landed at Motukauri, to be met at once by musket fire from the defenders. General fighting ensued, involving some twenty-two casualties. Moetara lost, among others, the chiefs Te Kakahi, Pahau and Taungahuru, and the defenders two important chiefs, Mariao and Taku.

Moetara then retreated with his forces to Captain Young's cattle-run at Koutu (One Tree Point), and built a large pa there enclosing Young's house and buildings, to protect them and his people from any counter-measures that the Motukauri or Whirinaki Maori might take. Munitions poured into this fortress, where the activity was being supervised by our warrior-tohunga Te Waenga, *alias* Te Manene. Sadly, though, he got too close to an accidental gunpowder explosion, which terminated his eventful career. Reinforcements crowded into Koutu. They included Jacky Marmon, who came with Nene (Tamati Waaka) and Patuone his brother, and 300 men. Marmon and about thirty of Nene's people crossed the river and fired into Orongotea pa, which was occupied by some Rarawa, but little harm came of this. The whole episode then ended tamely when the Koutu army demanded the *Fortitude*'s papers, and got them. Honour being now apparently satisfied, all parties dispersed, and on 3 May the *Fortitude* refloated and left the harbour little the worse for its harrowing experience. The final bloodless victory was no doubt due, as such events usually are, to a superior show of force, on this occasion by the Koutu army. But Nimmo and his partners lost possession of their land and a £900 investment at Motukauri. Returning to Koutu, they left their place and all their timber, burned, in ruins and tapued. So the *Fortitude* survived, but Hokianga had continued to take its toll. Less than a year earlier, the ship *Meredith* had been lost in attempting the bar for a load of timber. But this time the wreck had been in Moetara's territory and here the law of *muru* had apparently operated smoothly and without interference. How much effect then, did local rivalries have on the hostilities over the *Fortitude* incident?[17] It was fortunate indeed for Clendon in this early stage of his enterprise, that his vessel was not severely damaged or burned. Both he and his partner had committed themselves to residence in this country, and the *Fortitude* was then their main asset. Clendon, in fact, died at Hokianga some forty years later, ending an active and useful career, and his younger children were born there. It is interesting, then, that his second child had been born in the harbour in January 1830, when he was in command of the *City of Edinburgh,* loading timber.

Later in 1833, HMS *Buffalo,* with Captain Kent as trading-master, was sent to New Zealand for a load of spars, but again, as in the *Dromedary*'s case, the captain would not risk his ship on the bar. She was thus 'compelled to fill up on the East Coast, enhancing the cost of each spar two or three times'. The 'East Coast' Maori, whoever and wherever they may have been, 'were so enriched and spoiled by the *Buffalo* last year, that they positively refuse work', Gordon Browne, late of Horeke, wrote plaintively from Mahurangi. The British were not alone in seeking spars from Hokianga. One expedition on record is that of 1835 for the Brazilian Government, led by Commander Norton, who prospected the River and chartered the *Waterloo* to take spars from Hokianga to Rio de Janeiro.[18]

In 1831, prior to these events, the Bay of Islands missionaries, soliciting the support of a few Bay and Hokianga chiefs, had sent a petition to William IV advising him that the French had designs on New Zealand, and asking him to exert some control over his troublesome New Zealand subjects — that is, escaped convicts, runaway sailors and riotous workers of all sorts. These, of course, were no help to missionaries. The Hokianga signatories were Patuone, Nene (Tamati Waaka), Moetara, Matangi and Taonui (Makoare). A thinly-spread representation this, but the British Government had been aware of both the matters complained of, and had contemplated them with disfavour for some time. So it came to pass that on 17 May 1833 HMS *Imogene* disgorged one James Busby on to the beach at Paihia, the mission station at the Bay. This was our first public servant — His Britannic Majesty's Resident in New Zealand. This inspired stroke of diplomacy had the dual effect of response to the missionaries' petition, and the disposal of Mr Busby, an unemployed New South Wales public servant who had been canvassing influential people in England for a Government appointment. He had been given only one effective instruction — to 'conciliate the good-will of the native chiefs, and establish on a permanent basis that good understanding and confidence which it is important ... to perpetuate'. He was not provided with any means of achieving this, and having little natural ability to relieve the deficiency, he was not a success. But at least he opened a line of communication with the Government of New South Wales, which had been charged, unwillingly, with the responsibility of paying his salary and expenses, £700 in total. With him he brought a prefabricated house, some of which survives to-day on his former estate at Waitangi.[19]

Unfortunately for Busby, and to his surprise, his sole incumbency of the post of British Resident was rudely disrupted in 1835 by the appointment of that hyperactive Hokianga personality, McDonnell, as *Additional* British Resident at Hokianga, mainly as a result of his own dubious claim that Hokianga was too far from the Bay for Busby to do it justice. He also stated in support of his case that the European population of Hokianga at the time was 1000 — an estimate probably excessive by over 900. Busby had engineered his own appointment without the knowledge of Bourke, the Governor of New South Wales, who was to be in effect his employer. Now McDonnell had achieved much the same end by the same route and tactics, since Busby was to be *his* superior officer. Thus Bourke resented Busby and Busby resented McDonnell, and their joint tenure of the appointment did nothing but generate an incredible amount of ill-will between them, until McDonnell's resignation in 1837. In Busby we had an unattractive personality, honest but stubborn, an uninspiring and cautious public servant. McDonnell, on the other hand, was a man of action and an achiever of sorts, but he was also faulty in his judgements, devious, impulsive and arrogant. Much of the year and a half in which they shared the appointment was liberally punctuated by confrontation and by mutual recrimination, both direct and through Governor Bourke.

Being subordinate to Busby, McDonnell was instructed to act in consultation with the British Resident at the Bay. In the event he not only omitted to do this, but acted unilaterally, and embarrassingly, in many ways. The conclusion is inescapable that for quite different reasons both these men were unsuited to the offices they held. Nonetheless the appointment of an additional Resident at Hokianga hardly deserved the scorn Busby poured on it, since his own capability seems to have been fully extended at the Bay of Islands. And as commercial and industrial activity at Hokianga was of an entirely different nature from that at the Bay, it would have been reasonable to expect that Busby would welcome assistance. It could have been argued, however, that in McDonnell's case his contract with the Admiralty to supply spars might conflict with his duties.

At about this time, Hokianga certainly had a small but very active population, and an industrial significance that merited the attention of the British Government. But apart from McDonnell's contribution, no amount of capital was invested there large enough to justify such cries of distress as were being increasingly raised at the Bay. Industry at Hokianga was labour-intensive, and thus was not vulnerable to the pressures occurring at the Bay. It was also very definitely Maori-dominated, but few Pakeha seem to have suffered unduly because of this, owing largely, no doubt, to the influence of their Maori wives. Local wars and skirmishes occurred, but Europeans were not directly involved except insofar as they chose to be, or got in the way. Like the gangsters in Chicago in the 1930s, the Maori 'only killed each other'. Actually, drowning, often when intoxicated, seems to have been the commonest way for Europeans to take their departure.

As to McDonnell's appointment, it may well have been justified in Governor Bourke's view by what he considered to be Busby's failure. Ramsden, Busby's apologist, wrote, quoting Bourke:[20] 'The authority of the Resident ... is, I am sorry to say, almost totally disregarded by Europeans ... and he has failed to form so close a connection with the chiefs as to command their aid ... nor has he been able to accomplish any of the objects pointed out to him in my Instructions.'

7. The Early Thirties

McDonnell had been in residence at Horeke for three years, and his appointment had not yet been made, when Edward Markham, Hokianga's earliest and most ebullient resident annalist, entered the harbour on 18 February 1834 aboard the brig ***Brazil Packet,*** Captain Crow, anchoring off Pakanae. He was to enjoy six months on the River, socialising with the European settlers and the Maori and philandering with the Maori girls, on whose charms he dwells at some length and with appreciation.[1]

There were, according to Markham, about seventy Europeans residing on the shores of the harbour on his arrival. They lived in comparative peace and amity among 4000 Maoris, and, Markham says, all were much gratified when Captain Crow presented Moetara with a sword, a cloak and a letter from Colonel Arthur, the then Governor of New South Wales, in recognition of his action in recovering the *Fortitude*'s papers.[2] Markham was then taken up to Kohukohu by Captain Young, the owner of Koutu, who, as a matter of interest, was also the first purchaser of land at Opononi, where, for £69-13-0, or equivalent in goods, he acquired 41 acres in 1835 which he later disposed of to J. Webster.[3] Incidentally, the curious modern myth which suggests that Opononi is not the legitimate name, nor even a Maori one for this locality, merits little consideration, since the name 'Panoni' appears there on an 1827 version of Captain Herd's chart.

Young at that stage sometimes acted as pilot in the harbour, a function that was also undertaken by John Martin, who, in romantic circumstances and in Maori fashion, married 'Maori Kate', as we have seen. Martin had in 1832 acquired what he judged at that time to be 45 acres at Omapere (or A Mau Purrie, as he called it) and was settled there with his 'housekeeper Kate'. But sadly, on survey, the 45 acres turned out to be only 10.[4] Martin was later recognised as the official pilot, and accordingly in 1838, as already mentioned, he purchased the South Head, Araiteuru, 53 acres, and erected a flagstaff on it 'which I use for hoisting Signals to Shipping to direct them in taking the Bar'. Old Land Claims Commissioner F.D. Bell, in his 1863 report, recommended that this site be reserved, as it now is.[5]

Markham arrived at Kohukohu when negotiations for its purchase from Wharepapa, Tarewarewa and others were in their early stages. Wharepapa, by the way, was a name that a number of Maori chiefs took to celebrate the building of their first wooden house, as opposed to the nikau houses of their earlier days. Wharepapa means wooden house. Wharepapa's given name was Tohukakahi. One Oakes, who had travelled with Markham, had possession of Clark's house, which had been sold to Maning by Fishwick. Maning himself was present and did not impress Markham, who refers to him pleasantly as 'a double faced sneaking Thief' and 'a low minded savage'. Surely the illustrious author of *Old New Zealand* would turn in his grave if he knew of this affront. One Kelly was also there, and a gaggle of drunken sawyers, who obligingly went outside to fight, leaving their pork, potatoes and grog to the hungry Markham.

A man given to hasty judgements, Markham suggests that Maning was even then up to some shady deal to do Oakes out of the property. Oakes apparently had a lease of it from Wharepapa for six months, of which only two remained, but his intention to buy was being thwarted by a want of funds and the machinations of Maning and Kelly. These two did in fact succeed in acquiring the land, to the chagrin of Oakes. Purchase price, two 170-pound casks of tobacco, one 25-pound keg of gunpowder, a double-barrelled pistol and some lead. The 50-odd acres of land on which the town of Kohukohu was later located had a depth of 875 yards, and extended north from the Waihoura Creek for about 240 yards. Here was Clark's house, and later Russell's and Yarborough's. The Old Land Claim Plan, No. 65, defining this land, shows a bridge over the stream. This would be the famous Kohukohu stone bridge. The plan was made prior to 1862.

It seems that McDonnell and G.F. Russell, at Horeke, did all they could to prevent this purchase 'as they did not see the use of Rivals in the River'.[6] Kohukohu did, in fact, damage Horeke as a timber and trading base, since it was some miles down the River, and in a position to intercept incoming vessels. At that time Kohukohu was a shipping point for the timber brought down from the Mangamuka by the Maning and Kelly crew, and the brig *Amity* was loaded there during Markham's visit. Russell, recognising the potential of Maning's site, bought the property three years later, when Maning shifted down the River to Onoke, near Whirinaki, and this, perhaps, was the beginning of Kohukohu's career as a commercial centre. From here it grew, later in the century, to be the largest town on the River, and at one stage the third largest north of Auckland. But there was no sawmill at Kohukohu until 1879, when a Sydney firm, Greenfield and Stewart, built a large mill there, which in 1881 was taken over by Yarborough and Andrewes, as the Hokianga Sawmill Company.[7] Until then, only squared logs — baulk timber — and spars, were exported from Hokianga, but a little sawn timber was produced at Webster's water-driven mill on the Wairere Creek, near Horeke. Pit-sawn timber was, of course, available for local use.

New Zealand historians are indebted to both Earle and Markham for their accounts of life on the Hokianga, since together they describe the beginnings of European commerce there, and its remarkable progress over a period of a little over five years. And although many of Markham's uninhibited comments are coloured by his prejudices and his poisonous tongue, they do depict the social and commercial life of the harbour in a way that few of the more conventional commentators have. Where missionaries and their sympathisers dismissed Maori-European unions briefly as 'fornications' and so on, Markham observed, 'All the Sawyers live with the Native Women. In fact it is not safe to live in the Country without a Chief's daughter as a protection as they are always backed by their Tribe and you are not robbed or molested in that case; they become useful and very much attached if used well, and will suffer incredible persecution for the Men they live with.' This was probably fair comment, in spite of its faintly chauvinistic flavour. But he does concede that the mother and father of the 'bride' demanded gifts as the price of their daughter's compliance, and Markham himself quickly qualified as an expert in such transactions.[8] But in his case these liaisons were considerably more transient than most. As a result of this social phenomenon few of the present inhabitants of Hokianga, apart from recent or fairly recent immigrants, are without a proportion of Maori blood, large or small.

By this time, the Wesleyans had made some progress in

the conversion of the Maori people, particularly in the upper harbour. On a trip up the Mangamuka with Poynton, a sawyer working at Kohukohu, Markham observed about eleven others living there, and about twenty Europeans altogether. Poynton had land up there, between Totara Point and Tutekehua. Well up the River, apparently above the present Mangamuka bridge, 'the Native Settlements became thicker. They are all Missionaries as they call the Christians'. He records having seen ten or twelve canoe-loads going down the River on Saturday afternoon to Mangungu, to be ready for the Sunday service. Some had Bibles. Very observant, if deficient in other respects, Markham describes the prolific gardens of kumara, taro, maize and potatoes, and remarks on the peach trees bearing fruit. These were a feature of the Mangamuka district, growing wild until recent years. He also noted, and sketched, the *whata,* or storage places. Then, having in a burst of generosity presented his temporary Maori wife with a handkerchief for her services, and her parents with a shirt and a box of matches, he returned to Kohukohu.

Markham comments on the deterioration in the health and general living conditions of the Maori people, arising from the use of European clothing and to the recently adopted practice of living on the flats and near the water, instead of on the hills. This social change is confirmed by other observers, and was due, presumably, to a diminution of local tribal warfare and a wish to be close to the shore for trading purposes. On ill-health he writes, 'Another cause in my opinion for the prevalence of Consumption arises from their Blankets as I have seen a Man with three Blankets on almost all Summer, but a distant friend came, he gave him a Blanket, a relation came, he gave him a second, and when the Winter set in, He was ill from Cold, as he was worse provided for then than he had been in the Summer. They use them at all times for Clothing instead of keeping them for bed, and the Wind in the Winter blows through them.'

Trade was very brisk. Vessels came up the harbour and bought and salted as much pork as they could get at £3 or £4 a ton, selling it at Sydney or Hobart at £60. Similarly, potatoes bought at 12/- per ton were sold at £12. Up the Waihou River, an old double-barrelled gun could buy five large pigs. The bounteous nature of the Maori economy was amply demonstrated at a *hakari* or feast put on by Moetara at Pakanae, which Markham attended, and where, to his satisfaction, he found his temporary wife from Mangamuka. But her subsequent 'infidelity' led to her dismissal and the installation of a more permanent volunteer, 'Arungher'. The function was attended, so he says, by '3000 to 4000 New Zealanders all armed and scattered about'. There were 4000 bags of potatoes stacked in a line like a wall — about £2000 worth at Sydney, and these sustained the company throughout three days of haka by all the armed men and less violent but equally rousing performances by the women. Moetara's solitary horse was ridden by all those sufficiently courageous, some of whom had never before seen such a creature, and were 'thrown in every direction'. The horse, we are told, had been the purchase-price paid by Oakes to Moetara for 600 acres of land at Pakanae, but Markham, uncharitable as ever, voiced his doubts as to the integrity of the transaction with 'that griping Thief'. However, the Old Land Claim Commissioners, after 1840, approved Oakes' claim for 300 acres there — the first purchase at Pakanae.[9] All claims for purchases of land from the Maori prior to the Treaty of Waitangi, when Great Britain assumed power and Government in New Zealand, were examined by Commissioners, who determined the integrity of the purchase and the amount of land to be granted to the claimant.

Moetara's feast was in honour of one 'Apee', a chief of Waima, to whom he presented fifty gallons of rum and two elaborately carved and decorated war canoes, each sixty feet long. Truly an open-handed and munificent chief, this Moetara, and one who had plainly capitalised in a very short time on his commercial contacts with the outside world. His magnificent party was surely a triumph of organisation, and demonstrated a talent for this sort of thing that remains with the Maori people to this day. Markham's appreciative account of the women's dance is perhaps his best piece of descriptive writing, and merits quotation in full: 'The third and last day we had a scene very different, Eighty Women dancing a Slow Monotonous Step, but graceful movements of the Arms ... I never saw a finer set of Women or Girls in an Opera Ballet. They were in two divisions Moyterra's Tribe, and the Tribes about the Heads, and also Apee set, their Visitors, Forty in each division, Ten in each row, two lines advancing about two inches a time and two lines retrograding. Naked to the Middle and using the Arms with slow but graceful Movements, the People on the Ground keeping up a Monotonous Chaunt in good time. ... All the Chiefs Daughters danced it, and no Slave Girl was allowed to enter the Ranks. It lasted for hours; till the sun set they must not eat; ... they kept it up till sun Down, but the last few hours one Division sat down for half an hour, and they relieved each other; some of the women had flowers in their hair and even Combs as the European fashion of dressing the Hair is very prevalent, and some of the Women were nearly as fair as Europeans ....' Marmon told Markham that this dance was the *kanikani* and was religious. This, apart from the feasting, ended the three-day gathering, which had also included the scraping of the bones — the *hahunga* — of the eleven chiefs who had been killed at the fight at Motukauri in the previous year.

Returning to Kohukohu, Markham found a furore in progress arising from Maning's purchase of the place. Wharepapa, the prior claimant to ownership, had been satisfied, and probably Tarewarewa, but three others had appeared. One named Rivers announced that he would burn Maning's house down if he were not paid, and based his claim on the fact that he had been shot in the thigh on the land, and this had never been avenged. He settled for two new shirts and five pounds of tobacco. Another claimant's father had been killed there, and for this, recompense to the tune of a hoe, a spade, a shirt and five pounds of tobacco was demanded and paid. The father of the third man to claim payment had formerly set his rat-traps on the land — a valid claim in Maori terms. The Maori rat, or *kiore,* was 'more like a field Mouse,' as Markham explains, and was certainly a luxury item of food. The rat-runs were recognised as personal property, and this issue and the others having been determined, Maning was apparently possessed of an unblemished title.

There is no doubt that at this stage the Reverend William White and Thomas McDonnell exerted considerable influence over the upper harbour Maori, since they were demonstrably the European *rangatira,* or chiefs, in the River. White's influence was enhanced by his very close association with the Maori people both in religious and practical matters, and the success the Wesleyans were achieving in religious conversion. McDonnell's qualifications were rather more materialistic. Markham tells a story about the conversion of the old chief Matangi, mentioned earlier, whom he describes as being formerly warrior, murderer, cannibal and thief. Matangi went to White on three occasions, firstly with cancer of the lip, then with a swelling of the head and lastly with loss of sight. The implication is that White cured, or at least alleviated these horrendous symptoms, since the chief 'at last ... came to read, and write, and cipher: he had several Wives, he had not seen or spoken to his first Wife for years'; but, as a measure of his newly-gained religious fervour, Markham explains with his customary delicacy, he returned to that 'Beastly Old Hag, ... now a thoroughly changed Man ...'.

And so, after four months on the River, Markham left for the Bay of Islands, giving his darling 'Arungher' a garnet ring (rejected by an earlier love) as a token of his somewhat inconstant affection. Arungher was the woman who had replaced his earlier paramour, 'Awattie', dismissed, as he primly asserted, for infidelity. But judging from his own account, the moral stature of both was probably immeasurably superior to his own. He did momentarily contemplate taking Arungher to the Bay with him, but on sober reflection decided against it, correctly assessing the dubious wisdom of revealing such a relationship to the missionaries there. He finally settled by paying the weeping Arungher off for her devotion with his sheets, three blankets and a gown. Not an admirable character.

Many pitfalls await a settler among an alien race, which originate with his imperfect knowledge of its customs, particularly those relating to marriage, underlying which are, for him, unknown perils. The sad case of Harry Pearson demonstrates this. Harry may have been at Hokianga since the mid-1820s according to his own evidence, but he does not appear to have purchased land until 1835, by which time he had apparently accumulated sufficient capital, that is £160-6-6, to purchase two areas in the Mangamuka district totalling, by his own account, 2080 acres.[10] Here he had the company of 'the only Daughter of an Extinct Tribe ...'.[11] Unfortunately for Harry, her sister was married to Rangatira — Moetara's 'bloody minded Brother' in Markham's words — but she died, leaving Rangatira in the market for a new wife. Now, since in Maori custom a man had freedom of access to his wife's sisters, Rangatira exercised his rights to the ultimate extent, and by a trick lured Harry's woman away from him to Pakanae, where she was kept prisoner for more than a month. But she, having been with Pearson for four years, since about 1830, was in no mood to stay with Rangatira, and escaped back to Pearson at Mangamuka. He then unwisely indulged in a carousal away from home, leaving his wife unprotected. Impressed by Harry's promise to shoot him on sight if he appeared at Mangamuka, Rangatira had apparently been waiting for an opportunity of this sort, and whisked the woman away by stealth while Harry was in his cups. So the local law prevailed, and in due course the woman became Rangatira's wife. As Markham tells us, Pearson was the son of Major Doubleday of the Durham Militia, who had been exhorting the missionaries to influence his son to return home, to no avail. It was Pearson's apparently unquenchable thirst for liquor, which had brought him to Hokianga, and now, for the same reason, he had landed himself in this sad predicament.

Taking leave of Markham, we note his estimate of some seventy European settlers on the River in 1834, mostly sawyers, with a sprinkling of missionaries and mission workers — and McDonnell and his minions. The twenty living up the Mangamuka, then, may have been the largest concentration of Europeans. This would have been due to the heavy growth of kauri there, close enough to the River to be easy to get out, and with a strong tide to take it down to Kohukohu. The remaining settlers were distributed down the River, mostly on the east or south-east side.

It may appear strange that at this stage, *circa* 1834, the concentration of European activity in timber industry was occurring some twenty miles up the harbour, at Horeke and Kohukohu, and in the Mangamuka, Orira and Upper Waihou rivers. Although a few years later there was some activity on the west side of the harbour, in the Waireia River locality, opposite Whirinaki, a reluctance to settle in this area was probably due to the unhappy experience of Nimmo and his partners in 1832 at Motukauri, following the grounding of the *Fortitude*. In early times, the Rarawa people there do not appear to have been much involved in trading or other relationships with Europeans, and there were still problems with the Maori people relative to these west-side claims as late as 1860.[12]

Up the harbour a few miles on this side, McDonnell claimed to have purchased land at Motukaraka in the early Thirties, which he later sold to the New Zealand Company, but later still this, with much other land he claimed, reverted to the Crown. Dispute of every kind surrounded this land,[13] and, indeed, much of the many tens of thousands of acres he claimed to have purchased in Hokianga and Kaipara. He was still arguing the point with the Government over his land claims twenty-five years later, and in 1856 had petitioned Parliament concerning them.[14] He asserted that Papahurihia, the Maori seer of Waima, had stolen £15000 worth of spars from his Motukaraka land, at the instigation of 'unprincipled Europeans'.

Further upstream on that side, in the Mangamuka above Kohukohu, Poynton was located at Totara Point, where Bishop Pompallier's monument now stands. Markham informs us that he had been transported to the New South Wales penal settlement for his membership of the patriotic 'rebel' Irish organisation, the 'White-boys', but he was certainly a sound and reliable settler at Hokianga. Cochrane was located further up the River. Both were well established in 1834, and one Robert Hunt claimed to have purchased 3000 acres in 1830 with a boundary on the Mangataipa Creek, at the north end of the gorge. But after the Crown's assumption of the sovereignty of New Zealand in 1840, he took Government land scrip in lieu of this to the value of £2260.[15] After 1841, when the seat of Government was transferred from the Bay of Islands to Auckland, many claimants of land in Hokianga took scrip in this way. In effect, they surrendered their land to the Government, in exchange for paper which entitled them to select Government land elsewhere to the same value. These people rightly believed that land at or near the new capital would be more profitable than their Hokianga property, and there is little doubt that a large incidence of these transactions at Hokianga contributed to depressed conditions there. Indeed, the trade in timber and spars was even at that time declining. Poynton also took scrip for his land.

Other settlers in the Mangamuka in the early Thirties were Cassidy, Henry Pearson of the unfortunate marital difficulties, and Mitchell, adjacent to Cochrane, at Rahurahu. All these purchased land, but Hunt did not pursue his claim. Two Wrights, a Joseph and a J.W., also co-incidentally purchased land here in 1831, Joseph a modest twenty-five acres and J.W. an ambitious 1000, for which he later took scrip to the value of £1500. And, of course, there were speculative purchases in the River by McDonnell and Russell.

A notable settler in the adjacent Orira River was Thomas Styles, and there for a while he was in partnership with C. Harris.

In 1834, Markham visited him at Orira during his work on the construction of the ninety-ton schooner *Industry,* which a year or so later figured in a dramatic incident in the harbour. This land was at the mouth of the river adjacent to Marmon, with whom he was subsequently involved in a fight which led to his death. This mournful occasion arose from a dispute at Mangungu over a proposal by missionaries and some chiefs to prohibit the sale and consumption of liquor in the harbour. Davis describes the event leading to Styles' death: 'In a drunken brawl, one of them named Thomas Styles, received a blow, which, together with the poisonous effect of his excesses brought him to the margin of that great precipice that divides time from eternity.' A difficult way to say that the blow nearly killed him, which it ultimately did, upon which Davis, still as lavish with his words, remarked that, 'The poor fellow bid farewell to earthly scenes twenty-four hours after he had received the fatal blow.'[16] In 1834, Alexander Thomas (or Thomson) purchased 1800 acres of land in the Orira, also adjacent to Marmon, which the Government later acquired for the payment of scrip. One Samuel Egert, known as Dutch Sam, was also a boat-builder in the Orira. His land was alongside Styles', and at Rawhia, the peninsula between the Orira and Waihou Rivers, lived our redoubtable friend Jacky Marmon on his 523 acres. This he ultimately got title to after plaintive appeals and a bitter struggle with the Government. It was he, incidentally, who delivered the 'fatal blow' that laid Tom Styles low.

In the Waihou itself, Captain Young of Koutu purchased 640 acres in 1833, but he later exchanged this for scrip. It was on this river too, that Nimmo, McLean, Nesbitt and Gillies had first settled in 1827, sawing timber and making oars at Tarawaua, which, as near as we can locate it, was at the place now called Rahiri. McDonnell and Russell, as might be expected, also had land in this locality, and about their activities and those of Raine and Ramsay at Horeke we already know.

Apart from the mission station at Mangungu, no purchases of land appear to have been made prior to 1835 between Horeke and the Waima River, where, in 1831 Edward Fishwick and his partner David Clark, lately superintendent of the Horeke shipyard, purchased 1200 acres at Matakaraka, (on the opposite side of the harbour to Motukaraka). However, Clark died in that year, and apparently in the absence of any beneficiaries likely to object, Fishwick took this over as he had Clark's house at Kohukohu. But in the 1840s he got £1200 in scrip for the land, a substantial sum in those days. In 1831 he also purchased land in the Waima with Captain J. Stewart, the notorious participant in Te Rauparaha's destruction of the South Island pa Kaiapohia, and the massacre of its defenders.

We have already mentioned Koutu — Koutumongero, or One Tree Point — the name deriving from the gallows-tree on which slaughtered cattle were hung. In 1831, Young had stocked the land with sheep and cattle, but only the cattle thrived.[17] The sheep would have been fair game for the local dogs. Opononi and Omapere have also been dealt with, and so we come to the end of the purchasers of land before 1835 — only some twenty or so, including the speculators McDonnell and Russell — and nearly half of the transactions involving Mangamuka land. There were occupiers of land, and workers, mostly sawyers, present too — about fifty if we accept Markham's total of seventy all told — many at Kohukohu, which, as we know, Maning and Kelly got possession of about 1834. Although there had been some sixty-odd purchasers of land in the harbour prior to 1840, it was the pre-1835 people who were the pioneers of the timber industry here. All this, many thousands of acres, had been acquired solely for the timber on it, with no regard at all for the value of the land itself, and to this, in no small way, Hokianga owes some of its present problems. A tabulation of the Old Land Claims, that is, claims to land purchased before 1840 by Europeans, will be found in the Appendices.

8. Religion and Politics

Into the tidal estuary of the Waima River flow two major streams. From Taheke, the upper limit of the tidal waters, some twelve miles up from the harbour, the Punakitere penetrates some twenty miles inland, and probably drains more land than any other Hokianga river. Below Taheke, the Waima itself turns at Moehau and loses itself westward in the forested grandeur of the Waoku plateau, only a few miles from the west coast valleys of Taita and Waimamaku.

In the valley of the Waima stirring events occurred, some, such as the invasion by the Roroa people from the west, only dimly remembered. It was said the invaders killed so many that the bodies dammed a stream. The first drama to be documented occurred in March 1828, when two great chiefs went to their deaths.[1] From the commercially oriented Bay of Islands had come Tiki, the sole remaining son of the lately deceased Pomarenui, the Ngatimanu war chief slain at Pirongia in the King Country in 1826. Tiki's errand, however, was strictly a business one, but he had no better luck than his father. He was looking for pigs for trade with whalers at the Bay, and at Waima he found some which he appropriated without reference to their owners. In spite of Tiki's considerable support the outraged pig-owners reacted violently, and at the end of this episode eight men lay dead. These included Tiki himself, who had no-one left at the Bay to avenge him but the prestigious Ngatimanu chief Whareumu, Pomare's kinsman. So a little reluctantly Whareumu led a party to Waima, where the initially peaceful negotiation ended when a boy with the party fiddled with a loaded musket which discharged accidentally, killing a woman and a child. The woman, said in some versions to be Whareumu's wife, was apparently related to the Waima people, and her death was followed at once by another shot which wounded Muriwai — a wound from which he later died. General fighting now erupted, in which Whareumu himself died from multiple wounds.

Much to-ing and fro-ing ensued. Some of the Anglican

missionaries at the Bay, very alarmed at the possible effect on them of a war arising out of this, came over with the Bay chiefs Rewa (Maanu) and others to mediate if possible. There they found Pi, the Waima chief, and Wharerahi, Rewa's brother, already in conference on the matter, and a potentially dangerous situation petered out in talk, with only some legitimate ritual plunder by Whareumu's people. The issue was essentially one that had been precipitated by Ngatimanu people, a tribe tolerated at the Bay by Ngapuhi, but now, with the loss of their prestigious chiefs Pomare and Whareumu, they had little effective leadership. There was thus no issue as between the two great Ngapuhi groups at Hokianga and the Bay of Islands, and there is little doubt that this accounted for the relatively peaceful outcome of the affair.

Strangely, the death of Whareumu had been accurately prophesied by Hongi Hika as he lay dying at Pupuke, Whangaroa. After his attack on the Ngatipou people there late in 1826, he had pursued them through the Otangaroa valley and into the Mangamuka. Here, at Oporehu, at the fight known as Hunahuna, he received a chest wound from the effects of which he died on 6 March 1828. Among his last utterances was a prophecy that Whareumu would not survive him by more than a week. And so it proved to be.[2]

Waima, the stronghold of the Mahurehure hapu of Ngapuhi, was an ancient settlement, named Waimatuhirangi, it is said,[3] after a place in Hawaiki, the traditional homeland of the Maori. Moehau, another village close by, was also named for an ancestral home. But Waima was shortly to be the centre of a strange new belief — an amalgam in Maori terms of the ancient and the modern, and this brings us back to 1834, when the effect of this cult on events was to be felt.

The first of the many Maori prophets and teachers, the forerunner of Te Ua, Te Kooti, Te Whiti, Rua and others, was Papahurihia.[4] He appeared at the Bay of Islands in about 1833, where he seems to have got a rudimentary knowledge of Christianity from an Anglican missionary source, possibly John King, at Te Puna. There was some confusion as to whether Papahurihia was the name of his cult, or his own name, but it seems that the cult was called Te Nakahi (the snake) for the supernatural serpent who was supposed to visit him and inspire his teaching. In 1834, after disseminating his new faith successfully among his people at the Bay, he moved to Hokianga where he became known as Te Atua Wera — the hot god. Anglican and Methodist missionaries observed his success with some alarm. His doctrine, borrowed from Jewish, Christian and Maori notions and put together with ingredients of his own devising, clearly appealed to his people, to the detriment of both the mission organisations. The recognisable elements in the doctrine, the serpent and hell-fire, were obviously Judaic, but the delights of his heaven, such as guns, sugar, flour and ships — 'there too murder and sensual pleasure reign' — were certainly not those favoured by the missionaries.

A strange, enigmatic element of Papahurihia's teaching, apparently of his own invention, was described by Father Servant, of the later Catholic mission in Hokianga. 'He says that Tanakahi has compared the heretics to aotea's tree; this tree is placed in a straight line to which another tree leads placed along a curved line which begins at the foot of the straight tree. This tree is called the judgement tree. At the end of the curved tree are the heretical missionaries, in prayer; they are taking the path that leads to Satan's fire; the sound of the men of the fire is heard. Tanakahi, the new god, passes under the curved tree and goes to stir up the eternal fire; then he climbs the straight tree the top of which touches the sky; the heretics also try to climb but, when they think they are reaching the sky, the sky flees above them and they fall back into the abyss.' A gloomy prospect indeed for unbelievers. Father Servant, seemingly unmoved by the suffering of the 'heretics', was certainly not concerned that their fate might also overtake his own flock.

Papahurihia was apparently a competent ventriloquist, who devised miracles and customarily called up a spirit at night which communicated with him by whistling. All his services were conducted at night. His followers were called Hurai, perhaps a corruption of 'Jew', and, together with the later wiles of 'Popery' he was, according to the Methodist missionary W. Woon, a thorn in the Wesleyan flesh at Hokianga. In the course of time, and as Te Atua Wera's influence grew, the Hurai became an increasing nuisance in the River, and in 1837 initiated a minor war. But in the meantime, strange occurrences were afoot in the eastern Pacific, which cast Mr Busby and the Anglican missionaries into a flurry of consternation.

Since the Anglican church was a creature of Imperial statute, it is not surprising that it was closely involved in Imperial politics in New Zealand, and this element of its activities appeared in the furore surrounding the pretensions and actions of one Charles Phillipe Hippolytus de Thierry. By his own account de Thierry was a baron of the Kingdom of France,[5] but now a British subject. His father, Charles Antoine Thierry de Laville had, prior to 1798, been attached to the court of Louis XVI, and had been obliged to leave France in haste to evade the consequences of his unwise support for Louis and his Queen, Marie Antoinette. In 1819 his son Charles married the daughter of an English clergyman and was himself an Anglican, despite the later general and horror-stricken belief in New Zealand that he was an emissary of 'Popery'. In 1820, when studying at Cambridge for a degree, he had the misfortune to meet the Bay of Islands missionary Kendall who was then in England assisting Professor Lee in the reduction of the Maori language to writing. And with him were the Bay chiefs Hongi Hika and Waikato.

A strange, altruistic and idealistic man, de Thierry had ambitious plans that were by no means impracticable, but were beyond his own capacity, financial and practical, to achieve. He was interminably beset by creditors, but he had an over-riding ambition — to personally civilise and govern native tribal people and to mete out justice to them as their ruler. To this end, so he claimed, he entrusted Kendall with about £8-9000 in goods and money to purchase land in New Zealand, which would be the nucleus of the Kingdom he proposed to establish there. This may not have been as preposterous as it sounds, since in the early 1820s the Hokianga Maori could have been receptive to such a proposal, had it been executed with an impressive show of European organisation, and a supply of the goods coveted by the Maori people there. Be that as it may, Kendall on his return did obtain for de Thierry a deed of conveyance from the chiefs Muriwai, Patuone and Nene, for 40,000 acres of land on the east side of the Hokianga somewhere between Mangungu and Rangiahua, on the Waihou River. The price was a modest 36 axes, and therefore mystery will evermore surround the ultimate fate of the £8-9000. The most credible, if uncharitable explanation is that Kendall's friend Hongi Hika appropriated it to purchase muskets at Sydney on his return to New Zealand. Muskets in quantity he certainly purchased there, but there never has been a satisfactory explanation of the means by which this transaction was financed. Both Kendall and Hongi were long dead, of course, before de Thierry got to New Zealand and was confronted with the dubious nature of his land purchase. Muriwai was also dead.

It was some fifteen years after his meeting with Kendall in England that de Thierry found himself in some sort of condition to claim his New Zealand kingdom. In the meantime he was happy in the belief that all he had to do was raise enough capital to get here in appropriate style and initiate the necessary action. But first he turned his attention to other matters. One of these was his proposal to cut a canal through the isthmus of Panama in order to shorten the distance between the Atlantic and Pacific oceans, and particularly to his New Zealand estate. Time, of course, has proved this to be an eminently practical proposal, but it was derided then. So, thwarted by his own limitations and depleted finances, and the scepticism of the governments he consulted on the matter, the disappointed de Thierry set off from Panama in June 1835 for New Zealand and Hokianga. However, he was not a man who was ever without dreams, and another overtook him when he broke his journey at the Marquesas Islands, to the north-east of Tahiti.

If de Thierry failed in many respects it could not be said that he was wanting in persuasive talents, since at Nukuhiva, apparently with astonishing ease, he induced the people to accept him as their king, and indeed they executed a treaty confirming this, which was widely circulated. But soon, after enjoying a short and uneventful reign at Nukuhiva, and appointing his public servants, he set off with a few followers for New Zealand, via Tahiti, never to return to his Polynesian kingdom. No constitutional problems appear to have arisen from this casual and involuntary abdication, and in its own time Nukuhiva apparently reverted quietly to its former status, although de Thierry had added King of Nukuhiva to his New Zealand title.

At Tahiti he was delayed for about a year and a half by chronic financial and other problems, of which he had many, but he employed some of this time in corresponding with Mr Busby and others at the Bay of Islands, acquainting them in some detail with his plans for New Zealand. But since it was not until November 1837 that he landed at Horeke to claim his kingdom, we must leave him at Tahiti and look at the furore he was causing in New Zealand.

The effect of de Thierry's proposals for this country as

received by Busby and others was alarm, even panic. Describing his plans for his kingdom here, and still optimistic about Panama, he had written,[6] 'For the prosperity of New Zealand I am about to cut the isthmus of Darien, and am establishing a line of ships from Panama which will bring the mails from England and the West Indies direct to New Zealand and the Colonies.' To the missionaries W. Williams and King at the Bay he wrote, 'I have declared the independence of New Zealand — that is, my own independence as Sovereign Chief, including all who may find it in their interest to benefit by it, and who may prefer wealth to poverty, honour to degradation, liberty to slavery, happiness to misery.'

All this was taken seriously here, and came at the wrong time, particularly for both the Bay and Hokianga missionaries, whose well-being and progress was at this point being threatened by Maori followers of Te Atua Wera.

Because of de Thierry's French background, and the increasing French interest in the South Pacific, Busby suspected an interest in New Zealand, which he clearly believed to be exclusively a British sphere of influence. Maori at Hokianga were also split by disputes between the Reverend White and McDonnell, and Waikato, the anti-mission chief at the Bay who had met de Thierry in England. Waikato was now damaging the mission cause at Hokianga, where, owing to his Hikutu tribal connections, he was influential, and Busby was convinced that he would receive de Thierry with open arms.

Those horrendous possibilities were all transmitted by Busby to Governor Bourke at New South Wales, who was unimpressed. 'This looks like insanity,' he had commented on first hearing of the Sovereign Chief's proposals.[7] He did not believe that de Thierry would ever land, but if he did, the Governor had no intention of opposing him with military force. Any such invasion, he ruled, would have to be repelled by Maori alone — if they wished to do so. Busby and the Anglican missionaries, frustrated and still convinced of the threat, did succeed on 28 October 1835 in rounding up thirty-four Northern chiefs to declare the independence of New Zealand, under the authority of 'The United Tribes of New Zealand'. At that stage, of course, the practical possibility of union among the warring tribes of New Zealand was exceedingly remote. However, eighteen other chiefs signed the document over the next four years, but a total of fifty-two was a small proportion of all those concerned. Of this diplomatic manoeuvre, Gipps, a later Governor of New South Wales, commented, 'This silly and unauthorised act was a paper pellet fired at the hero of an even more pretentious fiasco.'[8] From Hokianga, only Nene, Patuone, Taonui and Tawhai attended and signed the Declaration — a poor coverage indeed — but the thirty-four gathered at Waitangi, having declared their independence, did assume the title of United Tribes. They also stated that all sovereign power and authority in their territories was vested in them — a bold claim — and agreed to meet in congress once a year at Waitangi for the purpose of framing laws and for the dispensation of justice. A provincial council was to be established under their authority consisting equally of Europeans and Maori, and an ecclesiastical establishment was to be formed and funded from the sale of Maori land. A military force and local government were also provided for.

If this quaint proposal to deal with Maori (and European) problems only on European terms had in fact been adopted, European-missionary domination must have resulted, and perhaps this was the intention. But due of course to official disapproval, nothing came of it. Nor could it have done, since the very idea of chiefs who harboured intense rivalries, and in some cases enmities, acting together in this way in concert with Europeans, was an incredible conception. Busby and the missionaries may well have been aware of this, but now they at least had a document to flourish at intending intruders such as de Thierry. However, he did not arrive until two years later, and by this time no one took him seriously.

Now at Hokianga the tension between White and McDonnell was beginning to assume serious proportions. Rivals for influence over the chiefs of the River, they had contrived to maintain a wary friendship, but there was not room in that part of the harbour for two such domineering personalities, particularly since both for different reasons wielded much authority. The abortive 'Temperance campaign' was the last occasion on which the two saw eye to eye, and as another futile gesture this event demonstrates the total want of effective authority or even agreement among the polyglot population at Hokianga.

On 21 September 1835, McDonnell chaired a meeting at

Mangungu for the purpose of devising procedures to prohibit the importation and sale of 'ardent spirits' in Hokianga.[9] Drunkenness was not only giving rise to riotous behaviour, but as we have seen, later resulted in the death of Thomas Styles, and, it seems, others who drowned from boats while under the influence — the early Hokianga equivalent of 'drunk in charge'. A number of resolutions were adopted at this meeting. It was decided that the British residents and 'natives' should agree to the importation and sales of ardent spirits being abolished; that Captain Young, Mr Oakes and Moetara be appointed as examiners of all vessels entering the harbour, to acquaint masters of the local rules, and to prevent the landing of spirits. A committee was to be appointed to determine measures to be taken in terms of the decisions of the meeting, and it was decided that the vendor and purchaser of spirits if detected in the transaction, be fined £25 each. McDonnell had already let all his barrels of spirits run to waste, or so he said, and the meeting congratulated Maning, now living at Onoke, and Captain Clendon of the Bay of Islands, for their determination to do likewise. This, after sober reflection, they may or may not have done.

About 500 Maori, influenced by White and his Wesleyans, and 'a few of the colonists' attended this meeting, the Mangamuka chiefs, hosts to most of the sawyers, being particularly concerned. Then, full of virtue and indignation, a deputation went aboard a vessel shipping timber to Australia and demanded that its stock of grog be delivered up to them. The astonished captain was heavily outnumbered and had no alternative, so he surrendered a barrel of rum which the Maori took to the gangway and emptied into the sea, doubtless to the horror and consternation of the crew. With dubious legality, this activity continued, McDonnell organising searches of ships and the confiscation of their liquor supplies, discharging the barrels into the harbour. All this generated both zeal and resentment, but the trade did not abate, and it was in a drunken riot at Mangungu some time after these events that Styles lost his life protesting against this arbitrary inroad into his civil rights.

The impossibility of enforcing such a prohibition must surely have been apparent to most Europeans, since, apart from their relationships with their Maori women, rum was the only solace of the undisciplined and often violent sawyers and timber-workers. Because of this, supplying it was an extremely profitable business worth taking risks for. Busby, and later even the Anglican missionaries at the Bay, had no illusions about the high-handed futility of the proposal, and the action soon lapsed, but strangely Governor Bourke approved. One may be forgiven, perhaps, for suspecting he did so to frustrate Busby rather than to support McDonnell. As for him, he was a land speculator and timber-merchant, and could afford to sacrifice a little rum to be seen by all as the champion of virtue in the community. But he was soon to be confronted by White, whose influence over the Maori chiefs he could not match.

However, a few months later a minor drama was acted out at Horeke that gave McDonnell's reputation a considerable boost. On 30 November 1835 the schooner *Industry,* presumably that built by Styles in 1834, arrived in the River from Launceston, and was boarded by Captain Young acting as pilot,[10] who was quietly informed by the mate, William Keys, that the crew had thrown the captain overboard. Young thereupon decided to take the *Industry* up to Horeke to consult McDonnell, which he did, anchoring her off the house. Here, Young's account and McDonnell's differ as to who did what, but it seems that among them, Young, McDonnell and Maning succeeded in arresting the perpetrators of the mutiny and murder by inviting them to the house to make statements concerning what they claimed was the accidental drowning of Captain Bragg. The prisoners were put in irons provided by Francis White, the blacksmith, William's brother, and confined on the *Industry.* The intention was to send them to Tasmania for trial in charge of Henry Oakes and a Maori guard provided by the Reverend White from among his converts. At this point the strained cordiality that had characterised his relations with McDonnell became over-stressed and the fragile cordial element evaporated entirely. Perhaps White saw this minor triumph of the Additional British Resident as a threat to his own prestige. In any case he refused to have his converts exposed to the wickedness and temptations of Hobart. He also demanded that McDonnell extract from Oakes a debt of £55 owed to him before he allowed Oakes to leave, and when McDonnell refused White threatened to muster a Maori force to prevent Oakes' departure. In retaliation, McDonnell, by threatening the displeasure of the British Government, tried to get other Maori to help him with the prisoners.

The upshot of all this manoeuvring was that the *Industry*

The caves at Ara-i-te-uru, South Head. *(George Andrewes Collection)*

F. E. Maning, Judge of Native Land Court, in later life. *(Auckland Institute & Museum)*

Maning's house at Onoke, used as his Native Land Court. *(Auckland Institute & Museum)*

John Martin's farm at Omapere, circa 1850s. *(Auckland Institute & Museum)*

John Webster's Maori Journal, 1847, showing his house at Rangiora. *(Auckland Public Library)*

Pakanae, Hokianga, 1853. *(Australian National Library)*

Koutu Point, Hokianga, 1853. *(Australian National Library)*

finally got away to Hobart with the prisoners, and with one Piritaihana, whom McDonnell 'deported' for his adultery with Raumati's wife. This probably preserved his life, since Maori chiefs regarded adulterous wives and their paramours with a very jaundiced eye. At the trial it turned out that three seamen, Smith, Harris and Hibell, had seized Captain Bragg and thrown him over the side after a dispute, and Sherrin graphically describes the captain swimming hopelessly after the schooner until he drowned. It appears that the mate, Keys, tried to lower a boat to pick him up, but he was prevented, and was obliged to take the vessel to Hokianga, where the men intended to settle among the Maori. Instead, they were finally hanged at Hobart.

McDonnell did not fail to make the most of this escapade, and figured heroically in the *Sydney Colonist,* which at the same time castigated Busby for his failure to co-operate in the temperance fiasco. These comments were undoubtedly prompted by McDonnell, who incidentally had omitted to consult with Busby at all on the *Industry* affair. But McDonnell's reign was coming to an end — even Bourke could not stomach the sort of nonsense he was generating. He had reported the *Industry* incident to Bourke over Busby's head, indicating how much more effective he was in dealing with such matters than Busby. In fact the brief remainder of McDonnell's tenure of office appears to have been devoted to a vigorous exchange of acrimony and accusation between him and Busby, mostly through Governor Bourke.

In December 1836 the brief but eventful career of the *Industry* ended when she went ashore near Hokianga, where she was plundered and hacked to pieces, but the crew were unharmed. This, of course, was the customary and legitimate procedure in Maori terms, but McDonnell seems to have used it to support his dramatic appeals for military intervention at Hokianga, to prevent the land from being 'drenched with the blood of his countrymen'.[11] Such grossly exaggerated statements from Horeke abounded, but how much of the disorder there was due to his own and the Reverend White's antics he appears to overlook. In any case wholesale disorder threatening the lives of Europeans never occurred, although Hokianga in the 1830s was prolific in riotous incident.

9. The White-McDonnell Feud

Unfortunately the protracted and bitter disputes between the Reverend White and Lieutenant McDonnell, and between McDonnell and Busby, border on the tedious. They were an inevitable consequence of the grossly undisciplined and disorderly life-style in the Hokianga of the 1830s. This involved untrammelled commercialism by both the Maori and Pakeha, with the Wesleyan mission influencing the former but having only a token effect on the latter, and itself having ambivalent objectives due to its poverty.

McDonnell had originally come to New Zealand with a contract from the Royal Navy to supply spars, and a commission to act for some London business houses, but got so involved in land and timber speculation and general merchandising that he ultimately lost the spar contract. It was in these activities that he came into conflict with White, the Superintendent of the mission, who had been obliged, so that the mission could survive, to trade in timber, pork, and other goods, and to employ his people to a large extent in these activities. He was thus in competition not only with McDonnell, but with other Europeans similarly employed. He also used the mission saw-pits to produce plank from Maori timber, thus allowing them also to compete in the market.[1] While this did him no good at all among the Pakeha sawyers, it certainly contributed to his mana among the Maori, and may also have had some small effect in minimising the alienation of Maori land, although White himself may have profited from this activity.

McDonnell accused White, apparently with some truth, of engaging in trade himself, and of buying land through the mission carpenter, Stephenson, and through his brother Francis White, a lay preacher who had arrived from England in November 1835, to join the settlement. Also of having timber on his land cut by 'native parasites' for his own benefit. 'Unless steps are taken ... to curb the authority of this sinister and overbearing minister ... anarchy and bloodshed will be the consequence!' McDonnell declaimed with his usual wild exuberance — a prophecy of doom that he used constantly with little discrimination and less effect. And the situation did not improve when Pi, the chief of Waima, complained that White had acquired land from Tawhai that in fact belonged to Pi — an unforgivable transaction in whatever culture it may occur.[2] Francis and William also purchased land at Mata, adjacent to the Mangungu mission station, and built their house there.[3] McDonnell clearly saw White both personally, and in his professional capacity, as a threat to his own commercial well-being.

In the hope of abating this nuisance, McDonnell now claimed that White's activities merited an immediate investigation and persuaded Busby, as the British Resident, to attend a meeting with him, White and Maori chiefs at Waihou, which Busby did on 8 March 1836. But McDonnell failed to appear, on the grounds of his sickness, and demanded that Busby go to Horeke. Busby quite rightly refused, and the meeting lapsed without the examination of White's conduct that McDonnell, for whatever motives, deemed so essential.

Busby was constantly embarrassed by McDonnell's gravely exceeding his authority, which, in fact, was extremely limited. His expedition early in 1836 to the Ngatiwhatua district of Kaipara was probably one of his most spectacular indiscretions. Upon hearing, so he said, of a British subject held prisoner there, McDonnell proceeded to the harbour in the little Horeke-built *Tui,* and at once summoned the prestigious Kaipara chief Tirarau into his presence and demanded that the man be given up. It is not quite clear that there was such a man, but regardless, Tirarau complained to Busby of McDonnell's behaviour in the matter.

The prisoner could, in fact, have been a pretext to get McDonnell into the Kaipara, which was virtually a virgin kauri timber mine at that time. Having got in, he attempted to get Tirarau's consent to take possession of land there, and at once became embroiled in a dispute. He claimed he had bought all the kauri land along the Wairoa from the Ngapuhi chiefs Makoare Taonui of Hokianga, with whom he was on fairly good terms, and Titore Takiri of the Bay. These, he claimed, owned the land from an early conquest — presumably at Te Ika a Ranganui, in 1826. Failing with this, he proceeded to mark trees with a broad arrow, and maintained that these were to be taken in satisfaction of his contract with the Royal Navy, the wrath of which would descend on the Kaipara people if the trees were not made available. Local chiefs again complained to Busby at Waitangi, who soothed them and once more warned McDonnell against making this sort of inflammatory and quite absurd threat to gain his ends. He was also told to deal with the Kaipara chiefs, since Taonui, Titore, and Ngapuhi generally, had no claim to the land, having made no attempt to occupy it when they drove Murupaenga's people out.

Thus McDonnell was obliged to back down, albeit with a bad grace, accusing the missionaries of intriguing against him. He now said his main aim had been to find an entrance into a place where no European had ventured before, and this was such a dangerous undertaking, that, for his trouble, chiefs had granted him some unoccupied land.[4] This tricky sort of behaviour, repeated on many occasions, casts grave doubts on McDonnell's general integrity. In the upshot, upon the assumption of government by the British Crown, the Old Land Claim Commissioners were not impressed with his story either, and rejected his claim for 23,000 acres of Kaipara land.[5]

An interesting sidelight on this expedition is to be found in a report of about 1841 by Felton Mathew, Acting Surveyor in William Hobson's brand new New Zealand Government. 'The accident that befell the *Tory* at the entrance ... procured to the harbour of Kaipara a bad name ... the *[Tory]* came on a shoal, which was not laid down on the chart of Mr McDonnell where a clear channel was given instead ....'[6] So much for the Kaipara survey. And again, a note by Hocken in his Bibliography concerning McDonnell's survey of the Hokianga is no more reassuring. 'Lieut. McDonnell was a settler on the Hokianga, and was appointed Assistant-Resident at New Zealand under Mr. Busby. He published a very incorrect chart of that river, now of great rarity, whereby one or two vessels were wrecked.'[7] McDonnell's publicised reputation as a marine surveyor, dubiously earned, perhaps needs revision in view of these opinions.

Such characteristics as were shared by White and McDonnell were unfortunately all bad. Both were arrogant, unyielding, violent and acquisitive, and the chiefs, depending on who they considered could best further their interests, favoured one or the other, or remained neutral. Early in 1836 the conduct of both came under scrutiny. As we have seen, White survived the abortive Waihou meeting, but McDonnell's campaign against him in official places and dissension in his own camp finally bore fruit, and the Reverend N. Turner was instructed by the London Wesleyan Committee to go to New Zealand to conduct an enquiry into mission matters,[8] and to take over from White, which he did in April. The enquiry opened on 21 June with a District Meeting of all missionaries, and on allegations of mismanagement White was found guilty. Which was not surprising. He was a hard-working man himself, and undoubtedly a hard taskmaster, generally disliked by his staff. The three new stations he had established himself in the Waikato were evacuated, and this seems likely to have been a sop to the Anglicans at the Bay, who considered that White had poached on their territory. So White was in bad odour there too, and to some extent may therefore have been the victim of internal resentment and external politics. Another matter at issue was whether the land he purchased at Mata and which he claimed was his own, had been paid for with mission goods. Whatever the case, the Land Claim Commissioners later believed White and awarded the 462 acres at Mata to him.[9]

White was now *persona non grata* at the Mangungu mission, but McDonnell was determined to destroy him completely. With this objective, he assembled a hand-picked European committee to enquire into the allegations of immorality, which he had been making persistently against White since 1831. These involved rape of Maori women — an unlikely proposition — and adultery with various others, which, although White denied them, appear more likely. This committee had no legality and little credibility, due to its composition, and it obligingly and unhesitatingly found White guilty. As his biographer, Gittos, wrote, 'Out of the fourteen people on the committee four are known to have been employees of McDonnell and a further seven could have been or [had?] been numbered among the disgruntled Mangamuka sawyers. One of these, Pearson, was certain to have been against White. In respect of the remaining three, Oakes was clearly an enemy, Poynton was a rival religious influence and Fishwick was apparently an unprincipled adventurer.' These people found White guilty of 'loose and immoral conduct'.

Gittos comments further, 'If the merchants, adventurers, sawyers and sly-groggers of the Hokianga thought they had disposed finally of the troublesome William White, events were to prove them very much mistaken. If the mission brethren felt relieved at the departure of their turbulent brother and looked forward to a period of tranquility and peace they too were sadly mistaken.'[10] White left for Sydney on the *Martha* on 28 July and there gained the support of the New South Wales Wesleyan District Committee, which considered him to be a wronged man, and reported favourably to London on his case. In December he returned to Hokianga on the *Tui,* to find that McDonnell had been relieved of the position of Additional British Resident, following his resignation by letter of 27 July, which seems only narrowly to have preceded a notice of dismissal. The resignation was accepted without significant comment.[11]

Both these turbulent fellows now contrived to get involved in an unseemly armed confrontation — an incident that has been glorified with the name 'The Battle of the Plank', which could not have done the tattered reputations of either any good.[12] It will be recalled that in 1834 the *Brazil Packet* brought Markham to Hokianga. The captain, Crowe, later acquired a kauri forest in Moetara's territory near Pakanae, where he engaged sawyers to cut the timber and to stack it at Captain Young's place at One Tree Point (Koutu). At the end of 1836 Crowe called with his vessel to load the timber, but his sawyers refused to raft it out to his ship until a dispute was resolved on the interpretation of their agreement with him. So, in the spirit now firmly entrenched in New Zealand industrial relations, Crowe announced that he would load the timber whether they liked it or not. The sawyers at once appealed to the 'settlers' along the banks of the River — all sawyers, no doubt — who raised a force of about one hundred armed with muskets and swords, to foil Crowe. In an armada of small boats they then descended on Koutu where they paraded in military order and marched to the timber-stacks. Now this was a delicate situation, since Crowe had the support of Moetara and Rangatira — 'men of singular distinction' as Davis says — while the sawyers from up the River were under the protection of Nene and Patuone.

Thus, in effect, a confrontation loomed between the two most powerful groups in the harbour. Crowe, at his timber-stacks, was undoubtedly in mortal danger during the altercation that took place there, but Moetara's people, his allies, 'lingered with their arms in the immediate neighbourhood, refusing to interfere unless Crowe or some of his party were fired upon.' Observing this, the riverside army no doubt became painfully aware that it was operating in hostile territory, and that a battle might result in which they could get severely mauled. At last, therefore, they settled for burning Crowe's timber-stacks, a solution that probably appealed to the keen Maori sense of justice on both sides. They then re-embarked, and with their flotilla returned up the harbour. The timber involved was no doubt from land at or north of Pakanae, purchased by Crowe in 1835 but which later reverted to the Crown.[13] Crowe himself survived this episode by only six months or so, suffering the common fate of drowning in the River in May 1837.

How McDonnell got implicated in this abortive war is not clear. At this stage he had been divested of such nebulous authority as had been vested in him by his appointment, and White believed him to have been involved in the raising of the sawyer's army — perhaps in the hope of eliminating a competitor. Whatever the reason, White is said to have induced Nene to arrest McDonnell in order to send him to Sydney for trial for his complicity in the matter. But the ex-Resident, apparently aware of this, threatened armed resistance and Nene, who had been lying in wait for him at Horeke, discouraged by this turn of events, abandoned his ambush. And so the Plank furore lapsed without further hostilities.

The dust raised by this incident had scarcely settled when White's unrelenting righteousness got him embroiled in another row, this time involving the little *Tui.* The activities of this craft, which are obscure, convinced White that he was justified in placing it under arrest, on a charge that could well have been related to sly-grogging. On what authority White acted is not clear, but the identification of authority was never a matter that concerned White or his arch-rival very much. Again Nene co-operated and on 2 January 1837 he boarded the *Tui* with forty followers, and assaulted the captain. Poynton, on hearing of this, from up the Mangamuka came to the rescue with a force that apparently outnumbered White's, since he desisted in his attempt to take the vessel by assault.[14] White, who now had little or no authority, even at the mission, other than the impact of his own personality, apparently continued to see himself as the only fount of justice in the harbour.

The champion of his Maori friends to the end, White also

figured in an incident at Mangamuka which arose out of a grievance cherished by the sawyers in the River against Ihutai chief Tohukakahi, alias Wharepapa, who was alleged to have ill-treated some of their number. About forty of these therefore assembled with the object of chastising Tohu, and fully armed proceeded by boat to Mangamuka to give effect to this. Among them was Thomas Styles, captain of the *Industry,* later to die in the brawl at Mangungu at the hands of John Marmon, as we have seen. White, forestalling these vigilantes, preceded the expedition and advised Tohu to retreat into the bush to avoid bloodshed. This he did, so that when the sawyers landed, they 'made a furious assault upon the Pah,' but found it empty. Frustrated, they looted the place and carried off many slaughtered pigs, giving rise to the name The Battle of the Pork for this 'heroic onslaught on the herd of swine'.[15] No repercussions seem to have arisen from this action, which the Maori people would have regarded as legitimate retaliation.

A great deal of turbulence seems to have been generated among both Maori and Pakeha in the Mangamuka. In its early stages the year 1837 saw another skirmish there, this being due to the growing mana of Papahurihia, the Nakahi seer. Kaitoke was a Mangamuka chief much influenced by this cult, whose effects at this stage were being felt mainly in the Waima, Omanaia and Whirinaki districts. Nakahi was, of course, inimical to the Christian missions. However, adherents were located in all areas, and the Bay chief Waikato, with connections at Whirinaki, was one of them. He had recently been involved in a fracas at Busby's house at Waitangi over a claim he made to land at Whananaki, on the east coast, which was bitterly opposed. However, he did get some compensation out of this, among which were two muskets and some gunpowder. These he gave to Kaitoke, who, as a matter of religious duty, shot dead in cold blood two Christian converts, Rihimona and Matiu, at a service being held at Mangamuka. One gun appears to have had 'certain hierogliphics marked on it, the sanguinary meaning of which, if not fully understood by Kaitoke, was to be explained by the bearer of the weapon'.[16] The instruction for this ritual killing, no doubt.

At Waihou and Utakura, Patuone and Nene, converts themselves, promptly raised an army and proceeded with some missionaries to Mangamuka, where, on arrival at the pa they were met by a fusillade which killed one chief and wounded another.

The expedition returned the fire and stormed the pa, killing twelve of the defenders and capturing the rest, one of whom was Kaitoke himself, who was wounded. Much discussion now took place, and on the advice of Patuone, noted as a peacemaker, the survivors were released on condition that they departed from the district, and presumably left the newly-hatched Christians in peace. Kaitoke appears thereafter as a Whirinaki chief.

With these incidents, White's career as a missionary, or even as a missionary associate, as he had recently been, came to an end. He left for England on the *Lord Goderich* shortly afterwards to be present at the enquiry by the London Committee of the Wesleyan Missionary Society into the evidence on his behaviour in New Zealand. He was there for the best part of 1837 and 1838, and returned to New Zealand strictly as a businessman, as the Committee had ruled him to be unfit to take any further part in ministerial work. In arriving at this conclusion it had, in fact, to find its way along devious routes, and no verdict could have been delivered with much confidence. Allegations had to be proved or disproved in the absence of wholly credible evidence on matters long gone stale, particularly in the area of sexual offences. The Committee confirmed the charges of mismanagement and misappropriation of mission funds, but on the charges of sexual misconduct they came to no consensus, only recording sorrowfully that they could not 'disengage their minds from deep and painful surmises'.[17] An inevitable view, bearing in mind the statements of women who confessed to having had 'connections' with him. Some are alleged to have occurred in White's house — and in a privy, of all unlikely places — but the possibility of the frail ladies having been encouraged by one of White's many enemies to make these heart-rending disclosures could not have been ignored.

Dismissed from the mission, White and his wife Eliza returned to Hokianga on the *Coromandel* on 2 December 1838 and established themselves with Francis on their Mata land, adjacent to Mangungu mission station — an unwelcome presence indeed to the people there. White had many virtues. With astonishing energy and endurance he had in his term of office disseminated the Wesleyan faith from its origins in Hokianga into the Manukau and as far as the Waikato and Waipa districts, grievously offending the Anglican missionaries at the Bay in the process. Also, to the accompaniment of plaintive protests from his fellow missionaries he made the organisation largely self-supporting by inflicting manual toil on his colleagues, which they disliked intensely, and by timber and other merchandising and agriculture. He grew wheat both in the Waihou on Patuone's land, and at Pakanae with Moetara's co-operation, and whether it was these activities or his alleged predilection for Maori women which precipitated his downfall is an interesting question.

His adversary McDonnell also suffered sad reverses, and in the final analysis it seems that neither of them won their war. McDonnell was finally deserted by his factotum G.F. Russell, with whom he had engineered many a crafty land deal. Russell, observing the ideal site and thus the business potential of Kohukohu, purchased it from Maning in 1837.[18] Married to a relative of Nene's he was in a strong position and in view of his activities there, it is he who deserves to be known as the Father of Kohukohu. Although others were there before him, he developed and made good use of its potential — even to the extent of outbidding his former boss for his contract for Navy spars. The Maori called him piwakawaka — fantail — for his small size and his quick-moving ways.

The island of Motiti, lying in the mouth of the Mangamuka midway between Kohukohu and Mangungu, has a curious history. Its area is given by travellers variously as low as half an acre, and by Commissioner Bell as eight acres. In 1819 Marsden described it as a little village full of inhabitants, and in 1827 Earle saw it as heavily fortified and a repository for provisions and ammunition. Markham appears to contemptuously dismiss Earle's description, particularly as to fortifications, but says that Moetara 'carronaded' Motiti for three days 'some years back'. This could well account for the difference between his and Earle's descriptions, since such a small island would be likely to come out of a three-day bombardment considerably transformed in appearance. Referring to the incident, Markham says, 'He [Moetara] has three 12 pounders, and got some sawyers to mount them, and built platforms in his War Canoes.'[19] Since there were no sawyers in the harbour before 1827, and few even then, this bombardment probably took place about 1830. The island was certainly of little consequence when White purchased it from Matu, Tiro and Potae in 1835, or he would not have got it for £23.[20] Yet whereas three years before Motiti had had a mission school with fifteen pupils, the largest school, Mangamuka, had only thirty.[21] Earle's 1827 sketch shows the *Governor Macquarie* aground off Motiti. It appears as a place of importance, crowded with buildings and elevated storehouses which could scarcely have survived Moetara's assault. Today it is an insignificant sandbank, almost awash at high spring tides.

10. New Directions

By the end of the 1860s much of the easily accessible kauri timber land in Hokianga had been acquired by Europeans. Most of these people were not interested in the land itself, since only the timber on it had any value for them. This, of course, was in contrast to many land purchasers in other parts of New Zealand, some of whom were simply unabashed speculators, buying in anticipation of re-selling at a big profit. At the head of the harbour, in the Mangamuka, Orira and Waihou rivers, much timber-land was purchased, but when the timber was cut out there, as elsewhere in the River, the land seems to have been regarded by many of its owners as worthless. Therefore, when after 1840 the newly-fledged Government gave them the opportunity of accepting scrip for it, valid for the purchase of land in other places, many Hokianga owners were quick to respond. The Government needed land to subdivide and sell to new settlers at a profit, for revenue, but the Hokianga people wanted theirs somewhere else. Even at that time the spar-trade was declining, and there was no significant milling of timber in Hokianga. As it turned out, then, those who took scrip got the best of the bargain, particularly when they invested it in the new town of Auckland. But the Government got a lot of land this way, too, and was thus encouraged in later years to build roads to service it.

The dynamic William White acquired a good deal of land in many places, and claimed to have made many of these purchases to preserve the land from exploitation by 'wicked Europeans'.[1] Although he retained little of this, he and his brother Francis exchanged a considerable amount of it for scrip.[2] In spite of his fall from grace, White still preached and affected clerical clothing, and remained the implacable foe of the rapacious exploiters of Maori land, who were led by McDonnell.

Down the harbour, too, the title to much more Maori land had been extinguished. At Motukiore, opposite Kohukohu, Russell and Birch now had land, and in the Waima the crafty

Fishwick was well established, as we have seen. William Trusted and the Wesleyan mission were also investors in the River, with Thomas Cassidy, and the Baron de Thierry, of whom more later. Many more who had bought here later settled for Government scrip, including P.G. Tuite, Russell's storekeeper and accountant at Kohukohu. Also in the Waima were James Pearson and Alexander Chapman, Nicholas and Chadwick, Strout, Harrison and Gundry.[3] Historian R. Ross has reported a Dr Cook resident in Hokianga in 1835 who treated the Waima chief Pi for an ailment that Pi later claimed to have healed himself with a decoction of tanekaha bark.[4] Cook seems to have disagreed with Pi's unprofessional therapy, and claimed the land the chief had offered him in return for a cure. Sadly, however, without success, and perhaps Pi's refusal raised a point that some still consider to be valid — no cure, no pay. A strange place this, to find a qualified medical practitioner bargaining for land with his services, and he may well have been the Dr Cook who was later official surgeon to de Thierry's polyglot entourage, which entered the harbour with appropriate ceremony during this period.

On the Omanaia River, Montefiore's Grant, 416 acres south of Rawene, was the only approved purchase there which was not exchanged for scrip. No doubt the suitability or otherwise of a river for rafting out timber had a bearing on its value to timber men. For the time being, however, Whirinaki appears to have evaded the activities of timber-hungry Europeans, except perhaps for a purchase of 600 acres at Te Kaka Keketahi, for which no Grant was issued to the various claimants. The exact location of this land is obscure, but it was apparently inland from the Koutu peninsula, and may indeed have not been classifiable as Whirinaki land. It was from here that Captain Crowe obtained the timber that precipitated the Battle of the Plank.[5] Leef, with 58 acres at Opara, on the south head of the Whirinaki, and Maning, late of Kohukohu, on his 100 acres on the North Head, at Onoke, were the two *bona fide* settlers on the River between Rawene and Koutu.[6]

The people named in the places described in this and earlier chapters were, then, those who up to this time had been prominent in the European exploitation of Hokianga's timber resources. Of those owners who accepted Government scrip for their land, few remained here, and the Old Land Claims Commissioner, F.D. Bell, had some interesting things to say in his 1862 Report on this subject.[7] A large proportion of the scrip-money paid out was used for the purchase of allotments within the City of Auckland, which, he says, were in 1862 worth at least ten times the value of the scrip paid for them in 1844. As for Hokianga land at that time, it is likely, in view of the limited opportunities in the sixties, that the land was worth less than the scrip the government paid for it. In Hokianga upwards of £32,000 ($64,000) had been paid in scrip to landowners who had proved their claims. Yet in 1859, after surveys had been done, Bell could produce only 15,446 acres to which the Crown was entitled in return for its scrip payments. And since the higher of these payments had been at the rate of £1 per (estimated) acre of land — in a few cases more but in most less — the Crown should have got say, 35,000 acres in Hokianga, and was therefore nearly 20,000 short. This was undoubtedly due to gross over-estimation, deliberate or otherwise, of the area of their land by those exchanging it for scrip, at a time when the Government did not have the resources to check the areas by survey.

On the gloomy saga of the Hokianga scrip lands, Bell reported ruefully: 'An instance of the great misconception that often existed as to the area of the claims, may be given in the case of those situated in the Orira Valley at Hokianga, one of which (that of William and Francis White) has at various times been the subject of much public notice. In the Orira claim Governor Fitzroy granted £6,099 scrip to William White, £250 to J. Marmon, £1,825 to A. Thomson, and £1,000 to J. Anderson. I had the valley surveyed, taking in the land to the top of the hills and every acre comprised in the original boundaries, and the contents of the whole were only 3,871 acres; of which 1,280 had to be granted to Francis White ... leaving 2,591 acres for the public, to represent £9,174 of scrip given 15 years before.' This was a convoluted transaction involving a number of people and matters, but Bell concluded that had the true area been known at the time the scrip deal was made, William White would have got no scrip at all, and Francis only 796 acres instead of 1,280.

The vexed question of the ownership of Rawene was one which remained unresolved until 1858. Herd had purchased it for the New Zealand Company in 1827, but as a result of an inspection by William Wakefield in 1839 the Company decided that it was not suitable for its purposes and therefore did not enter a claim for it with the Old Land Claims Commissioners. Previously, on his visit to England, White had carried a message from chiefs interested in the land suggesting that if the Company did not want Rawene they would buy it back, or just repossess it. One reason for the chiefs' dissatisfaction was that the land had been conveyed to Herd by a deed signed by Muriwai, whereas the Tawhai and Pi families of Waima claimed an interest in it.[8] And, in fact, the land was lying unused, although later various people occupied parts of it until the Government resumed it in 1858. It was apparently land not granted to Europeans by the Crown, but the Maori title for which had been extinguished by Herd's deed.

In 1837, the ageing Samuel Marsden tottered into this unruly scene of unbridled rapacity, exploitation, violence and lawlessness. He came on the timber-ship *Pyramus,* entering Hokianga on 23 February. 'The sea broke awfully on the bar. The captain was much alarmed, as we had no pilot and were in great danger of being overwhelmed by the heavy, violent waves constantly breaking aboard the vessel,' wrote Marsden, but next morning it dropped anchor safely near Mangungu. From there Marsden travelled 'about forty miles by land and water' to Waimate. Probably up the Waima River to Taheke and thence by land, but his only interesting comment on his experience concerned the considerable evidence of literacy among Maori wherever he went.[9] He came at a time of tumult, since at the Bay of Islands two factions were spoiling for a fight. But in the Bay was HMS *Rattlesnake,* commanded by Captain William Hobson, and Marsden was more interested in a jaunt with him than in the local hostilities. So off he went on the *Rattlesnake* south to Cloudy Bay, visiting mission stations on the way, and from there went back to Sydney, never to return. But only three years later, Hobson himself did come back to the Bay, and having negotiated the Treaty of Waitangi, became New Zealand's first Governor.

However, the Bay and Hokianga missionaries had to live now with this disturbance, which developed into a war of sorts between Ngapuhi allies of Titore Takiri, of Kororareka, and those of the Ngatimanu, Pomare of Otuihu, near Opua. Some seven years previously Titore had ousted Pomare from Kororareka, and this festering grievance was undoubtedly the underlying cause of the trouble, but according to Polack,[10] the killing and devouring of a woman at Long Beach, behind Kororareka, precipitated open warfare. This continued in a half-hearted, desultory sort of way for about three months. The very considerable European population at the Bay was not molested, and at times some thirty ships lay at anchor there within view of the furious but fairly innocuous military posturing, which in the upshot seems to have resulted in only a handful of casualties. However, Busby, the British Resident, was seriously alarmed at the situation, and both the Anglican missionaries at the Bay and the Wesleyans at Hokianga were unhappy as to the outcome.

This was the last inter-tribal battle at the Bay, and it came to an end in June, when Hokianga parties arrived to join in, but, says Polack, they were 'sorely puzzled which party to join, as they were equally related to both parties'. This knotty problem appears to have suspended military operations, which apparently fell into confusion, and owing to a general want of enthusiasm by all concerned, a peace was patched up. Such were the involuted relationships between the Bay and Hokianga Ngapuhi, which even included Ngatimanu. At Mangungu the Reverend James Buller noted,[11] 'A large number of natives from Whangape passed by in nine canoes. They were wild and savage, most of them entirely naked.... A party from Titore's pah went by this morning, having come for reinforcements. Several of the tribes are going from this river to join the fight. Pi, Moetara, and the Wirinaki people are preparing.' Buller then goes on to tell us that the war at the Bay was terminated entirely owing to the efforts of his Wesleyan Maori converts — the sort of claim that should be regarded with serious reservations and which is common in much missionary literature. It will be noted also that no credit in the matter is accorded to the resident Anglican missionaries at the Bay, but there is in fact no hard evidence to suggest that either group influenced the situation significantly. Buller's account also gains no credibility from his grossly exaggerated depiction of the sufferings of Europeans involved, so we must perhaps make due allowance for the good impression that missionaries were eager to make on their readers and employers. In the words of Dr A.S. Thomson, in later years Surgeon of the 58th Regiment in New Zealand, missionaries 'magnified and widely circulated' accounts of disorder,[12] and this is certainly demonstrated here by Buller.

White's contact with the New Zealand Company in England

seems to have convinced him of the merit of its proposed system of colonisation for this country, but he later changed his views on this. Although he continued with his land and general dealing, it does seem that he had the interests of the Maori people at heart. He certainly exchanged his land for scrip in large quantities, but the Government got his land, and he no doubt had confidence that it was therefore in good, and not unscrupulous hands.[13] The Wesleyan mission, owing almost entirely to White's efforts, had extended its influence widely in Hokianga. A sketch of the harbour in a Parliamentary Paper of 1838 shows sixteen chapels. All of them, except three in the upper reaches of the Mangamuka and one in the Whangape Harbour, are on the eastern or north-eastern side of the River. Apart from Mangungu itself there are three in the Waihou, one in the Utakura, three in the Waima and three between Pakanae and the Heads — one near Opononi being called Oakes' chapel. And there is one inland from there, at Waimamaku. There is a note on the plan that the population (presumably of Maori in the harbour) is about 5,000 and that the banks of the Mangamuka, Waima, Waihou and Whirinaki are 'partially cultivated'. Significantly there are no chapels on the twelve miles or so of the east side of the River between Pakanae and the Waima.[14] On this stretch is Whirinaki, with its settlement then called Waitemata, a place where the Wesleyans failed to make much progress. But, with the opposite side of the harbour, it was soon to be captured by the Catholics. At Mangungu, the New Zealand headquarters of Methodism, Turner was in charge until 1839, when John Bumby took over. The work was now expanding southward, and a year later, when returning from there, poor Bumby suffered the normal demise of the times, being drowned off Tiritiri Island. At which point John Hobbs took over.

Mangungu in 1838 may well have been regarded as the focal point of law and order in the Hokianga, and indeed, a strange manifestation of this did occur there in May of that year. In the upper harbour a European wished to travel downstream, and embarked with two Maori in a canoe to do so. But some days later his body was found on Kakaho Beach, near Whirinaki. These seem to be the facts that agree in all versions.[15] Davis says that the man, Henry Biddle, embarked at Herd's Point (Rawene), and 'met his death owing to certain violent acts perpetrated by the two Maoris'. Ramsden said that Henry Biddle's head was held under the water until he drowned, but Marmon, unreliable on his own personal affairs, gives a detailed account that seems unlikely to have been fabricated. And, of course, he was closer socially and physically to the action and the people. The unfortunate man, he says, was Henry the stone-cutter, (probably Biddle is also correct) who had been working as a sawyer for Cochrane, at Mangamuka. Wishing to go down to the Heads, he set off for Kohukohu. At some stage of this journey he came upon two Maori in a canoe, a man and a youth, and persuaded them to convey him to Whirinaki. But when they reached Papakawau, they demanded payment, which Henry could or would not give them, saying that they should have raised that question when they were in Kohukohu. Then when a blanket was demanded Henry again refused, so the canoe was paddled ashore and he was killed by the youth, who battered his head with a stone while the man held him. This, said Marmon, was the first cold-blooded murder he knew of in Hokianga.

The body was found and taken to Mangungu, and the missionaries sent to Waitangi for Busby, who came and presided over a sort of jury or committee of chiefs and Europeans which deliberated on the case. Now, the man was a slave, named Kite, and all versions agree that he was given up peaceably. However, Busby demanded the boy, who Marmon says was the actual killer, but this was another matter altogether since he was a chief's son, and the demand was refused. So poor no-account Kite, the accessory, was tried and convicted on his own confession, while no one was prepared to argue about the chief's murderous son. In due course Kite was sentenced to death and taken for execution to Ruapapaka Island, opposite to Mangungu, where, 'with little ceremony or concern,' as Marmon says, the chief Pangari shot him. And there they buried him.

A sort of half-baked justice was thus done, or at least appeared to have been done, and Busby seemed quite pleased with himself about it. In fact he had plainly exceeded his authority, as the European settlers also did, when they became directly involved. No European in New Zealand in 1838 had any right to involve himself in such a matter, since he was in a foreign country and subject to its laws, such as they were. But the committee combined to convict Kite in accordance with their own notions and let the chief's son go free in accordance with local rules. Scarcely a result to be proud of.

Busby reported the proceedings to Governor Gipps in New South Wales, who in turn reported to the Colonial Office in London, and upon the information being referred to the Attorney General, he remarked, apparently mildly shocked, that the whole of the proceedings were 'extraordinary'. But about a year later, for some obscure reason, Busby's action was approved by Whitehall. By this time, no doubt, it had become clear that no adverse reaction was likely.

This dubious venture onto the shaky ground of home-made Hokianga law had been made by members of a strange society. It comprised Maori people secure in their social and numerical ascendancy, a handful of European merchants and timber-men, many arrogant and misguided enough at times to contemplate chastising their Maori hosts, and missionaries totally convinced of their own righteousness. And collectively they were subject to no law but the will of the determined and powerful, and the custom of the 5,000-odd Maori surrounding them. But into this scenario came a man convinced of his own ability to put all that right, and to bring law and order to Hokianga territory, of which he claimed to be Sovereign Chief, and perhaps ultimately to the whole of New Zealand.

The Baron Charles Philippe Hippolytus de Thierry was an entrepreneur with much experience in promoting his own enterprises, but with a consistent record of failure, and only his personal charm, his unshakable confidence in himself, and his aristocratic and cosmopolitan background had allowed him to come as far as he had. But it does seem clear that while promoting his own interests he did genuinely hope to better the condition of the Maori people and the white settlers, and to offer them law and stable government. An incredible personality in fact. In Chapter 8 we left him in Tahiti awaiting funds, keeping his family and body and soul together by various means, and gratuitously meddling in Tahitian politics.[16] However, after about eighteen months there he had acquired sufficient finance to get himself and his family to Sydney. Here he met Governor Bourke, who had not been impressed by the furious charges and accusations levelled against de Thierry by Busby and the Anglican missionaries. He received the Baron courteously and did not actively discourage him from assuming his chiefly duties in New Zealand. So, having recruited a retinue of sixty 'colonists' at Sydney — some of doubtful quality — he and his family set off for his Hokianga kingdom in the *Nimrod,* arriving off Horeke on 4 November 1837. Relying on the deed given to him by Kendall, he was justified in believing that he owned 40,000 acres of land extending along the harbour from about Mangungu to the Waihou, although he had been advised that much of it had since been occupied by Europeans. However, he expected that all the inhabitants therein would accept his authority to govern them as their chief, and comply with such laws as he might promulgate.

But 1821, when Kendall was supposed to have purchased the land, was a very long time ago in terms of Hokianga events and the activities of the people. And their attitudes. Indeed, a campaign was mounted against de Thierry on his arrival at Sydney. Here the Reverend Henry Williams dined with him and his family, and according to the Baron undertook to give him letters of introduction to eleven colleagues in New Zealand, which de Thierry understood would be favourable to him. But when they were delivered they were found to be damaging. This, as his early biographer, Robin Hyde, observed, was a little astute, even for a missionary. In New Zealand the Baron was a lamb among wolves. Speculators, merchants, traders and missionaries were all intent on promoting their own interests, and enough conflict already existed among these. A further conflicting element was therefore not welcome, especially one which involved egalitarian notions for the government of the Maori people, and under the pressure of this massive opposition de Thierry's dreams quickly faded.

He had no force to support his pretensions, and worse, he had no money — in fact he was in debt. So, burdened with his self-imposed responsibilities, and shackled by his want of means and his inability to assume them, the Baron landed his entourage at Horeke. McDonnell appears to have been a little cautious with him, even deferential, no doubt because of his ignorance of the Baron's financial plight, and he allowed him the temporary use of his Horeke premises for his 'immigrants' and his family. But it quickly became clear that no-one had anything to gain or fear from the Sovereign Chief. After five days his colonists nearly all deserted him, de Thierry claimed, many seduced by apparently attractive offers of employment from the perfidious McDonnell. A riot then ensued among them against de Thierry, and nearly all in due course dispersed, leaving their

Chief with practically no retainers.

All this was bad enough, but the Baron now found to his dismay that the surviving chiefs, Patuone and Nene, two of the 'vendors' who had signed the Kendall deed of conveyance of the 40,000 acres to him sixteen years before, now repudiated the transaction. However, they did give the family some 814 acres of land — then thought to be 1,500 — at the junction of the present State Highway No. 1 and the Horeke road, now marked by a Historic Places Trust plaque commemorating this event. The land was an unattractive residue sandwiched between that then owned by 'usurpers' of the Baron's estate — Captain Young on one side, and Jellicoe and the first Wesleyan mission land, Te Toke, on the other. Pautone, in his evidence before the Old Land Claims Commissioners on de Thierry's claim,[17] stated 'I & T. Nene, made a present of a piece of land to the Baroness in consideration of the regard we had for her, but we received no payment for this.' And further, 'I and the other chiefs of the district immediately after the arrival of Governor Hobson sent a protest to him ... telling him that we had never sold land to Baron de Thierry.' All this Patuone explained elsewhere in this statement: 'Many years ago we were asked (on board the *Providence* by Mr Kendall) who were the proprietors of the district of Hokianga. Nene & Muriwai & I answered that we were — we were requested to sign a document not knowing for what except that we thought it a paper connected with the cargo of the vessel which we had furnished.

'It was not until some time afterwards that we received some axes from the hands of Thomas Hanson — these axes we thought were a present to us — and not for the purchase of any portion of our territories none of which did we sell either to Mr Kendall or to the Baron de Thierry.'

So, on this land, presented to the Baroness 'in consideration of the regard we had for her,' de Thierry, his wife Emily and their family, with a few loyal retainers, lived for a little over eight years, disillusioned but always kept afloat by the Baron's unshakable confidence in his own capabilities. They derived a bare living from the poor land, and high above the terrace on which the house was built is the hill Charles named after his beloved daughter — Mount Isabel. On this terrace, to the south of the Trust's plaque, he built a mud-walled, one-roomed house, and here, with gentle and courteous hospitality he entertained with great dignity a number of distinguished visitors. Only his son Charles has left descendants in the Hokianga, from a Maori woman he married between two other marriages to European women.

Although an Anglican himself, de Thierry clearly demonstrated his liberality and religious tolerance — an extremely rare and unpopular characteristic in those times — by his kindly and helpful association with the Catholic bishop, Jean Baptiste Pompallier, who arrived in the River only two months after the Baron. He came on the Tahiti-built schooner *Raiatea,* chartered there by the bishop to conduct him here to establish a Catholic mission in this hotbed of radical Protestantism. This he did pursuant to his authority as Vicar Apostolic of Western Oceania, and with the guidance of the Catholic Poynton in the Mangamuka, he established himself at Totara Point, at the junction of the Mangamuka and Te Karae rivers.[18] To the Methodists on the River and the Anglicans at the Bay this was a calamity of monstrous proportions, as bad if not worse than Papahurihia. Here in their midst was the Whore of Babylon — the Scarlet Woman — and commenting on this in 1844, H.H. Turton, a Methodist missionary who resigned in 1859, wrote in a letter to the Anglican bishop Selwyn, 'the missionaries of the CMS (Anglican) lived in a state of irreconcileable hostility with their christian brethren of the Wesleyan mission.... But when the Catholic mission arrived the two founding missions buried the hatchet and fell with redoubled and united fury on the common enemy.'[19]

Despite Poynton's well-meaning installation of the bishop at Totara Point, it was clearly a most unsatisfactory location, since all the upper harbour had been subjected to ten years of Wesleyan indoctrination, and at that stage was unshakably attached to the Mangungu hierarchy.[20] Pompallier, with his priest Father Servant and a lay brother, had arrived at Hokianga on 10 January 1838, but within six months the unsuitability of the site had become obvious. It was therefore decided, after visits to the Irish Catholics in the Hokianga basin, to approach the tribes of the River that 'heresy had not already sifted out'. Therefore, with Fr Servant and Bro Colomban, the bishop went down the River visiting Europeans, offering baptisms and episcopal blessings — but the great challenge was the Maori district of Whirinaki. Here, according to our informant, Monfat,[21] were 200 warriors, strong and audacious as well as evil, whose reputation made them famous not only among Europeans but also among the neighbouring tribes. This, he says, certainly made them impervious to the advances of the Wesleyans, and his account continues with a triumphant review of the manner in which all this wickedness was overcome. The party stayed overnight with the Whirinaki people and next day a brief service was held with the Europeans present, and the party returned to Totara to study the language with their 'dear Irish' (ses chers Irlandais). Soon, Monfat continues, the Whirinaki people asked them to go and live with their tribe, and in due course the bishop resolved to locate his central residence on land at Papakawau, on the western head of the Omanaia River,[22] where Poynton had acquired land for the mission. This is about two miles upstream from Whirinaki on the same side of the River, and here Poynton built the bishop's house, where, with due ceremony, he was installed on 29 June 1838. And this, as might be expected, was the occasion for a great hui.

All this had not been achieved, however, without some alarming demonstrations of hostility by the Wesleyans and their Mangamuka converts, who at one stage assembled at Totara, prepared to forcibly eject Pompallier and his assistants, together with the trappings of their religion, giving as their reason the 'counsel of the missionaries'. But after discussion they departed peacefully, having 'avowed regret for their hostile intentions'. De Thierry, aware of this state of affairs, and apparently not yet having come to terms with his powerlessness and total lack of influence, issued a Proclamation on 6 February 1838 in circular form, calling on all 'Christian men', pleading *'for all faiths and for all classes and conditions of men* ... to pause and consider the great responsibility they assume by leading the New Zealanders into acts ... which every honest man must deplore'.[23] There is apparently little doubt that at this stage vicious religious bigotry could have led to serious disturbance in Hokianga, but good sense ultimately confined hostile demonstrations to bitter and absurd expressions of rancour. In this forcing-bed of religious and nationalistic prejudice, de Thierry's support of Pompallier did him no good at all, and although he was by this time treated with contempt by the ignorant, he was not beyond suspicion. He was in correspondence with Captain Cecile of the French corvette *Heroine,* who, at the Bay of Islands, had accorded

Pompallier a deferential reception when he was sorely in need of support. There was a good deal of alarm at the Bay over the growing influence of the French in the Pacific, and this also did the Baron no good. For a long time he hoped for assistance from those who had backed his original colonising venture, and he carried on a copious but unrewarding correspondence with the French Government, interlarded with hollow promises and blandishments, with the object of gaining its support for his New Zealand sovereignty. Nothing came of this, in spite of his tentative innuendoes that a French naval establishment at Hokianga would be desirable,[24] given his co-operation.

Pompallier at Hokianga now at least had the support and loyalty of the Whirinaki people, who despite their naughtiness had the healthy respect of their neighbours, and the bishop's headquarters was now on their doorstep. De Thierry on the other hand was without friends or supporters, although it was unlikely that the family would come to any harm owing to their location on land presented by Nene and Patuone. De Thierry, a pathetic figure, with his family reduced to poverty, was visited by the Reverend W. Wade in 1838. Wade, having landed from his boat in the Waihou on his way from Mangamuka to Mangungu, 'came upon a level open road, extending in a direct line before us, but not more than twelve feet wide. A walk of nearly a mile along this road, which had evidently been made with much labour, enabled us to remark on it, as we knew it to be the Baron's first attempt at roadmaking in New Zealand.... No-one was at work upon it. Nor did we see anyone, till, approaching the ascent to the Baron's mud cottage, we observed half a dozen white men clearing a piece of ground.... The Baron came out to meet us: his dress was old, and shabby in the extreme, but his address free and gentlemanly. He received us in the politest manner, made a score of apologies for the state in which we should find his dwelling, and then ushered us in.

'The cottage, a long gable-ended building, constructed of white clay, and covered in with very inferior native thatch, stood in a well-chosen and commanding situation. Its interior was comfortless and deplorable in the extreme ....' Thus de Thierry's situation in about January 1838, and, sadly, it did not improve.[25] So, two quite new elements, an unwelcome religion and a powerless Sovereign Chief, had now been introduced into this barbarous community, which for ten years had been dominated by Maori, timber-men and struggling Wesleyans.

As to Pompallier, he soon found his location at Papakawau to be unsuitable also, and in 1839 the mission headquarters was moved again, across to Purakau, directly opposite on the north side of the harbour, where it remained until the early part of this century.[26]

11. Prelude to Government

There can be no doubt that de Thierry ranks highly in early New Zealand affairs as much for the total ineffectiveness of his political aspirations as for their incredibly ambitious objectives. Apparently quite out of touch with reality, powerless, and living in poverty on charitably donated land — totally defeated in fact — he continued to correspond with the French government and influential personalities and to describe his prospects in glowing terms, soliciting French support for his chieftaincy and colonisation scheme. Schizophrenia may have accounted for his confident, breathtaking misrepresentations, since he was otherwise an honest, kindly and well-intentioned man. As Raeside comments:[1] 'Above all, when de Thierry had a pen in his hands he could transport himself into a world of fantasy.... He could write and believe the most outrageous fancies and indulge in the most unscrupulous inventions.' But a man who later numbered Sir George Grey, Bishop Pompallier and Colonel Wynyard among his close friends cannot be lightly or entirely dismissed.

In every way de Thierry had left his run too late. If he had promoted his schemes in 1821, the French Government might have been receptive to his proposal to establish a base in New Zealand, even at Hokianga. Probably it was just as eager in 1838 but the chance was gone and could hardly be recalled without embroiling France in conflict with Great Britain. That this was well understood was demonstrated when in 1840 the Nanto-Bordelaise Company backed off from any claim of French sovereignty for its settlement at Akaroa.

In his letters to France, de Thierry clung to his status as a 40,000-acre landowner in Hokianga, and this illusion was not dispelled in official French circles until after 1840 — in fact Pompallier could well have been encouraged to settle there. And relying on the Baron's letters, an Anglo-Belgian company also had plans for a settlement at Hokianga. Such schemes were encouraged by preposterous letters to his brother Francis long after total failure was painfully apparent here. Clearly the intention of these letters was to extract financial and political support from the French Government. In 1838 Captain Cecille of the French corvette *L'Heroine* had reported cautiously to the Minister of the Navy on de Thierry, and at that time Francis was actively planning the colonisation of his brother's non-existent 40,000 acres. But the end was near for Charles. Reports received in France were becoming cautious to the point of disbelief, and the Baron's pretensions were finally laid to rest when in April-May 1840 Captain Lavaud of *L'Aube* interviewed him after the assumption by Britain of the sovereignty of New Zealand, and uncovered at last his true situation. This was no doubt very embarrassing for Charles, but to Francis and his family the exposure of the truth was disastrous. The loyal and tireless brother, reduced to poverty, finally took his own life.[2]

As an epilogue to the great de Thierry debacle it might be suggested with some justification that the integrity of the denials of Patuone and Nene of the sale of the 40,000 acres to Kendall for thirty-six axes may have been as questionable as Kendall's unexplained use of the balance of de Thierry's alleged £9000 purchase-price. After all, two years before the transaction at Hokianga, both Marsden and the vendors, Hongi and others, were content to settle for axes for 13,000 acres for the mission at Kerikeri. But both at Hokianga and the Bay the Maori conception of the value of the land had undergone a very considerable rationalisation in sixteen years, and rapacious and bigoted Europeans had also been at work for ten years. For de Thierry to have taken over such a large area of land and assumed any authority at Hokianga, particularly if, as suspected, he had French sympathies, would have jeopardised the aspirations and activities of all the Europeans there, be they missionary, land speculator, timber merchant or worker. And it is possible, therefore, that the combined pressures generated by these groups, and the enhanced value of the land, could have induced the two chiefs to give further consideration to what they actually had meant sixteen years earlier when they accepted Kendall's axes and signed his deed. After that lapse of time they were no doubt surprised that de Thierry had materialised, when, embarrassingly, perhaps, they had re-sold much of the land involved. As for Kendall, he appears to have emerged from it all with a considerable credit balance.

Raeside's comment on the sparseness of historical information coming out of Hokianga in this period is sadly a very true one: 'For the seven years de Thierry spent in the Hokianga between 1837 and 1845 the history is poorly documented. It is true that there are missionary journals and letters, but they are surprisingly arid. The missionaries were not particularly interested in the day to day life of the settlers, and much preoccupied with conversion, baptisms and the trivialities of the mission.'[3] This difficulty, in fact, extends beyond those dates, but the remarks on the mission people are very true. They were also extraordinarily obsessed with sexual morality and tended to avoid the polluting contact with many of the settlers, who generally had a light-hearted approach to alcoholic excesses and sexual relationships. The Wesleyans shared this sort of paranoia with the Bay missionaries, and to them the doings of most of the settlers were therefore unsuitable for comment.

White, however, now himself 'unfrocked', undoubtedly partly for reasons connected with his alleged extra-mural sexual interests, continued to be a focus for disruption in the upper Hokianga, due to his violent opposition to the settler faction. He owned land in the Orira River from which he was taking spars, and it seems that he was sending them down to holding booms constructed in the adjacent Mangamuka ready for rafting downstream into the harbour. Apparently convinced that White had taken these spars from his land, Poynton marshalled a force of forty settlers armed with guns and cutlasses, broke open the booms and carried off twenty-one spars. All this arose from a boundary dispute between the two which had been arbitrated earlier by G.F. Russell and R.B. Smith, of Kohukohu, but since their opinion did not favour White's view of the position, he had continued to take spars off the disputed land. Poynton had acted promptly with his small army, being aware that White was attempting to raise a Maori force to oppose him. However, according to Poynton, the chiefs Nene of Utakura and Raumati of Orira both expressed their horror that a minister of the gospel should contemplate such violent action. Apparently this sort of thing was acceptable if you weren't a minister. Anyway, since Poynton seems to have forestalled him, White's counter-measures did not eventuate.[4] This confrontation, and earlier incidents, demonstrate White's continuing influence over the Wesleyan Maori, which was then particularly evident with Nene and his brother Patuone. But his hold over these two was later to diminish.

Nene had previously been willing to engage in hostilities on White's behalf, as we have seen, but his virtuous attitude on this occasion may well have been in deference to the Wesleyan hierarchy, and also, perhaps, to Busby, who was drawn into this unresolved dispute. Nene was ever the astute politician, with a sure eye for winners, and it is unwise, in fact, to accept at their face value eulogies of the two brothers, particularly of Nene, which are still current in certain quarters. Both, with whatever motives, demonstrated an early predilection for things European, Nene to the extent of allying himself to the British forces in 1845-6, in their campaign against Hone Heke, which we shall soon come to. By many Maori this is still deplored and it is perhaps significant that after Heke's war, Nene did not return to his home in Hokianga, but lived out his life in a Government house at Russell. Patuone, also at the Government's behest, lived at Takapuna, near Auckland, as a watchdog for the Crown on the northern approaches to the town.

As to White, on his return from England on the *Coromandel* in December 1838, he had set up a small colony on his own land, adjacent and to the south of the Mangungu mission land. This consisted of eleven unemployed men from Sydney, with four women and seven children. The men were carpenters, sawyers and a schoolmaster and they were the nucleus of a labour-force he built up for the prosecution of his timber business, upon which he now relied for his living. With him on the *Coromandel* had come an Irishman, Dr Richard Day, who served for a time as tutor at the mission station, and a T.S. Forsaith, who also boarded at the mission and later entered the timber trade at Kaihu, on the Kaipara, later known as Dargaville.[5]

Strangely, when in England in 1838 White had a very large Maori-style house built for him at Rawene, then known as Herd's Point — the first European residence built there — but he does not seem to have occupied it himself. This may have been a reflection of his changing attitude to the New Zealand Company. Plainly he arranged for the building of the house before he left for England, when his views on the Company's colonisation scheme were very favourable, and he may well have anticipated organising some sort of settlement at Rawene on the Company's land, with its consent. But on his return to New Zealand with a very jaundiced opinion of the Company's sponsor and organiser, E.G. Wakefield, and ultimately by association, of the Company itself, he probably abandoned the idea of using its land, and set up his little colony on his own. By this time he was convinced that the Company would exploit the Maori and his land to his ultimate sorrow. In December 1839 William Wakefield, as we know, did inspect the land the Company believed it owned at Rawene and Motukaraka, but took no action on its development, and White had already circumvented McDonnell's attempt to sell land at Kaipara to the Company, on the grounds of his faulty (or non-existent) title.[6] So White's was probably the influence that kept the New Zealand Company out of the North.

Of Rawene, which until now had failed to attract Europeans, a story of ancient Maori times is told, and concerns Te Wairua, Hongi Hika's great-grandfather. It seems that when he flourished, the Rawene people, that is, those of the pa Rawene, just below the present hospital, were at war with the Panguru (Whakarapa) and Mitimiti Maori across the harbour. Te Wairua, who at that time was married to a Kapotai woman called Ngakirikiri at Waikare, in the Bay of Islands, had come to their assistance but was drowned off Rawene in an encounter with the enemy. To avenge this, a Waima chief Te Kiripute, sent to Waikare for Te Wairua's brother-in-law, who came and was successful in killing the offending Mitimiti chief, and took his head back to Waikare. Te Wairua was a much married man. Inland he had three more wives, Tutu and Waikainga, sisters, and Wharetoru, but he had in late life married Ngakirikiri and lived with her at Waikare.[7]

The areas of Maori jurisdiction in the Hokianga are at this stage fairly clear, but it is interesting that the influence of Muriwai, who died following the skirmish at Waima in 1828, apparently extended far beyond what was apparently his home in the Utakura valley. It was he alone who in 1827 signed the deed of sale of Herd's Point to the trustees of the first New Zealand Company, and later complaints made by Arama Karaka Pi, Mohi Tawhai and Papahurihia concerning the sale were only that they also had an interest in the land — Muriwai's interest was not disputed. Onoke Point, too, the south head of the Whirinaki River, is shown on Herd's 1827 chart of Hokianga as 'Moodiwy's Point', and Cruise in 1820[8] described 'Mootu Kraka' as 'one of

Moodywy's Pahs'. This can hardly be anything but Motukaraka — well down the harbour, opposite to Rawene. It will be recalled, too, that Nene, Patuone and Muriwai told Kendall when he was purchasing land for de Thierry, that they were 'the proprietors of the district of Hokianga'. A bold claim, perhaps, but surely one with some element of truth.

However, in 1840 the most influential chiefs in the harbour were: at Kohukohu, Wharepapa (Tohukakahi) and Tarewarewa; in the Orira, Pangari and Raumati; in the Waihou, Patuone; in the Utakura, Nene (Tamati Waaka) and Makoare Taonui; in the Waima, Arama Karaka Pi and Tawhai; in Omanaia, Papahurihia; and at Pakanae, Moetara and Rangatira. The west and north-west side of the harbour had still failed to attract Europeans, and at this time little was known of the people or chiefs on that side, downstream from Kohukohu, that is, at Motuti, Whakarapa (Panguru), Te Karaka and Waireia. These seem to have been allied in some way to the Whirinaki people, who were equally shy of Europeans until the advent of Bishop Pompallier.

Clearly, the chiefs most amenable to the sale of land were domiciled upstream from Rawene, where the three big operators in the timber business were located — G.F. Russell at Kohukohu, White at Mata, a little downstream from Horeke, and McDonnell at Horeke itself. It seems also that Moetara had now regretted his sale of Pakanae land to Henry Oakes and this may have been due to the aftermath of the wreck of Thomas Styles' vessel the *Industry* on the coast, in December 1836, when, as described earlier it was plundered and destroyed. Moetara's people seem to have been involved in this, and Gittos[9] suggests that the *Industry* and Oakes may have been sly-grogging, an activity to which Moetara was implacably opposed. Whatever the cause, the destruction of the vessel generated great ill-feeling between the Pakanae people and the Europeans in Hokianga, which made Oakes' position in Moetara's territory untenable, and he left the country in 1837. However, he apparently retained some sort of possession, since in 1840 David Rough, at the Bay, reported from Paihia to him in Australia that the cottage on the land was in good condition and that the land had a fine flock of goats on it, into which, no doubt, Moetara's people were making regular inroads. Rough also refers to the 'likelihood of a town being formed at Captain Young's Point' (Koutu). Vain hope.[10]

Therefore, despite the many thousands of acres owned and

occupied by Europeans up-harbour as the end of the 1830s approached, only comparatively small areas had passed out of Maori hands below Rawene. Captain Young was in possession there of only a few hundred acres at Koutu and Opononi, and Martin had very small areas at Omapere and the South Head. Maning and Leef were similarly and modestly established near Whirinaki, and across the harbour a few small holdings at or near Mata totalled about 1000 acres. In all, 2000 or so acres had been acquired by less than 10 purchasers.[11] Mata, by the way, is one of three places so named in the harbour — this, one a little north of Kohukohu, and another adjacent to Mangungu.

The big dealers up-river, however, according to Commissioner F.D. Bell's report, claimed to have acquired between them:[12] Russell by himself 750 acres and with White 10,470 acres; White by himself 1153; McDonnell 68,300. Other large acquisitions above Rawene were made by J. Baker, 3200 acres; J.R. and G. Lacourt, 25,000; H. Pearson, 2080; Poynton, 4000, and with Hunt 800; and R. Anwyl, 3500. Although the Lacourts' claim later lapsed, at this stage there were nearly 120,000 acres in claims above 2000, and a great many more below this figure.[13] And it is a strange coincidence that the Maori deeds of sale of the two biggest operators, White and McDonnell, were destroyed— White's in the wreck of the *Aurora* at Kaipara Heads on 27 April 1840, and McDonnell's when fire destroyed his house at Horeke in July 1842.

While White and McDonnell were feuding, across the harbour at Kohukohu G.F. Russell had established himself on land now occupied by the township, where Markham had lived in temporary domestic bliss with 'Arungher', his paramour. Fifty acres of this he finally acquired in 1837 from the Reverend Nathaniel Turner, whose flexible conscience had permitted him to invest in the land in defiance of the Wesleyan Mission's firm rule forbidding land purchases by its missionaries. Oddly, although this misdemeanour of Turner's invited comment, it seems, in fact, to have attracted very little, whereas White's similar activities had caused an enormous uproar. The bulk of Turner's adjacent property he had previously sold to Marriner.[14] So Russell was very well placed — when McDonnell's irresponsible wheeling and dealing in the harbour and at Kaipara resulted in the failure to meet his obligations under his Royal Navy spar contract, Russell had acquired it, and was making

Kohukohu the timber-trading centre of the Hokianga.[15] His wife, reputed to be related to the crafty chief Nene, may have been one of Patuone's daughters or his sister Tari's. Maning was now married to the sister of the Whirinaki chief Hauraki and living near her home, at Onoke.

Thus, while in Hokianga the two most influential settlers, McDonnell and White, were creating a leadership vacuum due to their intemperate behaviour and their preoccupation with personal issues, the nucleus of a stable European community had emerged at Kohukohu. And throughout the remainder of the century commercial and social influence in the harbour grew and prospered here unchallenged, since Horeke never regained its lost industrial pre-eminence. At the end of the decade, then, the 200 or so Europeans at Hokianga were mostly located upstream from Rawene, while the lower harbour remained firmly in the control of the Whirinaki chief Papahia, and the Pakanae brothers Moetara and Rangatira. Apart from Wharepapa at Kohukohu, the chiefs at the head of the harbour, Nene, Patuone, Taonui, Pangari, Raumati and others were much under the influence of the Wesleyan missionaries and other Europeans. This inevitably tended to diminish the authority of the chiefs.

At this stage, his fears of de Thierry having been allayed, Busby was confronted with the menace of the French bishop at Hokianga, who was now actively seeking land for a headquarters at Kororareka in the Bay, which he did acquire in 1839. After discussion at Waitangi with the Whirinaki chief Papahia, who had accompanied Pompallier on his visit to *L'Heroine* at the Bay, Busby was of the opinion that the bishop was soliciting active French naval support. And indeed, Pompallier would have been justified in doing so, and Busby in believing this to be true, in view of the continuing venomous verbal attacks on the French prelate by the Protestant missionaries. French influence here was now an extremely sensitive political issue, since arrangements were already in hand to strengthen British influence in New Zealand.[16] At the same time French whalers were operating on the coast in numbers equal to the British, and in 1839 the land purchased at Akaroa in the previous year was the subject of a treaty for its colonisation, between the Nanto-Bordelaise Company and the French Government.

Clearly, the unscrupulous and undisciplined progress of the

merchants, traders, timber-men and land speculators in New Zealand was approaching its end. As a trauma, this oncoming event was to affect the Hokianga economy to a much lesser extent than it did the capital-intensive activities at the Bay. Particularly as so many on the River were to exchange the land they had already divested of its easily-worked kauri for scrip with which valuable town-land could be acquired in the new capital at Auckland.

12. The Treaty at Mangungu

The Hokianga economy, as opposed to that at the Bay of Islands, was labour-intensive. The shipping using the harbour did so for the purpose of taking away timber, flax and the garden produce of the Maori, and it brought in only goods incidental to the production of these things. But at the Bay a commercial economy had emerged servicing the whaleships, which were there for rest, recreation, refitting and re-victualling. Ships there were birds of passage and they took away little that was locally produced other than food. As early as 1834, when Markham dallied at Hokianga, up to thirty vessels would lie at anchor in the Kawakawa River in the hurricane season, between Kororareka and Opua. These, and the floating population associated with them, which could have amounted to 1000, had to be serviced, and they were the reason for the money and consumer goods economy at the Bay of Islands. But the few Europeans at Hokianga were working, not playing, and in the first half of 1835 thirteen vessels arrived there to take on timber produced from the land there, and nine departed loaded.[1]

Nevertheless, timber and flax were not the primary reasons for the British Government's increasing interest in New Zealand. As ever, there were the invested money and the military considerations, which themselves involved the protection of accumulated national investments in capital and people. In 1839, perhaps as much as £4,000,000 in whale oil alone passed through the Bay,[2] and an incalculable amount went direct from the South Island and the Chatham Islands. This, with the produce of the land, represented very substantial New Zealand, Australian and British investments and generated much commerce at the Bay, which could be threatened by foreign intervention, uncontrolled violence and retaliatory action by aggrieved Maori. But that was not all. By the time political action had resulted in the arrival of Captain Hobson in New Zealand as Consul and potential Governor, land almost equal to the area of the whole of this country had been claimed as having been purchased by *bona fide* buyers or speculators.

Old Land Claims Commissioner F.D. Bell, who in 1862 finally cleared up the chaos created by these claims, pointed out that the majority of the purchases were made in 1837-9 and that in some claims 'the contents were estimated in round numbers, by millions of acres, or by degrees of latitude and longitude, or by the expression "as far as a cannon shot will reach". So far as can be estimated, however, after excluding the last mentioned classes, the particulars as given in the Return show a total of 10,322,453 acres.' This area comprised the *bona fide* claims, and of it 292,475 was awarded to the claimants of various categories.[3] But if we were to take only the largest of the excluded classes mentioned above, which did not comply with the Government's criteria and were rejected, and were to add these to the *bona fide* ones, not too much of New Zealand would be left for them, many of which were not very small either, and very little for the Maori people. Here are some of the rejected claims for a share of New Zealand, which is now known to contain a total of 65,948,160 acres:[4]

E. Weller (New South Wales)	1,781,360 acres.[5]
G. Weller (New South Wales)	1,425,260 acres.[6]
W. Wentworth (New South Wales)	20,036 acres. (North Island)[7]
W. Wentworth (New South Wales)	10,000,000 acres. (South Island)[8]
Guard & Co. (New South Wales)	1,280,000 acres.[9]
P. Williams (New South Wales)	1,141,500 acres.[10]
G. Green (New South Wales)	1,024,000 acres.[11]
W. Webster (United States)	145,000 acres.[12]
The New Zealand Company	20,000,000 acres.[13]

Other offshore partnerships — Jones and Co., Peacock and Co., Catlin and Co. and Guatel and Co. — are reputed to have made dubious claims for over 11,000,000 acres among them, and these, with the above, total about 48,000,000 acres. The Church Missionary Society missionaries, Taylor, Fairburn, King, Matthews, H. Williams, Shepherd and Clarke, and Busby also, all claimed 5-figure estates totalling over 250,000 acres. So, since we name here only 20 claimants out of a total of 1050,[14] we have a breathtaking demonstration of the frenetic activity and rapacity of the land speculators operating in New Zealand.

Since the New Zealand Company was marginally involved in Hokianga, as we have seen, and influenced events here, a brief account of its career will not be out of place. It was the brain-child of E.G. Wakefield, a strange and able, if unscrupulous man, but it had been preceded by a previous company formed in

London in 1825 to colonise New Zealand. This we know financed an expedition under Captain Herd who purchased land at the Thames and Rawene (Herd's Point) in 1827, but owing to the apparent hostility of the Maori in both places the project was abandoned. Then, in 1837 the New Zealand Association was formed to disseminate information on E.G. Wakefield's theories concerning emigration and colonisation. In short, these involved transporting to New Zealand a cross-section of English society and establishing it *en bloc,* social gradations and all, on land to be acquired there. This Association gave birth to the New Zealand Company, which absorbed the 1825 company, and in May 1839, without British Government support or approval, it despatched the vessel *Tory* to New Zealand to purchase land. In August she arrived at Cook's Strait and very quickly the Company's agents 'purchased' its 20,000,000 acres on both sides of the Strait. The *Tory* was followed by the *Aurora* with immigrants, and a great deal of development took place at the chosen town site, now Wellington.[15]

The British Government could scarcely fail to be influenced to a considerable extent in its decision to acquire the sovereignty of New Zealand by these and the preparatory activities of the Company in England. It was led by the Earl of Durham as Governor and had on its Scots and Irish Committees such people as the Dukes of Hamilton and Argyle, the Earls of Glasgow and Eglinton and the Lord Archbishop of Dublin. And £400,000 of influential people's money was invested in the Company — a very large sum in 1839. So, although Captain William Hobson had already been appointed to take up the post of British Consul in New Zealand, the decision was taken within days of the unexpected departure of the *Tory,* to appoint him also as Lieutenant Governor in New Zealand of any land there, the sovereignty of which might be ceded by the Maori people to Queen Victoria.[16] Hobson's success in this respect was to be of great embarrassment to the Company.

The arrival of Hobson in New Zealand, the meeting of the chiefs and Europeans he presided over at Waitangi on 6 February 1840 and his ultimate success in persuading many of the influential chiefs in New Zealand to sign the treaty of cession, is documented *ad nauseam.* But all this had an immediate and traumatic impact on those who had purchased land here, and the furore which the Treaty generated at the Bay of Islands was much greater than elsewhere, since the independence of the urban community there evaporated overnight with the advent of a Governor and his public servants. And from the Bay the Government was administered until early in 1841.

But in the meantime, recognising that Hokianga was next in importance in the settlement of New Zealand, Hobson proceeded there immediately after Waitangi in his quest for further signatures for his treaty from the important chiefs. The Hokianga politician Nene had attended the Waitangi meeting, and indeed had exerted a most significant influence on Maori opinion, but many local chiefs had not attended. So, on the way to the harbour the new Governor called a meeting at Waimate and having obtained all the signatures he sought there, went on his way with two of the Anglican missionaries.[17]

At the Waihou he was met by a deputation of Wesleyan missionaries and settlers from the district, which would have included those from the Orira and Mangamuka, and received fulsome assurances of their devotion to the Queen. From there the party went down the river by boat, passing Horeke, where McDonnell's people, asserting his pre-eminence in the district, treated Hobson to a salute of thirteen guns from his private battery. And so to Mangungu, to more felicitations and congratulations from mission personnel and settlers. Here, Buick tells us,[18] a crowd estimated at 3000 gathered, including 400 to 500 chiefs — a grossly inflated tally of these, with little doubt, since he notes only thirty-four as signing the Treaty on that day. However, chiefs or not, they did not all appear to be impressed with Hobson's blandishments and his explanation of the benefits of British rule.

This meeting is fully reported by Buick, from Lieutenant Shortland's notes, and is of sufficient significance to the history of Hokianga to be recorded here:

> The debate was opened by Aperahama Taonui, who rose and said: 'We are glad to see the Governor. Let him come to be a Governor to the Pakehas. As for us we want no Governor; we will be our own Governor. How do the Pakehas behave to the black fellow at Port Jackson? They treat them like dogs! See a Pakeha kills a pig; the black fellow comes to door and eats the refuse.'

'What is the Governor come for?' exclaimed Papahia. 'He, indeed! He to be high, very high, like Maungataniwha ... and we low on the ground; nothing but little hills. No, no, no! Let us be equal; why should one hill be high and another low? This is bad.'

MOSES (Mohi Tawhai) — 'How do you do, Mr. Governor? All we think is that you come to deceive us. The Pakehas tell us so, and we believe what they say; what else?'

TAONUI — 'We are not good (or willing) to give up our land. It is from the earth we obtain all things. The land is our Father; the land is our chieftainship; we will not give it up.'

'No, no,' cried Kaitoke, 'no, Mr. Governor, you will not square out our land and sell it. See there, you come to our country, looked at us, stopped, came up the river, and what did we do? We gave you potatoes, you gave us a fish-hook; that is all. We gave you land, you gave us a pipe, that is all. We have been cheated, the Pakehas are thieves. They tear a blanket, make two pieces of it, and sell it for two blankets. They buy a pig for one pound in gold, and sell it for three. They get a basket of potatoes for sixpence, sell it for two shillings. This is all they do; steal from us, this is all.'

Here Buick comments on the influence of Europeans on some Maori views.

'Ha, ha, ha, this is the way you do,' cried Taonui, 'First your Queen sends Missionaries to New Zealand to put things in order, gives them £200 a year. Then she sends Mr. Busby to put up a flag, and gives him £500 a year, and £200 to give to us natives. Now she sends a Governor.'

Then Maning, whom Taonui admitted had informed him on these matters, was interrogated and reprimanded on this by Hobson.

The Lieutenant-Governor then proceeded to tell the chiefs that their Pakeha friend had given them advice in utter ignorance of the most important

> principle that British laws could not be enforced on a foreign soil, and that their only hope of protection against unscrupulous Europeans was to become a party to the treaty.

He does not, however, tell them how to protect themselves from unscrupulous governments. After further comment, the debate continued.

> 'Welcome, welcome, welcome Governor!' cried Ngaro. 'Here are the Missionaries; they come to the land, they bought and paid for it, else I would not have them. Come, come! I will have the Governor. No one else perhaps will say "Yes", but I, Ngaro, I will have him. That is all I say.
> MOSES (Mohi Tawhai) — 'Where does the Governor get his authority? Is it from the Queen? Let him come; what power has he? Well, let him come, let him stop all the lands from falling into the hands of the Pakehas. Hear, all ye Pakehas! Perhaps you are rum-drinkers, perhaps not; hear what is said by us. I want all to hear. It is quite right for us to say what we think; it is right for us to speak. Let the tongue of every one be free to speak; but what of it? What will be the end? Our sayings will sink to the bottom like a stone, but your sayings will float light, like the wood of the Whau-tree, and always remain to be seen. Am I telling lies?'
> Kaitoke, who had previously delivered a hostile speech, again openly maintained his opposition by interjecting, 'Let us choose our own Governor.'

Rangatira, Moetara's brother, then spoke.

> 'Welcome Mr. Governor! How do you do? Who sold our land to the Pakehas? It was we ourselves by our own free will; we let it go, and it is gone, and what now? What good is there in throwing away our words? Let the Governor sit for us.'
> MOSES (Mohi Tawhai) — 'Suppose the land has been stolen from us, will the Governor enquire about it? Perhaps he will, perhaps he will not. If they have acquired the land by fair purchase, let them have it.'

Taonui then spoke again.

> 'Lo, now for the first time my heart has come near to your thoughts. I approached you with my whole heart. You must watch over my children; let them sit under your protection. There is my land too; you must take care of it, but I do not wish to sell it. What of the land that is sold? Can my children sit down [stay] on it? Can they — eh?'

Now Nene, after chanting a song of welcome, with his brother Patuone, and Rangatira, proceeded to justify his refusal to let de Thierry have his 40,000 acres.

> 'Listen to me, Governor; all of you listen to me. This is my speech. If the Baron de Thierry wishes to claim my land, why is he not here to-day? No, no; it was never sold to him. Does he think he will have it? No, no; he shall not have any of it. That is all I have to say.'
>
> A chief, Hone Kingi Raumati, whose baptismal name was John King, next delivered a sympathetic address: 'My speech is to the Governor. This is what I have to say. It was my father, it was Muriwai, told me to behave well to the Pakehas. Listen, this is mine; you came, you found us poor and destitute. We on this side say, "Stay and sit here." We say, "Welcome, welcome"; let those on the other side say what they like. This is ours to you. Stay in peace. Great has been your trade with our land. What else do you come for but to trade? Here am I. I who brought you on my shoulders. I say come; you must direct us, and keep us in order. This is all mine to you. If any one steal anything now there will be payment for it. I have done my speech.' A chief whose name does not seem to have been preserved by the chronicler of the meeting, but who had support for the Governor in his words, said: 'How do you do? Here am I, a poor man; and what is this place? A poor place, but this is why you have come to speak to us today. Let the Pakehas come and I have not anything to say against it. There is my place, it is good land; come and make it your sitting-

place — you must stay with me. That is all.'

The last speech was that of Daniel Kahika: 'What indeed!' he said in indignant tones. 'Do you think I will consent to other people selling my land? No, truly. If my land is to be sold I will sell it myself. But no, I will not sell my land. I do not like the Pakehas to tease me to sell my land. It is bad. I am quite sick with it. This is my speech.'

So closed the debate at Hokianga.

Buick says that ultimately Hobson got 120 Hokianga signatures on his Treaty, in spite of the considerable opposition that he encountered, and Hobson himself notes also that there was difficulty in restraining those from signing 'who were disentitled by their rank from inserting their names'. So the signatories from his 400-500 chiefs were apparently selected by someone — one wonders upon what basis, or on whose advice. However, this finished the business here, but instead of proceeding down-harbour as he had intended, he went next day, 13 February, to Horeke (which he calls 'Hauraki') by appointment, and there met '1000 as fine warriors as were ever seen'. McDonnell's guns were again discharged, together with the muskets of the assembled 'warriors', who partook 'all in perfect harmony' of the free feast and tobacco ration he provided. All of which was predictable. As to the projected trip down-river, it seems likely that it was cancelled due to the anticipated hostility of Bishop Pompallier's growing congregation at Whirinaki and environs, and on the opposite side of the harbour. No doubt it was considered that the Wesleyan vote was adequate for the Governor's needs.

On this matter, Hobson wrote, as might be expected, 'The influence against me was entirely traceable to the foreign Bishop of the Roman Catholic persuasion, and to a set of escaped convicts and other low ruffians who have congregated on the river in considerable numbers.' In assessing Hobson's dilemma at Hokianga, it must be borne in mind that he was entirely in the hands of the Wesleyan missionaries, whose record of venomous sectarianism hardly qualified them to advise him on Hokianga matters as a whole, and in particular on who should sign the Treaty, and on what others there were who should be canvassed. Bigotry at Hokianga had reached heights unknown at the Bay, and any hostility or want of docility by Maori there could conveniently be ascribed to the machinations of the 'Popish Bishop'. Hobson, who was scarcely in a position to know this from his own knowledge, had been told, it seems, that in the whole of the Hokianga only two 'head chiefs' had refused to sign — a bold claim, perhaps, which, if true, tended to weaken the argument that the bishop was frustrating his efforts there. However, at this point Treaty proceedings at Hokianga ended.

The quest for further signatures to the Treaty proceeded through New Zealand, punctuated by minor and major crises for Hobson, who, overcome by the strain of the events for which he was wholly responsible, suffered a stroke shortly after his return from Hokianga to the Bay. But sufficient signatures were shortly obtained to justify Hobson's issuing a Proclamation taking possession of the whole of New Zealand in the name of Queen Victoria, including the territory of the frustrated French settlers at Akaroa. This process being well in hand, Hobson, his condition greatly improved, approved the purchase of Clendon's trading-post at Okiato, in the Bay of Islands, a few miles upstream from Kororareka, for a temporary 'capital'. This he called Russell, and until early in 1841, when the new town of Auckland was ready for him, he administered the New Zealand Government from there.

A cruel blow had by now, however, descended on the land purchasers in New Zealand, struck by the Governor of New South Wales, to whom Hobson, as a Lieutenant-Governor, was subordinate. On 14 January 1840 Gipps had issued a Proclamation to the effect that all purchases of land in New Zealand subsequent to that date would be null and void and those made previously would not be deemed to be valid until confirmed by a grant from the Crown. Hobson, as Lieutenant-Governor designate, then issued a similar Proclamation in New Zealand on 30 January 1840.[19] This, as can be imagined, was a horrifying trauma for the speculators and the big buyers, but worse was to come. In May 1840 Gipps introduced a Bill into the New South Wales Legislative Council which, among other things, limited grants in New Zealand, regardless of the magnitude of the claim, to 2560 acres (4 square miles) and this was passed. But before this could get to England to receive the Royal Assent, Hobson had been appointed autonomous Governor in New Zealand, and Gipp's Act lapsed, but Hobson enacted an ordinance here in the same terms.

Further, grants in respect of land claimed to have been purchased from Maori vendors were to be made in proportion to the money or goods paid for it, and a schedule of arbitrary values of land purchased at certain dates was to be adhered to.[20] This varied from 6 pence per acre in 1815 to 4 to 8 shillings per acre in 1839, which tended to favour the Anglican missionaries, and the maximum area to be granted, other than in exceptional cases, was, as decreed, 2560 acres. Goods paid for land were to be assessed at three times the Sydney prices. Predictably, there were howls of pain and wrath at all this, and in response to pitiful pleas from grievously wounded speculators, various amendments were made to these rules, and the pressure from such people continued until Commissioner Bell's inquiry into all the claims and grants in the late 1850s, and even beyond this.

In the meantime Commissioners Godfrey and Richmond had been appointed in 1840, and a new element was introduced by a Proclamation of 26 March 1844 by Fitz Roy, then Governor of New Zealand, authorising the purchase from claimants with Government scrip, of land to which they had established their title to the Government's satisfaction. Such land, for the purpose of issuing scrip, was valued at £1 per acre, and the scrip was good for the purchase of Crown lands.[21] The inquiry of the Commissioners extended over some years, and many Hokianga purchasers, as we have learned, eagerly grasped this opportunity to acquire scrip. The process had the effect later, however, of passing problems of disputed boundaries over to the Government, since in many cases boundary definitions accepted by the Godfrey-Richmond Commission left much to be desired. Therefore, plans of Hokianga land, although called Old Land Claims Plans, are often surveys executed by the Government to define its acquisition of 'scrip' lands.

Now began the dreary saga of the validation or rebuttal of these European claims to land, which, as noted above, extended into the 1860s. This not only soured the claimants, but appears in some cases to have shaken Maori confidence in the judgement of Queen Victoria's administrators, who appeared to be questioning the integrity of those Maori who had signed deeds of sale, or at least their understanding of what they were doing. Few of them denied these contracts but they did object to the principle adopted by the Government, that the area of land in any claim over and above that awarded to the claimant by the Commissioners should be vested in the Crown. So it happened that one man shortly emerged as the focus of Maori discontent in these and other areas. He was Hone Heke Pokai, who had been one of the more promising of the Anglican mission pupils. He had married Hariata Rongo, Hongi Hika's daughter, which had enhanced his own considerable mana, and he soon became the leader of those Maori people disenchanted with the effect of British rule on their well-being and prestige, and, indeed, on their very status in their own land. Robert Fitz Roy, who became Governor in December 1843, following the death of Hobson and the Acting-Governorship of Willoughby Shortland, was aware of growing Maori discontent and the reasons for it.

Writing in 1846, after his dismissal, Fitz Roy observed that the Maori were threatened 'even on trifling occasions, with the punishments of English law; (To them unintelligible),' and were told by equally discontented Pakeha that they were now Queen Victoria's slaves. They could not, in the terms of the Treaty of Waitangi, sell their land to whom they pleased, but they also found that land they had sold for trifles was now being resold for 'perhaps more than thirty times the value which they had received'. The chiefs felt that their authority was dwindling, and Maori generally found the increasing European population was becoming 'averse to their company' and they were being treated with less caution and kindness than previously.[22]

Europeans and Maori at the Bay of Islands and in the North generally were now suffering from economic depression following the transfer of the Government to Auckland, to where a large proportion of the Bay and Hokianga people had followed it. Disaffection had emerged before this, however, as the New Zealand journal of the Colonial Surgeon, John Johnson, reveals.[23] Only a few months after the Waitangi Treaty ceremony a dispute was provoked by the sons of the Reverend Henry Williams on his inland estate at Pakaraka, where some local Maori proposed to build a pa. The Williams boys threatened to burn it down, and this, and no doubt other underlying grievances, led to a serious conspiracy in the district to murder the Europeans at Pakaraka and Waimate, and launch a general attack on the English in the following December. This became widely known and although the attack did not eventuate, general discontent smouldered until offensive action was taken by Hone Heke in 1844.

Some back-sliding of mission Maori was also taking place. De Thierry relates a specific instance of this which occurred at Hokianga, when in 1842 two of his sons on a pigeon-shooting expedition came upon a Maori man well known to them. He had a fire going, and his son, aged eight, lay nearby tied hand and foot. As no food was in sight the two boys asked what he was going to cook. Cheerfully he replied that since his son was fat, visitors were expected and the son was all he had to offer them, he would have to do. Horrified, the boys took the two home to their father, de Thierry, who bargained with the child's father and redeemed him with a gift of pork. This man who proposed to cook his son was a psalm-singing church-going convert.[24]

In this troubled climate of affairs, then, unrest grew and finally erupted into violence not five years after the signing of the Treaty.

13. The Aftermath of Waitangi

The foregoing events all had their impact at Hokianga, and although Hobson had given Pompallier an undertaking at Waitangi that his New Zealand Government would deal even-handedly with all religious persuasions, his remarks and activities at Mangungu were hardly consistent with this. At Hokianga religious bigotry flourished unabated, so clearly this was not the place from which the Vicar Apostolic of Western Oceania could best administer his charge. Pompallier had, as we know, satisfied himself after only a year at Papakawau, that Purakau, across the harbour, was the most suitable site for the Hokianga mission, and the establishment had therefore moved to there in 1839. The personnel, headed by Father Servant, then consisted of three further priests and three brothers of the Society of Mary. And there the old presbytery can still be seen, albeit in poor condition. A cross stands above it on the point and on the foreshore are the remains of a tidal mill, built and operated by Father Petit. These relics, and an ancient oak supporting a grape-vine, are the remaining evidence of the existence of the old Marist mission there.

Pompallier was thus now in a position to locate his headquarters at Kororareka, where he had purchased land, this being the centre of such civilisation as existed in New Zealand at the time, and there he established himself in 1839. At this stage it could be said that if the Wesleyans excelled in sectarian acrimony, Pompallier was a long way ahead in extravagant claims to success. 'For 35 or 40 leagues around my residence at Hokianga the people expressly ask the same favour [of baptism] after receiving sufficient instruction. The most distinguished and powerful chief of New Zealand has declared for the Catholic faith. Heresy makes no proselytes and is even losing its own followers. Quite recently an entire tribe which was in its flock chose to enter the true sheep fold of Jesus Christ.' This in a letter to Cardinal Fransoni in Rome, at the end of 1838 — a claim which could scarcely be sustained by the realities of the situation.

This unrestrained optimism was the one characteristic he shared with his compatriot, Charles de Thierry. But equally with all missionaries he was under the necessity of presenting such favourable reports to ensure an unfailing flow of finance.[1]

But at Hokianga, it could well be said that the impetus of Wesleyan progress had been impaired by White's behaviour, and, paradoxically, by the loss of his dynamic leadership. Early in 1840 he was exploiting the kauri land he had acquired at the Kaipara and was loading spars on to the *Navarino,* which he had chartered to transport them to England. Both the Wesleyan missionaries and the New Zealand Company were interested in the settling of the Kaipara for the expansion of their respective empires, and it was in January 1840 that the *Tory,* the Company's vessel, entered the harbour for an inspection of the land offered to it by McDonnell. He claimed to have purchased 23,000 acres there, but since the Old Land Claims Commissioners later thought otherwise, the Company was fortunate that it did not fall into the same trap here that it had done with the land that McDonnell had earlier unloaded onto it at Motukaraka, in the Hokianga. It was at Kaipara that the serious deficiencies of McDonnell's chart of the harbour resulted in the *Tory*'s going aground on a sandbank at the entrance, so the whole Kaipara saga could scarcely have enhanced his standing with the Company. As to White, his spars loaded, he went post-haste to Taranaki in pursuit of his implacable determination to thwart the Company's intention to acquire land there — an objective that he did not entirely achieve.[2]

The irregular and questionable antics of these two gentlemen were now, of course, subject to the law and order that had lately come to New Zealand, tentative and thinly-spread though it was at this stage. In their frenetic and undisciplined progress they were also being overtaken by events, as some degree of stability came to Hokianga. The first evidence of officialdom arrived in the person of a post-master. A petition from Hokianga in May 1840 by seventeen Wesleyan missionaries and thirty-three others requested a weekly postal service costing no more than one shilling (ten cents) per letter, and this was duly provided. The mail was delivered first by Maori carriers, but when 'native chiefs' refused to carry the mail from the Bay to Waimate for less than four dollars, a mounted trooper delivered it, and from there it was taken to Horeke, the mail 'terminal' for Hokianga.[3] But there does not appear to have been an official post office there until 24 August 1840, when Thomas Beckham was appointed as Postmaster, and also Resident Magistrate.[4] Presumably some building of McDonnell's was used. It is interesting too that Horeke got a licensed hotel sometime in the 1840s,[5] but even more interesting is information from the same source that long before this the gardener's house on McDonnell's property, believed to date back to the early 1830s, had been used as a hotel. If this is indeed true, it casts some doubt on McDonnell's early condemnation of 'demon rum'. At Taheke, the upstream limit of water transport in the Waima district, the Taheke Terminal Hotel was also licensed in the 1840s.

Despite his unfrocking, White continued to dominate the missionary faction at Hokianga through his influence with the important Maori chiefs, but he now made his living from his timberlands at Hokianga and Kaipara. He chartered ships to export his timber and travelled frequently to Australia until he had disposed of all his land. But in the upshot he apparently did not prosper from all this, since eventually his occupation was given in the census as a carpenter.[6] His young nephew, John, the son of his brother Francis, was destined to become a celebrity in his own right. Born in England in 1826 and brought to Mangungu by his father in 1835, he became an authority on Maori tradition and customs, a fluent Maori linguist, a magistrate and the author of novels and valuable ethnological texts on Maori life and legends. But the fiery White-McDonnell domination of upper Hokianga affairs now burned low, as men of maturer and calmer temperament emerged as leading personalities. One such was John Webster, who landed at the Bay of Islands on 1 May 1841. A Scotsman who had spent the previous few years in Australia on cattle-drives and other adventures, he joined his brother William, who had a small water-driven sawmill on the Wairere Creek, a little south of Horeke. This mill William had earlier set up at some unidentified place at the Heads, where it pre-dated sawmills generally in Hokianga by over thirty years. John stayed with his brother at Wairere until in 1844 he made the acquaintance of John Logan Campbell, one of Auckland's early business tycoons. Campbell had come to Hokianga to purchase timber from G.F. Russell, at Kohukohu, for the English market.[7]

This event in itself brings into focus McDonnell's loss of the initiative in business matters at Hokianga. His Horeke house and other buildings were destroyed by fire in July 1842, a disaster that seems to have coincided with a general decline in his fortunes. He became a dedicated petitioner to both Houses of the Legislature in support of his land claims, and, with James Busby, an untiring litigant before various Land Claims Commissions. He quarrelled violently with the tribes from whom he claimed to have purchased land, and 'insulted every magistrate ever stationed in the north'.[8] In the process his influence dwindled, and he ceased to be a power in the land.

Webster, whose business activities certainly contributed to McDonnell's downfall, and Russell, his father-in-law, were between them the founders of Kohukohu as the earliest 'civilised' township in the Hokianga, although this distinction is often awarded to Yarborough. He, however, did not come to the place for another thirty or thirty-five years after it had become the commercial centre of the River. And the sawmill that boosted this pre-eminence in the 1870s was built for an Australian firm, not for Yarborough. Until the end of the century Webster certainly exerted the greatest influence, socially and otherwise, on events at Hokianga, and it appears that in the early 1840s he had a friendly association with the de Thierry family. He claimed that he and young Charles de Thierry were the first Europeans to visit Herekino, where there is a shallow west coast harbour some twenty miles north of the Hokianga. Interestingly, he too suggests that Kendall mis-appropriated the funds entrusted to him by the Baron to purchase Hokianga land.

By December 1842 Russell had expended £3000 on his property at Kohukohu —[9] a very substantial sum at that time. Even on the occasion of Wakefield's 1839 visit to Hokianga, he remarked that the *Tory* had to share the Kohukohu anchorage with two barques loading timber, and that ashore there was the house and store of a 'timber-dealer and general store-keeper'. Although it has been suggested that the sketch of Kohukohu done during this visit by Heaphy, the Company's draughtsman,[10] is a composite of Horeke and Kohukohu, this is a very dubious theory. The sketch of Kohukohu in John Jolliffe's 1851 Journal[11] is drawn from a different angle, but it depicts a house similar to that in Heaphy's. On the other hand, Heaphy's background topography is not recognisable as that of either place. This is a not uncommon feature of sketches hastily outlined and completed later at the artist's leisure. In any case, the evidence suggests that Russell built his quite pretentious house between 1837, when he acquired the land, and 1839, the date of Heaphy's drawing. Jolliffe visited Russell, and walked 'through his sweetly pretty garden which is the [sic] by far the prettiest I have ever seen out of England it is a perfect garden of Eden in the Wilderness'.

A sketch-plan on OLC File No. 971 shows Russell's house on the terrace now occupied by Yarborough's twentieth-century dwelling. One of those a little upstream was no doubt Captain David Clark's 1831 house from Horeke, and downstream, Dr Smythe's is shown across the bay. Further down still, probably near the present Marriner St, is Marriner's house. And the small inlet between Russell's and Smythe's, at the mouth of the Waipoura Creek (here shown as Waihouuru Creek), is marked 'Dock Yard' — probably the landing-place and storage-yard for goods imported for Russell's store. It was a little distance up this stream that the surviving stone bridge was built by Russell, prior to 1851, since it is shown on the Jolliffe sketch, which was made in that year. Somewhere on or near the dockyard area would have been a saw-pit and general workplace, and the timber brought down from up-river would be held within floating booms offshore.

Marriner, as we have seen, accepted Government scrip for his Kohukohu land, and the portion downstream from the present township of Kohukohu to the Waihoehoe Creek was reserved by the Government for the family of Captain David Clark, pursuant to their claim on Kohukohu lands. Marriner's land, purchased from the Reverend Nathaniel Turner, had a frontage of some two miles along the River from the Konoke Creek in the north, downstream to and a little beyond the Waihoehoe Creek at Tauteihiihi. The claim comprised about 1000 acres, and excluded Russell's fifty-three acres on which most of the township later developed. Marriner had been McDonnell's storeman.

In 1844, Dr Campbell, later Sir John Logan Campbell, went to Kohukohu to arrange with Russell for a cargo of 'hewn kauri spars and baulk timber for the Home market. (London). All squared by the Maoris'.[12] It was on this occasion that he met Webster, who became Brown and Campbell's agent at Hokianga.

Trade at Kohukohu was thriving at that time, but the coming war was already casting its shadow over the North.

Throughout the early 1840s examination by the Commissioners of the Old Land Claims proceeded, and some sourness was generated in this process, but the people generally suffered most from the flight of business from the North to the new Government town at Auckland. And at the Bay of Islands, where before 1840 indigenous Maori authority had survived despite intense indoctrination in European ways of behaviour and commerce, the withdrawal symptoms were traumatic. British law now prevailed over Maori custom, but European business had largely evaporated. It is also unlikely that the chiefs who had signed the Treaty had anticipated the flood of immigrants that followed, although they mostly went to Auckland. Out of these things, and the new arrogant attitude of some Europeans toward the Maori people observed by Fitz Roy, arose a growing bitterness.

This syndrome seems to have affected the Hokianga Maori to a lesser extent than elsewhere, and they divided there on a different basis. By marriages this was essentially an inter-racial community to a much greater extent than the Bay of Islands had ever been and the Maori people as a whole had not come to be so dependent on a European economy, although they had derived considerable benefit from it. At Hokianga, those chiefs who enjoyed close European relationships, and had gained from them, supported the Government in the war that was brewing, and conversely, the people at Omanaia, and the Ihutai hapu, between Kohukohu and Mangamuka, who were always somewhat aloof, favoured the disaffected element. The Catholic Hikutu of Whirinaki confounded the Wesleyan suspicions about Pompallier's malign influence by favouring the Government cause, but according to Maning's *Old New Zealand,* they became involved only 'to practice war, and elevate their names ... and many young men came from different tribes (hapu) to join Walker, [Nene] and to perfect themselves in the practice of war'.

Inevitably, then, war was coming to the North, with the Hokianga chiefs divided on the basis of intra-tribal jealousies and grievances. As to the Maori people of Hokianga generally, another passage in *Old New Zealand* by an old chief present at the Mangungu treaty ceremony demonstrates the dim understanding that many — perhaps most — of the people there had of the object of Hobson's appeal for their signatures.

Then many other chiefs began to speak, and there was a great noise and confusion, and the people began to go away, and the paper was lying there, but there was no one to write on it. The Governor looked very vexed, and his face was very red. At this time some pakehas went amongst the crowd, and said to them, 'You are foolish; the Governor intends to pay you when all the writing is done, but it is not proper that he should promise to do so; it would be said you only wrote your names for pay; this, according to our ideas, would be a very wrong thing.' When we heard this we all began to write as fast as we could, for we were all very hungry with listening and talking so long, and we wanted to go to get something to eat, and we were also in a hurry to see what the Governor was going to give us; and all the slaves wanted to write their names, so that the Governor might think they were chiefs; and pay them; but the chiefs would not let them, for they wanted all the payment for themselves. I and all my family made our marks, and we then went to get something to eat; but we found our food not half done, for the women and slaves who should have looked after the cooking were all mad about the Governor, so when I saw that the food was not sufficiently done, I was aware that something bad would come of this business. [See Chapter 1]

Next morning the things came with which the Governor intended to pay us for writing our names, but there was not much tobacco, and only a few blankets; and when they were divided some of the chiefs had nothing, others got only a few figs of tobacco, some one blanket, others two. I got for myself and all my sons, and my two brothers, and my three wives, only two blankets. I thought it was too little, and was going to return them, but my brothers persuaded me to keep them; so we got into our canoe to go home, and on the way home we began to say, 'Who shall have the blankets?' And so we began to quarrel about them. One of my brothers

> then said, 'Let us cut them in pieces, and give every one a piece.' I saw there was going to be a dispute about them, and said, 'Let us send them back.' So we went ashore at the house of a pakeha, and got a pen and some paper, and my son, who could write, wrote a letter for us all to the Governor, telling him to take back the blankets, and to cut our names out of the paper, and then my two brothers and my sons went back and found the Governor in a boat about to go away. He would not take back the blankets, but he took the letter. I do not know to this day whether he took our names out of the paper. It is, however, no matter; what is there in a few black marks? Who cares about them?

This incident is confirmed in Hobson's own account of the Mangungu treaty meeting.

But the most divisive factor at Hokianga was the re-emergence of old grievances. Hone Heke, the deceased Hongi's son-in-law, was irreversibly identified with indignities inflicted on Hokianga people by Hongi, which occurred on his hostile incursions into the harbour, to avenge a foray by the Ngatikorokoro people of Pakanae into the Bay of Islands. The Ngatikorokoro had also been associated earlier with a humiliating defeat of Hongi's people by the Ngatiwhatua at Moremonui, on the west coast, south of the Waipoua forest. So Hongi had raided into the lower Hokianga and laid siege to Whiria, Moetara's massive and ancient pa at Pakanae, but was repulsed. While this was going on, however, Tuohu, an ally of Moetara, went inland and struck swiftly at Hongi's pa at Pakinga, near Kaikohe, which he took. Hongi, hearing of this on his retreat from Whiria, turned back and attacked and took the pa of Te Tihi, on the opposite side of the harbour to Pakanae, killing Te Tihi and swallowing his eyes — an unforgivable indignity. He then re-crossed the harbour and took Maererangi, Tuohu's pa.

Since Nene was related to Te Tihi, this old campaign was a factor in his decision over twenty years later to oppose Heke in his campaign against the Government.[13] The Ngatikorokoro people, essentially Ngapuhi, were ambivalent in their loyalties, being closely related to Ngatipou, who were no friends of Ngapuhi. Similarly, the Roroa at Waipoua had loyalties to both

Ngatiwhatua and Ngapuhi. Thus cracks were appearing in the powerful Ngapuhi nation which led eventually to bitter factional military confrontations.

Thus, when war did eventuate, such was the influence of Nene, Moetara and Te Taonui — those in Hokianga who had probably gained most from European contact — that a large proportion of the people accepted their advice and followed them into battle against Heke and his allies. Inland Bay of Islands, on the other hand, was solidly behind Heke, and there was some harrassment of Europeans there by an unruly element of his followers. At Hokianga, however, there was little of this, since, with few exceptions, such as de Thierry, McDonnell, and of course the missionaries, this was essentially an inter-racial community, whose households were conducted by Maori women. The sensitivity and regard the Maori people had, and still retain, for blood relationships, had protected Maori women and their families since the first European took a Maori wife at Hokianga.

So the unrest at the Bay continued until a truculent Heke, on the pretext that a Kororareka butcher had taken a slave of his into his household, went there with a party and took the woman away by force.[14] Then, after considerable uproar which was beyond the resources of Beckham, the Police Magistrate, to control, and inflammatory speeches by Heke on the subject of grievances arising from British rule, the flagstaff on Maiki Hill, above the town, was chopped down. Thus the outward and visible sign of the new British dominance was laid low, and as a result of all this, the new Governor Fitz Roy convened a meeting at Waimate to discuss these events. Having negligible military support, he could do little but make soothing noises concerning the adverse effects of his Government on Northern affairs. But he was preaching to the converted since Heke did not attend. However, Nene kindly assured Fitz Roy that he would see to it that Heke behaved himself. A provocative gesture indeed, which was followed by further harrassment of Pakeha in the district. By this stage, Te Ruki Kawiti, the Bay of Islands Ngatihine chief of Waiomio, a non-Christian Ngapuhi, had joined Heke, but Fitz Roy was reassured by Nene's words at Waimate, and the 150 men of the 99th Regiment that had arrived on loan from New South Wales were sent home again.

A few months later, in January 1845, Heke again visited

Kororareka and the re-erected flagstaff suffered the fate of its predecessor. Fitz Roy then offered £100 reward for Heke's capture but got no takers, so Heke offered the same reward for Fitz Roy and went on his way unscathed. The Governor, now convinced that he had a real problem to deal with, again appealed for troops from New South Wales, and, with dubious wisdom, renewed his sorry flagpole. Whereupon Heke paid another visit to the town and climbing Maiki Hill pushed past a guard of Nene's men unopposed, and personally chopped the thing down again. No Maori was going to shoot down one of his own people for the sake of a wooden pole.

It was now apparent to Fitz Roy that the troublesome incidents in the North had inflated into a major crisis, and owing largely to Heke's courageous action, some vacillation was occurring among Nene's followers — even Nene himself wavered. However, following urgent appeals from the Anglican missionary, the Reverend Henry Williams, and his solemn assurances that the Treaty of Waitangi was not the 'trick' that Heke had declared it to be, Nene and his followers recovered their composure. Their attitude to Heke having then hardened, he knew exactly what he was up against. Faced with the almost limitless military resources of Great Britain, he plainly had no chance of ultimate success, but unlike Nene he was an idealist rather than a politician, and he clung to his resolve to oust British rule. Anglican missionaries continued to point out to him the error of his ways but he was obdurate, and as a defiant gesture flew the Stars and Stripes on his canoe when at the Bay.

Inevitably a confrontation came to pass. Early in March 1845 Heke and Kawiti gathered a force of 600-700 at Uriti, a little bay south of Kororareka, prepared for a conflict with the defenders of the town. These were troops of the 96th Regiment, ninety marines and sailors from HMS *Hazard,* the ship's guns and 110 civilian volunteers. Action commenced on 11 March, when Kawiti launched a diversionary attack from Matauwhi, adjacent and to the south of the town. The defenders of the new iron-clad flagpole on Maiki Hill were so preoccupied with this that they forgot what they were there for. When the guards were outside their blockhouse enjoying the spectacle of the Matauwhi battle, Heke's men came by the ridge from Long Beach, behind the town, routed them, killed four or five — and in spite of its iron sheathing, the flagstaff was felled once more. In this melee the signalman was unintentionally killed, and a little half-caste girl, the daughter of Captain Wing, formerly of Clendon's *Fortitude*.

Shortly after this, Lieutenant Philpotts, the acting captain of the *Hazard,* ordered the evacuation of the town — a strange decision, since militarily the defending force was by no means defeated. However, as far as Philpotts was concerned the incident was closed, and Heke's and Kawiti's people, having nothing better to do, roamed at will through the town. Indeed, they may not have planned on taking Kororareka at all, since they had downed the flagstaff, the object of the exercise. But looting proceeded, and in the best tradition of non-rancorous Maori warfare the invaders assisted some householders to salvage their belongings, and even ferried refugees to ships anchored in the bay. Soon these were gone, taking the homeless people to Auckland, and the town burned merrily. Heke and his men then returned inland to Hongi's old pa Tapuaeharuru, on the Omapere lakeside, and Kawiti to Waiomio. And at the lake, sporadic skirmishing now took place between Heke's men and Nene's, who were encamped at a pa at Okaihau.[15]

Loyalty or otherwise to the Queen had little to do with whose side the protagonists fought on in Heke's war. There can be little doubt that the astute Hokianga politicians, Nene (Tamati Waaka, or Thomas Walker) and Moetara, picked the winners of the coming conflict and influenced Hokianga opinion accordingly. Here was an opportunity to settle old scores, with professional British assistance. Maning, in his section of *Old New Zealand* devoted to Heke's war, quotes his old chief:[16]

> Now, when Thomas Walker Nene heard that the war had actually begun, and that Kororareka had fallen, he called together his family and all his friends, and said he would fight against Heke, and seek revenge for his friends and the pakeha people. Walker had always been a friend and protector to the Europeans; and also Hongi Ika, Heke's relation, had killed in former times Te Tihi, at Hokianga, and swallowed his eyes, and Te Tihi was a matua (elder relation) to Walker.
>
> And Te Tao Nui came to join Walker, and brought with him all his family and relations, many

> fighting men; only one man of his family did not come — that man went to help Heke. Te Tao Nui had always, like Walker, been a good friend to the Europeans, and he was also an ancient enemy of Hongi Ika.
>
> And the tribe of Ngati Pou came to help Walker. Formerly they had been a great tribe, but Hongi Ika had driven them from their country and slain most of their warriors; but they in return wounded Hongi, and he died of that wound some years afterwards. They came to help Walker, in search of revenge against Hongi Ika, for Heke and Hongi are the same. This tribe of Ngati Pou brought forty men to help Walker, which was all left alive by Hongi, but they fought well, for their hatred to Hongi was great....

The Hikutu, as we have seen, joined Nene for the fun of it. Later, in a speech to one of Heke's emissaries, Nene said that this was not 'a war for Te Tihi, but for Kororareka; but if you remember Te Tihi also, how can you help it?' And after the early battles, Heke's ally, Te Ruki Kawiti, in a letter to Sir George Grey, the new Governor, wrote that Nene was constantly 'naming his dead' — recalling old grudges and using this war as an opportunity to avenge them. 'You do not understand this. Walker's fighting is not for your dead, no it is on account of those killed long ago, on account of Kao of Tuahui, Tihi and Poaka: These were killed long ago.'[17]

14. The War in the North

Since Heke's and Kawiti's hopeless war against British rule in New Zealand is adequately dealt with in many published works,[1] only accounts that are relevant to our narrative are included here. In fact, Hokianga was affected directly only insofar as its Maori or Pakeha populations voluntarily involved themselves in the hostilities or chose to evacuate their homes in anticipation of attacks by disaffected Maori. In the event, serious disturbances of this sort did not occur there, since the most influential and powerful Hokianga chiefs came out on the Government side. Only Papahurihia — that is, Te Atua Wera of Omanaia — and Wharepapa (Tohu Kakahi), the chief of Ihutai, effectively assisted Heke. Indeed, the solid support of the Government by the chiefs there minimised the possibility of harm coming to Europeans, and this immunity was strengthened by a declaration by both Heke and Nene that they would regard Hokianga as neutral ground.[2]

However, the de Thierry family, largely on Nene's advice, abandoned their home following Heke's attack on the flagstaff on 10 January.[3] There appear to have been two reasons for this, one being that de Thierry no longer owned the land, having already accepted £1500 in Government scrip in exchange for it. Even then there does not appear to have been any great urgency to leave, but Nene, for reasons not altogether clear, advised the family to do so, on the pretext that with war impending little spare food would be available on the River for Pakeha. No evidence has been found that he advised other Europeans similarly and it is perhaps significant that Nene's ally, Makoare Taonui, later occupied the de Thierrys' home-site. Nene seems to have had some motive for wanting the de Thierrys out of it, but whatever this was, the family sadly complied *en masse,* abandoning its home of eight years in the Waihou on 6 March, eight days before the destruction of Kororareka, never to return. Not, however, before Heke had visited the house uninvited, and indulged in an unseemly scuffle with de Thierry only, it seems, for possession of Charles' musket; he accepted failure in the contest gracefully. As gracefully, in fact, as he later entertained the de Thierrys at his pa at Lake Omapere, on their journey to the Bay. The subsequent voyage from Kororareka to Auckland on the *Sir John Franklin,* from the deck of which the family watched the battle for the town, was, then, the last sad incident in the Baron's ambitious plan for a New Zealand kingdom. But his descendants survive on the River, from a later marriage of young Charles to a Maori woman.

In contrast to the situation in the Hokianga, the Kororareka debacle left the Bay of Islands almost bereft of Europeans. As Henry Williams wrote from the Bay, to Mair at Whangarei, 'Waitford is still here with the Pikopos [Catholics]. Mrs Clendon is here. Mrs Wright [,] Hingstone *Heio ano* [that's all]. The Bay is clear and on the appearance of any military the remainder of my family will remove somewhere I hope to stand my ground.'[4] Hokianga, shocked and watchful, awaited the Government's response to the calamity at Kororareka.

Heke was now camped at Mawhe Kairangi, on the shore of Lake Omapere in Hongi's old pa Tapuaeharuru. Anticipating an attack by British military forces, he was building a new defence work on a slight rise about half a mile north of the pa, at Taumatatutu, in a position which commanded approaches both from the north and the south, since at that time it was not clear from which direction an attack might come. Any attempt to pass this new pa could only be made in full view and range, between it and the lake on one side, and a swamp on the other, so that heavy casualties might be expected from any attempt to outflank it. Of unusual construction, the pa had a stone base, or *pekerangi,* in which the outer palisades were embedded. Upon its completion it was named Te Kahika, and its invincibility was assured by appropriate *karakia,* or prayers, devoted to it by Te Atua Wera. Nene, some miles north in his own pa at Okaihau, nearly opposite the present hotel, was supported by Tawhai of Waima and Makoare and Aperahama Taonui of Utakura.

The Hokianga settlers seem to have had a light-hearted attitude to these preparations, being aware, no doubt, of the Heke-Nene agreement on neutrality. Some of the youths played at soldiers, instructed by Webster, who claimed to have 'learned the sword exercise'.[5] He trained a number of these lads, among whom were Francis White's three sons, John, William and

Joseph, William Gittos and young Charles de Thierry. Some of these later took part on Nene's side in the battles at the Bay, along with Marmon, Maning and Webster. Webster, Maning and Russell were supplying Nene with arms and ammunition, and also military advice, if, indeed, they were competent to do this.[6]

So, Heke and Nene, sallying out from their respective bases, now engaged in sporadic skirmishing on the land bordering the lake. In doing this, of course, both were in breach of the Queen's peace, and by the same token Webster, Maning and Russell were guilty of gun-running. Shortly, however, when the Government became aware that Nene's actions were to its advantage, it sent him an official letter of approval, together with supplies and powder. Unfortunately Taonui got information on this second-hand, from Nene, a diplomatic oversight which imposed serious stresses on their relationship. But soft words from Nene averted a breakdown and the two remained allies throughout the campaign.

Ultimately, the Maori forces ranged against Heke were led, among others, by Mohi Tawhai and Arama Karaka Pi of Waima, Makoare and Aperahama Taonui of Utakura, Rangatira of Pakanae, Moehau of Whirinaki, Wiremu Repa of the Upper Waihou, Nopera Panakareao of Kaitaia and Pukututu of Kawakawa. Thus Heke was encircled by enemies except to the south, where the Mangakahia people were neutral. Most of the Bay of Islands chiefs, Hongi's former allies, supported him. Prominent among these were Pene Taui, Te Haratua, Whe, Hare Te Pure, Hautungia, Te Awa, Kuao, Heta Te Haara, Tahua Hori Kingi, Maru, Kokouri, Hikitene, Haumere and Tukerehu. And, of course, Te Ruki Kawiti of Waiomio, Papahurihia (Te Atua Wera) of Omanaia and Wharepapa (Tohukakahi) of Kohukohu, Hokianga.

Nene's decision to oppose Heke in his idealistic bid for Maori independence may have averted an attack by the 'rebel' forces on the infant capital of Auckland, since it was known that this was Heke's intention. But apart altogether from Nene's intervention, an economic factor intruded — a sudden overseas demand for kauri gum sent many of Heke's men off to the gumfields, ignoring his call to arms in their eagerness to take advantage of this rare opportunity to make money.[7] And in another direction, too, Heke was thwarted, since the Mangakahia chiefs, although not actively hostile to him, refused the passage of his men through their territory to advance on Auckland.

This, then, was the situation when in March and April 1845 HM Ships *North Star, Velocity* and *Slains Castle* landed some 500 troops of the 58th Regiment, borrowed from New South Wales by Fitz Roy, at Auckland. The Governor had not in fact been very upset by the destruction of Kororareka, since he considered Heke's and Kawiti's activities there had 'removed the most blighting house of corruption in the colony' — surely a strangely philosophical view of a major political and military affront.[8] But in due course, with 470 men at his disposal, Lieut. Colonel Hulme sailed for the Bay, where as an opening gambit he attacked and burned Pomare's undefended pa at Otuihu, near Opua. Then on 3 May, after a bloodless victory here the soldiers were sent on their way to Okaihau to join Nene at his pa. Landing at Onewhero, the expedition marched in foul weather by Kerikeri to Okaihau, arriving wet, miserable and dispirited on 7 May. The next morning, although there was no improvement in the weather, this bedraggled army went forward to attack Heke and Kawiti, and the pa Te Kahika, at Taumatatutu.

The Hokianga lads who witnessed the ensuing action plainly regarded it as a welcome episode in their otherwise uneventful lives. Young John White, present throughout, has left an account of this military fiasco in which he appears as a singularly insensitive youth. 'It was on May the 7th Wednesday 1845 that myself and a few others of my age [19 years] determined to go and see the first attack on the New Zealanders by British soldiers.'[9] Fourteen youngsters, Maori and Pakeha, walked up the Utakura valley, talking loudly as they approached settlements 'as if we were a party out on a murdering expedition', apparently for the sheer joy of terrifying the inhabitants. On arrival at Nene's camp on the day before the battle they had dinner with him and watched the troops preparing for the action, singing 'all the songs that have been written for 60 years'. White seemed particularly amused at a conversation between a junior officer and Taonui's wife in which both appeared entirely engrossed, but in which neither had any idea what the other was saying. John had a 'hearty laugh' at this evidence of pre-battle nerves. So, having had more hearty laughs at the Catholic priest ministering to soldiers, and mimicking his accent, the youths bedded down and slept the sleep of the just.

In the morning the soldiers were given hatchets 'to cut the

railing of Heke's pa if they rushed it,' which mercifully they did not do. The boys, with Webster and Maning, accompanied the troops to the pa, watching the skirmishing around it and the firing of the twelve rockets which had been brought up. Some of the soldiers, having passed the pa, looked back and saw the Union Jack raised on the staff inside, White relates, and thinking that it had been taken they approached, only to face a heavy fusillade. This trick, says White, resulted in the heaviest British casualties of the action. It appears too that to pass the pa safely on the lake side the troops had to take to the water, and some did this to bring the wounded back. The most lively engagement of the day was apparently a hand-to-hand encounter at the rear or south side of the pa, in which Kawiti's son Taura was killed. Thereafter, sporadic fire was kept up on the pa until the troops withdrew and retired to Nene's camp, protected by the covering fire of his men. In another strangely callous passage, White describes wounded soldiers being assisted by Maori women: 'the women pitied them, some of the women offered to assist those who were badly wounded, which offers the soldiers accepted, it was most laughiable [sic] to see a fine looking young fellow about 6 feet leaning on two old women one under each arm, all three looking as solem [sic] as death.'

White's assessment of those killed among the defenders of the pa — seventy to one hundred — was certainly a gross overestimate. Clearly in the minds of the young Hokianga men the whole episode ranked rather as a rugby match might — but was not, perhaps, taken quite so seriously.

The pa had, in fact, been impregnable to anything but artillery. Hulme had only his Congreve rocket-launcher, an anti-personnel weapon incapable of breaching Heke's strong palisades. Supported by Nene's men the troops could only skirmish around the pa, engaging Kawiti's men who were in support at the rear, and dealing with a sally from the pa. Both sides sustained heavy losses before Hulme, conceding the impossibility of entering and taking Te Kahika, withdrew his men to Okaihau, and on 9 May retired with the force by way of Kerikeri to Kororareka. He had lost thirteen men killed and thirty-nine wounded.

The wet, weary and battered troops, having returned safely to their base at the Bay, were left under the command of Lieut. Colonel Bridge, who decided to engage in a little war of his own at Waikare, at the head of the river of the same name which penetrates rough country in the south-west of the Bay. The Kapotai people there were known to be in possession of plunder taken at the destruction of Kororareka and this action had relevance to Hokianga, since it developed into a fight between Kapotai and Hokianga people under Repa, Tawhai and Hauraki, a young Hikutu chief of Whirinaki, a brother of Maning's wife.[10]

Following an ill-managed advance up the Waikare in boats, which stranded inopportunely on mudflats, the Waikare pa was attacked, plundered and burned on 16 May. There was apparently little opposition to the 300-odd force attacking the pa, whose occupants took to the bush, pursued by the Hokianga people. Desperate hand-to-hand fighting among separated groups then took place in the bush, where Hauraki, with thirteen men, found himself opposed by sixty Kapotai led by the young chief Hari. The fight and its aftermath is described with much feeling and effect by Maning's old chief, in *Old New Zealand.*[11] It was a close fight, but Hauraki's group prevailed.

> Then Hauraki cried out to the retreating Kapotai, 'Fly away on the wings of the wood-pigeon, and feed on the berries of the wood, for I have taken your land.' Then a certain slave of the Kapotai said, 'That is Hauraki, a very noble born man. He is a chief of Te Hikutu, and of Te Rarawa, and of Ngati Kuri.' Now when Hari the young Kapotai chief heard this, he cried aloud to Hauraki, saying, 'Swim you away on the backs of the fish of the sea, there is no land for you here.' Then these two young warriors drew nearer to each other. Hauraki had just loaded his rifle, but the caps which he had were too small, and he was a long time trying to put on the cap. While he was doing this Hari fired at him, and the ball struck him on the breast and passed out at his back; but so great was his strength and courage that he did not fall, but took another cap and fixed it, and then fired at the Kapotai chief, and the ball struck him on the side under the arm-pit, and went out the other arm-pit. So Hari staggered and fell dead. When Hauraki saw this, he said, 'I die not unrevenged,' and then sank gently to the ground.... Then Hauraki said, 'Do not remain with me to die, but hide me in the fern and

Kohukohu, showing Russell's house, 1853. *(Australian National Library)*

Webster's house at Opononi. *(Auckland Institute & Museum)*

John Webster at Opononi, circa 1890s. *(Auckland Institute and Museum)*

John Lundon, contractor, hotel-keeper, entrepreneur at Hokianga, and politician at Auckland and Wellington.

Gumdigger's camp. *(Courtesy of Martin Smyth)*

Rawene, showing Lundon's Harp of Erin Hotel (formerly Hardiman's) at right.

The Rangiahua Hotel and Store, circa 1900. The bridge was built in 1886. *(Northern Advocate)*

> escape yourselves, and go to my relation Walker, [Nene] and tell him to muster all his people, and come and carry me off.'

But the Kapotai were returning to the attack and Nene and the Maori allies were anxious to get away: Hauraki was thus left dying in the forest. Finding himself abandoned, Hauraki said:

> 'I am a mere man, not like unto my ancestors, half god and half man.' Then the spirit said, 'In the mind is the strength of the body. Arise!' So Hauraki arose, and travelled a long way in the night till he found a small canoe by the river side; then he pulled down the river towards the Bay of Islands till the canoe upset; then he swam on shore, and when he got to the shore he was almost dead; but near to where he landed was the house of a pakeha, and the mother of this pakeha was Hauraki's cousin, so that pakeha took him and concealed him in the house, and took care of him, and before the middle of the day a party of Walker's men arrived there in search of him. So they took him to the Bay of Islands, and the doctors of the soldiers did what they could to cure him, but without success. So his tribe, who had arrived at Okaihau, carried him home to his own place at Hokianga, where he died.
>
> When Hauraki died, and his body lay at Wirinake to be seen for the last time by his relations, there was a great gathering of the Rarawa and Ngapuhi, to fulfil the last rites due to a chief.... At this time it was night, and the sister and also the young wife of Hauraki went in the dark and sat beside the river. They sat weeping silently, and spinning a cord wherewith to strangle themselves. The flax was wet with their tears. And as they did this the moon arose....
>
> At this time men came who were in search of these women, and prevented the sister of Hauraki from killing herself at that time. They watched her for several days, but she died of grief. But the wife of Hauraki consented to live that she might rear her son, so that he might fight with the Kapotai on a future day. So she called his name Maiki, which is the name

of the hill on which stood the flagstaff, the cutting down of which was the cause of the war. He was, therefore, called by this name, that he might always be reminded of his father's death....

So Hauraki was taken to Te Ramaroa, a cave in the mountains, behind Wirinake, where his ancestors are buried.

After this unrewarding excursion up the Waikare, the British force returned to Kororareka, and the sorry campaign continued under the direction of Governor Robert Fitz Roy, but with a new field-commander, Colonel Henry Despard, whose achievements proved to be even less impressive than those of his predecessors. His first encounter in the field was at a place near Kaikohe now called Ngawha, but which is the true and original Ohaeawai. Action commenced here about a month after the Waikare incident, with 880 men, including 250 of Nene's force. This time artillery was employed.

At Ohaeawai, Saint Michael's church now stands on the site of the pa at which this encounter took place, some three and a half miles from Kaikohe. This stronghold was extended and strengthened by its Ngatirangi chief, Pene Taui, assisted by Wharepapa of Hokianga and Kawiti, to meet the next inevitable attack. Since blood had been spilt there, Heke had by now abandoned Te Kahika, at the lakeside, and had retired to a camp on the south side of the two volcanic hills, Te Ahuahu (or Pukenui) and Maungakawakawa. Nene had therefore advanced and built a pa just north of Te Ahuahu, using materials from Te Kahika, and from these positions the opposing sides finally met in a fierce fight at which Te Atua Wera officiated as Heke's tohunga. Webster and Marmon took part in this engagement, in which Heke was badly wounded while carrying off his grievously stricken old friend and lieutenant Te Kahakaha from the field of battle, supported only at this stage by Wharepapa's men. Te Atua Wera, unarmed, was then attempting to stop the retreat of their own people, and shouted to Heke to give him arms. Heke did so, but in his frantic haste took a cartridge-belt from a slain man and fastened it around the tohunga's waist. Since it was blood-stained, they had now both 'touched the bloody spoils of the slain'. A powerful tapu had thus been broken, ensuring the failure of the engagement.[12] But both sides were so badly mauled at this stage that there was no further military activity here until the British brought up troops from Kororareka to attack Pene Taui's pa.

Because of his wound, Heke was not present at the siege of Ohaeawai. This further ill-conceived and ill-directed action resulted in the deaths of forty-one and the wounding of seventy-three British troops, many of these falling in a frontal attack. The pa was later abandoned voluntarily, while almost unscathed, ten defenders, according to British figures, having died in the action. Clendon, Webster, Marmon and Maning were all present at Ohaeawai with Nene's men, who advanced on Heke's home at Kaikohe after the pa was found to be empty. The house was burned, but the man himself and his family had retired to Tautoro, some five miles to the south, to where no one, apparently, was prepared to follow him. Kawiti also retired south to his home at Waiomio, above which, in the Akerama hills, he started work on his own pa, Ruapekapeka.

Domestic and military events in New Zealand had by this time conspired to discredit Fitz Roy. On 1 October 1845 he was advised by despatch that he was to be withdrawn and replaced by Captain George Grey, the Governor of South Australia, who arrived to take up his appointment about six weeks later.[13] The troops were now camped at Waimate as a garrison, where the only serious diversion accorded them was the destruction of Haratua's empty pa near Pakaraka, a few miles south, and the even less heroic and gratuitous destruction of much property at the Waimate mission station. By this time, Nopera Panakareao, the Rarawa chief of Kaitaia — another victim of Hongi's family — had joined Nene and his allies at Waimate, and much verbal sparring and negotiation ensued there between the Nene and Heke factions, with the missionaries, and by correspondence with Fitz Roy.

Within days of Grey's arrival at Auckland on 18 November, Waimate was evacuated and the troops retired to Kororareka. The new Governor, who, unlike Fitz Roy, had also been appointed Commander in Chief in New Zealand,[14] was a man given to decisive action, and he quickly determined to attack Kawiti's pa at Ruapekapeka, the last pocket of resistance. And perhaps with the ineptitude of previous commanders in mind, he took care of this campaign himself. At the end of December Kawiti, high in the hills some seven miles south-east of

Kawakawa in his cleverly constructed pa, faced a force of 1110 British military — infantry, artillery, engineers and volunteers, with a sprinkling of East India Company personnel — and 450 Maori allies under various Hokianga chiefs and Panakareao. The attack on the pa was opened with artillery fire on 11 January, and on the next day, Sunday, a sufficient breach was made in the heavy palisades. Infantry attacked, entering the pa when the Christian Maori were outside in the bush at their Sunday devotions. The 500 or so defending the pa were thus effectively split, but within, Kawiti's people put up a brave fight, although against such odds resistance was hopeless. The pa was taken, although Heke, Kawiti and most of their people escaped into the bush.

The War in the North was over, but the bitterness between the Bay and Hokianga Maori persisted. 'Where is Kaharau?' Heke had said bitterly when the Hokianga people failed to support him in his defiance of British rule — a reference to the age-old bond between the descendants of the Hokianga and Bay of Islands wives of their common ancestor Rahiri. Nene, on the other hand, was well rewarded for his support of the Government, which built him a house at Kororareka, now Russell, and awarded him a pension of £100 a year ($200). To many of the Maori people this was the price of betrayal, and he never returned to live at Hokianga, dying in this self-imposed exile in 1871. The losses of Nene and his pro-British men during the war have not been assessed, but Heke's and Kawiti's total losses were said by their own sources to be sixty killed and eighty wounded, although by British Army records, there were 94 killed and 148 wounded. This was no doubt guess-work, since no certain means of assessing these losses was available to them. British official casualties were 82 killed and 164 wounded.[15]

Serious discontent among the Maori people in New Zealand was in fact only beginning, although resistance in the North had now been effectively put down, owing in some degree to the internal dissension there. Military action continued with little remission in some part of New Zealand until the 1870s — or even the 1890s if the Dog-tax War in Hokianga is taken into account, and the harrassment by the Government of Te Whiti's people in Taranaki. Successive Governments therefore kept a close eye on the activities of chiefs and people.

At the time of the action at Ruapekapeka the Bay of Islands

had been practically cleared of its European inhabitants. Grey was not prepared to leave it undefended, however, and against the possibility of further disturbances he left 300 troops there as a garrison, where they remained for eleven years. After Ruapekapeka some uncertainty still remained as to whether the uprising had been entirely subdued, which could hardly be dispelled while Fitz Roy's earlier statement of policy remained unrevoked. This was to the effect that the Government would reward 'friendly' Maori for their assistance by giving them land confiscated from the 'rebels', a course which could well have led to continued hostile activity. Grey therefore revoked this order, and by a Proclamation of 23 January 1846 issued a free pardon to the defeated allies.[16] Although Kawiti submitted unconditionally, Heke accepted the position with reservations, so that the possibility of further disturbances, and in yet other localities, could not be lightly dismissed. Therefore, seventy-two apprehensive Europeans departed from Hokianga rather precipitately and were taken to Auckland in the Government brig *Victoria* shortly after Ruapekapeka. William White's family went, although he himself returned, but his brother Francis' family remained at Hokianga until 1850.[17]

There had been three Resident Magistrates at Hokianga since 1840. They were Messrs. Beckham, McDonogh, and the last of these, Lieut. St. Aubyn,[18] who had lived at Rangiora, in the Narrows, about a mile or so south of Kohukohu.[19] Perhaps because of the isolation of Hokianga during the war, the magisterial duties for the district were withdrawn from 30 June 1845 onwards, and assumed by the Bay of Islands Magistrate. This was J.R. Clendon, who early in the year conducted a census, dated May 1846, of the European inhabitants of the districts of the Bay of Islands, Hokianga, Whangaroa, Mangonui and Kaitaia, the total of whom was 537 plus 92 half-castes.[20] Of these Europeans only 104 were at Hokianga — a small total for the second-ranking industrial settlement in the North — but the count of half-castes there in mixed-race families is disproportionately high at 36. In Clendon's rather confused list it seems that there were eleven (or twelve) families in which both parents were European, and these had thirty-nine (or forty-one) children. There were twenty families in which the wives were Maori, and fifteen single men, including one priest. A lone female servant appears — McDonnell's — and two others of unspecified gender, one

Russell's. Thus, little less than half the Europeans were children at that time — a very shrunken population of adults. Clendon may have encountered problems in defining the term 'married', but he credits none of his single men with children. Our friend Harry Pearson, whose Maori wife, Markham informed us, was snatched from his bosom in 1834 by Rangatira — Moetara's 'bloody-minded brother' — appears sadly in the census as unmarried after twelve years. Was he inconsolable, between wives, or had he simply discovered that marriage interfered with his carousing?

15. The Population Stabilises

With Clendon's 1846 post-war census a pattern of the future population of Hokianga and its activities begins to emerge. The spar and baulk-timber business was declining, and the wheelers and dealers and those who for various reasons were attracted to urban life in Auckland, where all the action was now occurring, had gone there. Two factors influenced this. Many of the thirty-odd Hokianga land-buyers who among them accepted over £31,000 in Government scrip for their land had pocketed this and skipped off delightedly to Auckland to take up land there. Those remaining, therefore, were the other thirty or so *bona fide* settlers who had retained their land, together with those without land who had elected to stay. Some too, seventy-two in all, had been scared off by the prospect of escalation of the war, and, as we have seen, were taken to Auckland. These included most of the mission families,[1] although the Reverends Hobbs and Warren appear on the census in May, with their eleven children, together with Stannard, at the Pakanae station, called Newark. Strangely, however, HMS *Pandora*'s chart of the survey of 1851 has a note on the site of this station, 'R.C. Mission (Deserted)', which was perhaps made on the Protestant assumption that only a Catholic mission would be deserted. But the note at least establishes that Newark had by that time been abandoned. But the Waima station, started in 1840, still survived.[2] Nevertheless, as Wesleyan mission activity expanded southwards, it declined in Hokianga.

So, apart from refugees who may have returned, it was mainly those in Clendon's census who remained as the hard core of European settlement on the River, and many of them were the older settlers. Among them were McDonnell, who remained at Horeke until the late Fifties, the three Webster brothers (John, William and George), Russell, Poynton, Lloyd, Trusted, Harris, Cochrane, Pearson, Marmon, Maning, Baker, Dunne, Young, Nimmo, Leef, Hardiman, Birch, Dr Smythe, Anderson and Martin. And the descendants of many of these people, and of others who stayed on, liberally contribute their names and descendants to Hokianga's present population. In fact this is perhaps the only truly bi-racial place in New Zealand, since an extremely high proportion of its population derives from these people and their Maori wives of the early 1800s.

For twenty years Hokianga kauri had been exploited. Only the timber was wanted — scarcely anyone was interested in the land it grew on. In the 1850s Commissioner Bell dealt altogether with land claims by over 700 applicants, and those of them who took Government scrip in lieu of the land they had purchased from Maori vendors received a total of some £109,000.[3] But the Hokianga claimants who took scrip — only some thirty of them — got more than one quarter of all the scrip paid to the 700-odd, which is a measure of the low regard they had for Hokianga land. For this land they had paid the Maori vendors in cash or kind, less than £4000.

Of all the claims Bell dealt with, 459 were by buyers purchasing land before 1840 — the Old Land Claims — the remainder being the so-called Pre-emptive purchases after that date. These, of course, were in direct breach of a provision of Article 2 of the Treaty of Waitangi, which reserved for the Crown the exclusive right to purchase Maori land — a provision which was calculated to protect the people from unscrupulous speculators, but which did not, however, protect them from subsequent unscrupulous Governments. Governor Fitz Roy, at his wit's end to finance his Government had in 1844 waived this Crown right of pre-emption, but charged land purchasers a fee of ten shillings per acre for land acquired under this waiver. However, ten shillings per acre could in many cases have been more than the Maori vendors were getting for the land, which obviously did not please them, so the scheme was soon reduced to futility by the lowering of the fee to one penny per acre. There had been 1049 Old Land purchases by 459 claimants throughout New Zealand, and 305 Pre-emptive purchases by 245 claimants.

Apart from its population loss Hokianga suffered from economic depression affecting its timber industry, aggravated by the flight of business from the North to Auckland, so that it could scarcely have supported its earlier population anyway. To fill the gap created by the deficiencies induced in the economy by other events, gum-digging — which had depleted Heke's manpower in 1845 — offered a little relief. The spar trade languished progressively both because of the reduced expenditure on the Navy by the British Government and the innovation of steam power in Naval vessels. Nevertheless, the export of baulk timber hung on tenaciously if unspectacularly, and was augmented by minor quantities of sawn scantling and boards from the Hokianga saw-pits, and, no doubt, from William Webster's water-driven mill at Horeke.[4]

So post-war Hokianga entered into a phase of suffering, resulting from its recent pre-occupation with war and politics and the shifting of the centre of gravity of commerce from the North to Auckland. This had started in the early 1840s, and had dramatically emptied the Bay of Islands after the destruction of Kororareka. No such physical damage occurred on the River, but at the time of the Ruapekapeka battle, when the hasty partial evacuation of Hokianga took place, Captain Patten, with HM Brig *Osprey,* came up to defend the harbour.[5] Apparently frustrated upon finding his services unnecessary, he proposed to liven things up by attacking an Ihutai pa belonging to Wharepapa, he being the only Hokianga chief effectively supporting Heke. Patten was only dissuaded from this by an alarmed deputation of settlers. Having sat out the war unscathed, protected by the Heke-Nene neutrality pact, they contemplated with dismay having a military crisis brought to them gratuitously by this trigger-happy British Naval captain. But his presence, and a force of Taonui's men who had undertaken to watch over Hokianga after Ruapekapeka, reflected official apprehension of continued unrest. And Clendon's census some months later established the number of Europeans at risk in the North. In the event they did not suffer, in sad contrast to the impetuous Captain Patten. Patrolling the coast on 10 March 1846 in thick weather, he attempted the impossible — to enter the Hokianga through the Herekino Heads, having mistaken this entrance for Hokianga. This was disastrous in every way, since Herekino, some twenty miles north of Hokianga, has little enough water inside or at its approaches for reasonable sized yachts. The brig became a total wreck at the Heads, providentially without loss of life, but in commemoration of this traumatic experience, Herekino has since often been called False Hokianga.[6]

A feature that distinguished Hokianga from some other areas of settlement was the absence of roads. The River was the road and all communications were by boat until late in the century, and this accounts to a large extent for the horrendous incidence of drowning there, which in Hokianga was the standard way of death. Nevertheless, a few roads of a sort — bridle-tracks — were made, one notably by de Thierry in the late 1830s. White also made a track between Mangungu and Waima, to connect the two stations, parts of which may still be seen, and another up the Utakura River.[7] This, and de Thierry's, were beginnings of links with the Bay of Islands. For other than these there was little purpose until in the 1880s the Government, to provide access to land it had acquired for farming, undertook a considerable roading programme.

Gum was first exported from Hokianga about 1836, when it was fetching one penny per pound in the United States, but it was not until much later that its usefulness was better appreciated overseas, and in 1854, 107 tons, valued at £1712, or seven shillings a pound, were exported.[8] However, prices fluctuated very considerably, and gum-digging was not a reliable way of making a living until late in the century. In the interim, and perhaps at all times, gum dug in Hokianga may have been sent out through the Bay of Islands, so that the figures of tonnages exported from Hokianga may not accurately reflect its total production.

White and McDonnell remained in Hokianga after the war. But since they were men of large enterprise there was no longer scope for their particular talents, and their influence on events became negligible. When White died in 1875, a section of his obituary in the *Herald* seems to have dealt fairly with him:[9]

> He possessed those qualities which the natives were and still are especially quick to discern and appreciate — power of physical endurance, absolute fearlessness of personal danger, and a tenderness of disposition combined with a strength of will, in a very rare degree.

McDonnell's public image, on the other hand, was coloured by his violent insistence on the integrity of his numerous land purchases and by their excessive acreage, and the refusal of the authorities concerned to accede to his claims. Having explored all other avenues, he petitioned both the House of Representatives and the Legislative Council in 1856, but from them gleaned only conflicting decisions. By the 1850s his claims had settled at 91,300 acres.[10] But his Hokianga race was almost run, since few of his subsequent activities are of any note except the final disposal of his Motukaraka claim, which will be examined in its place. He was otherwise distinguished as the father-in-law of one A. Spofforth, whose son was Australia's Demon Bowler, the first of the notable ferocious fast bowlers in Australian cricket. McDonnell is also reputed to have been the first to introduce Norfolk pines into New Zealand and to have given Mrs Mair, at the Bay of Islands, the remains of a box of seedlings, one of which grew into the famous many-headed tree at Te Wahapu, Mair's establishment at the Bay. The large pine at the Horeke Hall was probably from this batch, planted about 1836-7. McDonnell was a very enthusiastic horticulturist and rivalled Busby in viticulture. Otherwise, he was notable for his breathtaking statement in support of his application for his appointment at Hokianga as Additional British Resident: that at that time the European population of Hokianga was nearly double that of the Bay of Islands — an estimate astray by some 1000 per cent.[11]

But he did bring fame of sorts to Horeke, since in his time he made it the focus of early European industry and commerce in the Hokianga. Seemingly Horeke has little future, but it did indeed have a stirring past that extended back far beyond McDonnell, Raine and Ramsay, Clark, Stewart and the others, to and beyond the heyday of the great Popoto chief Muriwai, who died in 1828 as a result of the fracas at Waima over the pig-stealing episode. For, according to Yarborough,[12] the Ngatiawa pa Puketutu, overlooking the village, was the last to succumb to the aggressive Ngapuhi assault by Rahiri's great-grandsons, Tauratumano and Toma, which finally expelled Ngatiawa from Hokianga. Seven or eight hundred feet above Horeke they then built the great pa Karewakirunga, and near it Tutehe. Two more guarded the entrance to the Narrows, and, with another at Kohukohu, these protected the whole of the upper harbour, as Taurapoho before them had protected the Waima with his numerous pa.

The last great military event at Horeke occurred in Muriwai's time, according to Lieutenant Colonel McDonnell, the son of Thomas, following a great *hui* and feast given by the Popoto people.[13] In those times, toward the end of the eighteenth century, Popoto could muster 1500 fighting men, and six villages stood in the shadow of Karewa, Tutehe and another nearby pa, Makauekaue. These villages — Otaehau, Te Horeke, Parepare, Mangatete, Mangaraupo and Waikahanganui — were prosperous enough to invite 2000 men and women of Ngatiwhatua to their feast. Accepting this, the Kaipara people embarked on a leisurely progress, from Mangawhare, near Dargaville, to the head of the Hokianga, which occupied a month. Here, the fully-armed party were met by Popoto in a fleet of canoes and conducted to the Karewa villages, where the three pa, in spite of the festivities, were strongly garrisoned. And under the direction of Muriwai the host was entertained and fed for a week, carefully watched by the garrisons.

However, all this hospitality and gluttony, instead of inspiring gratitude, only aroused the cupidity of the Ngatiwhatua chiefs Te Koukou and Ngahe, who, observing the bounteous produce of the land, coveted it for themselves. So, announcing their departure, they said that they would take their party home by way of Mangakahia, and requested an escort to lead them on their way. The remainder set out to return by the route by which they had come, but when both parties had travelled a little way, Ngatiwhatua fell on their escorts. All those with the Mangakahia party were killed except a girl, Ponaiti, who escaped back to Te Horeke. From the other party a few of the escort escaped, and they and Ponaiti told of the Ngatiwhatua intention to return and overcome Popoto. Return they did, but to have their massive attack met with such furious opposition from the defenders of the well-prepared pa that few Ngatiwhatua survived, since those fleeing from their defeat were met and slaughtered by ambush parties lying in wait for them.

In 1845-6 Karewakirunga and Horeke were again put in defensive array during Heke's War, when Thomas McDonnell had two 32-pounder cannon dragged to the summit of the pa and placed in position. An armed garrison of 300, supported by 17 other cannon lower down the pa, defended Horeke, but these defences were never tested. So ended the military glory and industrial pre-eminence of Hokianga's first European settlement.

Apparently Ngatiwhatua did subsequently dispatch a war-party to Hokianga in an attempt to avenge their shocking defeat, but it was unsuccessful. Jackie Marmon claimed to have been with the party which met and turned back the raiders on this occasion, but at the time of Heke's War and afterwards he was having troubles of his own. He had received scrip for land he claimed at Hokianga but was rebuffed by successive Governors and Land Claims Commissioners when applying for a grant of the land at Rawhia, opposite Horeke, upon which he declared he had lived since 1829. Claiming that he had purchased this six years later, in 1835, he applied to the Commissioner for a grant, but was unsuccessful, since he offered no evidence in support of the purchase.[14] However, after Fitz Roy's waiver of the Crown's right of pre-emption, Mr Atkins, Marmon's agent, applied for a grant under this provision, and in 1845 the Governor issued Marmon with a Pre-emption Certificate for 300 acres on condition that he produced evidence of a 'fresh and distinct purchase'. In January 1846 Atkins therefore produced a document of conveyance from vendor Maori to Marmon and requested a grant. But he was advised that until a survey was made and the prescribed twelve months had afterwards elapsed, (Gazette 1844, p. 139, Clause 10) no grant could be issued. In September 1849 he again applied for a grant, but was refused on the grounds that he had not produced the survey. But Marmon was told that he would be allowed to purchase as much of the land as he had improved. This, of course, would have involved making further payment for land he had already purchased, and again the matter lapsed.

Having taken scrip for all other land he had purchased, Marmon was now in the position of having no title to the land on which he had lived for 20 years. So in 1858 he applied to Commissioner Bell at the Hokianga Court of Claims, with an affidavit witnessed by J. White and the chief Pangari, for the title to Rawhia on the evidence of his 1835 purchase, having by now surveyed the land. He also produced Pangari as a witness to the purchase, and to his occupation of Rawhia since 1829. Very sensibly, therefore, Bell directed in 1862 that a grant be made to Marmon for Rawhia, an area of 523 acres, which was duly made in 1865, thirty years after the purchase, and after thirty-six years of occupation. The mind boggles at this very early evidence of departmental intransigence, as much as at Marmon's apparent ineptitude. At Hokianga, only McDonnell's difficulties exceed Marmon's in their complexity.

White and McDonnell having been obliged, owing to their self-inflicted problems, to relax their firm grip on public affairs in Hokianga, Russell and J. Webster became the men to be reckoned with there. Russell was well established at Kohukohu in the late 1840s. He was involved in a partnership with Dr Campbell, of Auckland, (later Sir John Logan Campbell) who, with John Webster, inherited his Kohukohu property upon his death in 1855.[15] Webster had previously been Campbell's agent in Hokianga, but had married Russell's daughter in that year.

By 1847 a small community had developed between Kohukohu and Rangiora, where there is a small bay a little to the north of the present vehicular ferry landing. Russell and Dr Smythe were at Kohukohu itself, and Marriner a little further downstream, near the present Marriner Street, at the place then called Rakaupara, while John Webster had set himself up at Rangiora, where some time later his brother William had a sawmill. But even in 1847 it was a place of some importance, since the Customs-house and Post Office were located there, presided over by Lieutenant St Aubyn, who was also the local policeman.[16] St Aubyn had been appointed Police Magistrate at Hokianga in 1843 but the position was abolished on 30 June 1845 and he was instructed to hand Magisterial papers over to J.R. Clendon who was Police Magistrate at the Bay of Islands.[17] Although late in 1846 he seems to have wandered off to Sydney, a new incumbent was appointed in January 1847, and the Customs-house and Post Office appear at Rangiora on HMS *Pandora*'s 1851 survey of Hokianga. Matthew Marriner, as we know, then owned about 1000 acres which extended about four miles up the coast from Rangiora, but excluded Russell's fifty-three acres. The property, when later exchanged for scrip, passed to the Crown, which vested the land extending from about Rakaupara almost to Rangiora in Maori owners, under the name of Tauteihiihi.

In the 1840s Webster ran quite a thriving business from his home at Rangiora, purchasing kauri gum, wheat, potatoes and onions for re-sale and export. Much of this came from the Maori people in the Omanaia valley, whence little timber seems to have been taken in early times. Here he made the acquaintance of Te Atua Wera, or Papahurihia, Hone Heke's tohunga, who became his firm friend.[18] At this time, Webster had sources of baulk timber, mostly supplied by Cassidy, who had sawyers working up the Waima River, and by Cochrane, in the Mangamuka. Webster acted as agent in this trade for Russell and

Campbell.[19] Rangiora was not, in fact, part of Marriner's land, but was within the Motukaraka block, which McDonnell claimed to have purchased and later sold to the New Zealand Company, but which, to his discomfiture, was later taken over by the Government.

Webster's timber business involved very hard physical toil, since the squared or sawn timber from the rivers was brought only to the banks for him. Here it was made up into rafts, which he and his men then towed to his holding-booms at Rangiora with rowing-boats. But Webster was clearly a tough man. On one occasion he rowed from Rangiora to Horeke, and from there he walked the whole distance to Paihia, at the Bay of Islands, all in one day. This was about four miles by water and some thirty by land, over some rough going in the Utakura valley. But Webster was also a gentleman of some compassion and gallantry, as we shall see.[20] In the first week in January 1847, William White Junior brought two young Maori women down to Rangiora. They were cousins — slaves of Ngapuhi captured in the Waikato — who had been working for William's mother, but in the cold-blooded way captors then had with their slaves, their owners announced that they intended to take one of them away and kill the other. So, after discussion with young White, Webster undertook to hide them in the bush around his place until they could be smuggled on board a vessel for Auckland, and from there returned to their Waikato relatives.

The girls apparently made themselves relatively comfortable in the Rangiora scrub, living off the land and watched over and partly fed by Webster until young White was able to take them secretly into the Orira River, whence in February he was able to arrange for their passage to Auckland. All this was done in great secrecy, since both Webster and the Whites risked serious utu, or retribution, from the girls' callous keepers. So successful in fact was the operation that these people were still diligently searching for their slaves a month after they had been spirited away to Auckland — one searcher even claiming that he had stolen into Heke's pa at Kaikohe at night and had heard the voice of one of the girls *kua moe tane* — married to a man. This was no doubt a liberally embellished episode recounted to draw the attention of listeners to the daring of the searcher, venturing into what, in 1847, was still enemy territory to Hokianga people.

Webster notes that even at that time the law scarcely

applied to Maori people in the Hokianga at all, where atrocities such as a husband murdering his pregnant wife quite casually by spearing her through the body, went unpunished and almost unremarked.

A pleasanter chord is struck, however, in Webster's account of the doings of his friend, A. Motte Esq. He had come from London to Hokianga to enquire into the fate of £3000 that his brother, 'one of McDonnell's victims', had sent to the Horeke tycoon in advance payment for a cargo of timber, for which he had waited in vain. Motte soon quarrelled with McDonnell, but seems to have emerged from the contest with neither money nor timber. He was dealing with a professional. However, he does not appear to have allowed the incident to interfere with his social activities. As Webster says, 'he is a very quiet, gentlemanly fellow, he is greatly devoted to the fair sex he is sadly put out because he cant talk Maori so as he can say a sweet word to any fair lady he meets'. Judging from A. Motte Esquire's subsequent activities, he did not find this an insurmountable handicap.

At Hokianga in 1847 there was no certainty that the last had been heard of Hone Heke. He was still threatening Nene, who, installed by the Government in a house at Kororareka, was building himself a pa there. At the Bay of Islands in January 1847 Governor Grey had sent a message to Heke to meet him on board his ship, which Heke refused to do, demanding that Grey come to see him. And Heke's Hokianga allies, Wharepapa and Papahurihia, remained a law unto themselves at Kohukohu and Omanaia. But in 1848, only two years before his death, Heke did meet with Grey, and they at least shook hands, even if they did not resolve their differences.

Nene, or Nene Waka, as Webster called him, seems to emerge at this stage as Governor Grey's message-boy for Maori affairs, living in his Government house at Kororareka and commuting hither and thither at the Governor's behest. He was expected at Hokianga in 1847 for various reasons, but did not show up. He did complete the continuing saga of the absconding slave-girls, however, by making a special journey to Auckland to get Grey's consent to re-take them and to restore them to their slavery in Hokianga. He got this consent, but the girls evaded him and got a passage back to their Waikato homes.[21] There, apparently, Nene was not inclined to follow them.

Among the evocative items in Webster's journal is his translation of a philosophical and in places enigmatic letter from Heke to his ally Wharepapa, at Hokianga. This is dated 15 October 1845, that is, three months after his first assault on the Kororareka flagstaff and five before the destruction of the town:[22]

> Sire Wharepapa I salute you. I hope you and your children are all well. I have not a thought my sire. only rest where we are. tis for Hokianga to give us some work. what work I care not then we shall know the meaning of all things flinch not if you or your sons are made sport of. revenge not but take it as good. heed it not. what is it to be jeered at who will wonder at it. Altho' it has been said what has Heke done he has killed no man himself. yet am I not alive on the face of the earth the only thing the foreigners have against me is the destruction of their property. The only thing I like it for (with regard to the land) I have the preference The Taonui [a so-called 'friendly' chief] was born there. My ancestors were New Zealanders. and the land is my second father. heed not my sire the news of this peace making. it is groundless. it is on account of the tears of my *matua* (Kawiti) this is all from your son.
>
> Heke Pokai
>
> Living at Tautoro

16. Settling Down

Now the memories of the war — exciting, fearful or bitter — were drifting away into the past, but the claims of Nene and his allies to Heke's land persisted for some years, and further fighting on this issue seemed likely. Disgruntled at having gained nothing from their active assistance to the Government against the 'rebels' other than revenge for ancient intra-tribal grievances, these covetous chiefs were demanding his land as payment for their services. Grey, to his credit, would not allow this, and all of Heke's and Kawiti's land that had been occupied by the British was restored to them.[1]

At Hokianga, in the aftermath of the war, a certain social and industrial stability had been achieved among the European population and in the late 1840s a recognisable social structure and pecking-order became apparent in the upper harbour. Although down-stream from Rawene European commercial and social activity remained minimal.

Upstream from the Narrows, social pre-eminence undoubtedly reposed in George Russell at Kohukohu, and his coterie of peers included Webster, Marriner, St Aubyn, the Postmaster and customs agent, Dr Smythe and Dr Day — all of Kohukohu or Rangiora except Day, who lived at the Mangungu mission station. Smythe, Day, Gundry, Maning, Russell and Captain Young had purchased land from Marriner — Russell ten acres in addition to his own fifty-three — before 1844, when Marriner had accepted Government scrip for all his land, including that sold. Therefore the portions they were now in possession of belonged to the Crown. However, this was later sorted out satisfactorily. Day's and Young's portions were to the north of Russell's fifty-three acres, while Dr Smythe's was in the Kohukohu bay, adjacent to Russell's additional ten acres.[2]

Now living at Matakaraka, at the mouth of the Waima River, Cochrane also qualified as a member of the Russell peer-group, being a minor potentate in his own way, and the Mangungu missionaries appear as associate members, with the group but not of it. Ex-missionary White at this period seems to have been spending much time on his timber business at Hokianga and Kaipara, but his family now lived permanently in Auckland. Brother Francis, with his family, remained on the White land at Mangungu, and retaining a certain neutrality, socialised with the Russell people. Gundry and his partner McDonald, with Maning and Young, do not appear much in accounts of this period at Kohukohu, and apparently did not occupy their land there. Young and Maning, although they lived down the harbour, certainly qualified for inclusion in the Russell group, if only on a visiting basis. And, of course, visiting captains were honorary members. As to Maning, Webster makes the interesting comment that he lived on an independent income of £200 from Tasmania, which seems to identify him as a remittance-man.[3] He lived quite comfortably at Onoke with his wife, Moengaroa, sister of the chief Hauraki, whose death in the war, it will be recalled, affected her so deeply. Strangely, Maning avoids mention of his Maori wife in his later writings. Captain Young, with a European wife, lived close to them, at Koutu.

Martin, the pilot and signalman at Omapere, near the Heads, was an independent institution in his own right, and this description also applied to Father Petit, of Purakau, now the sole Catholic priest at Hokianga, and held in high regard by all there. Webster described him as 'a most persevering man. He will be seen at all times during rain and storms pulling up and down the river. He is charitable and self-denying. He will give the last shirt off his back to anyone he sees more in want of it.'[4]

Next in the pecking-order were those who owned land and exploited the timber on it with Maori labour, mainly in the Mangamuka, Orira and Waima rivers, of whom Trusted, Cassidy, Pearson, Poynton, and Harris were examples. Then came the sawyers they employed — a tough, roiling, roistering band — so many thorns in the side of the Wesleyan missionaries. And lastly, in a category of one, by himself, was John (Jacky) Marmon, whom Webster describes, without rancour, as the 'white savage', probably due to his former reputed cannibalism. His home, Rawhia, about which so much dispute revolved, was on the north side of the harbour, opposite to Horeke, at the mouth of the Waihou River.

Rawene, later the metropolis of Hokianga when it became the County Town in 1876, appears in the late 1840s to have had no permanent European inhabitants. By Maori deed it had been conveyed to the New Zealand Company in 1827, but the Company never pursued its claim to the land. Ross[5] states that Captain McDonough, who was appointed both Postmaster and Resident Magistrate in Hokianga in 1840 and 1841 respectively, lived there during his term of office. He purchased the house William White had built while he was in England in 1837-8. However, there is no record of subsequent functionaries having resided there until about 1861, and we know that Robert St Aubyn, who followed McDonough in 1843, was located at Rangiora. And from there the local officials, including one H. Aubrey, seem to have operated at least until the mid-1850s. In 1861, Sir George Grey convened a meeting of 1500 Maori at Rawene, when it was decided that the Resident Magistrate should be located there,[6] since hitherto a serious incidence of unchecked lawlessness had prevailed in Hokianga. With regard to the name Rawene, some authorities believe, mostly on the evidence of Magistrate von Sturmer's documents in that period, that it was not in common use until the 1870s. But in his 1847 Journal Webster refers quite consistently to the point as 'Rawini'. And the plan of the township produced by the surveyor W.G. Clarke in 1864, was headed in very large and ornate lettering, 'Rawene', and beneath that in small print, 'Herd's Point'. From then onwards, the official names were, in succession, Township of Hokianga, and finally, in 1947, Town of Rawene.

In the late 1840s then the focus of commercial and social activity was still in the upper harbour, where it was to remain for many years. All was not peace there, however. Cochrane and McDonnell had upset the balance of the local labour market by importing Rarawa Maori from north of the harbour — Whangape and Herekino people. No doubt these offered their service cheaper, but they were hostile to the Hokianga Ngapuhi, and on one occasion a party of them robbed Webster's people at Rangiora. This gave rise to a tense situation there that had a potential for serious trouble. After an ugly scene at Webster's place, the Rarawa retired with their loot, much to the disgust of the Motukiore Ngapuhi across the Narrows from Rangiora, who had been unaware of the incident and now craved retribution. Resentment simmered for a while, and in due course a Hokianga party went up to the Mangamuka in force to deal with the Rarawas. But at the mouth of the river Wharepapa, with commendable restraint and good sense, stopped them and sent them back. He had had enough of war, and was having no private battles in his territory. Webster had the incident reported to Major Bridge at the army garrison at the Bay of Islands, since it embodied all the ingredients necessary to incite a tribal war in the North, but no further action was taken,[7] either by Bridge or the protagonists.

Episodes such as this disturbed the peace in the North, and there was little evidence of law and order. In fact, a detachment of soldiers had to be sent up to Mangonui, north of Whangaroa to apprehend five unrepentant cannibals for making a meal of a woman and some children. These were taken and hanged, apparently with little reaction from the local people. But old habits were dying hard, and passions aroused by the war were slow to cool.[8]

In this unstable environment the Wesleyans were not flourishing. In May 1847 Webster observed timber being taken down to the Heads with a raft of palings for a new mission station. But several years later a station at Pakanae, where Rangatira was now presiding, was, as we know, shown on HMS *Pandora*'s chart as 'abandoned', and even in 1847 Webster observed that the Pakanae people had a firm belief in Te Atua Wera, whose influence was clearly spreading from Omanaia to the lower harbour.

Te Atua Wera, or Papahurihia, had been Hone Heke's lieutenant, in a cause which had both political and spiritual undertones. History has devoted little attention to the reasons behind Heke's war, or to the intensity of the feeling of the people who rallied to him. Heke is merely a 'rebel' and Nene is still regarded indulgently by Europeans as the 'friendly' chief. The war had ended at Ruapekapeka a little over a year before Webster wrote, but the bitterness and dissension that had been encouraged and nurtured by the Government for military purposes lingered, and is found written into a letter of 1845, written by a chief, Te Heira to a woman at Hokianga:[9]

> Tautoro October 19 — 1845.
>
> My friend the Werupu how do you do, my love is great for you. I have received your letters and have seen your thoughts. they are right. they make my heart weep for love. they are right but what my friend can

be done. you are at a good distance. when at the Kahika [Heke's pa at Lake Omapere] the Taka and I were fellow workmen in building the Pah of the Kahika and the return for our work was the death of some few of the soldiers and at Owhaeawae [Ohaeawai] the Wharepapa and the Ngawa assisted us in building the Pah. the return was the death of the soldiers. that is all paid — The Werupu listen to my thoughts. twas you who just asked of us our thoughts. it would have been right if you had gone and joined Nene Waka. should Waka ask why you prefer me and Heke tell him that Heke, I and yourself have but one ancestor Te Pakiana. if he says it is not so I tell you then he is judging falsely why? does he not remember it is a war in which a man may do as he likes. he must not think that all must go to join him. let every man choose for himself and act without prejudice. it is well if a man takes to the Waka and the Governor and England. it is also good if a man joins us to defend the land of New Zealand. why has Nene Waka brought up the things of other days. he did it that you might turn against Heke and I. did this work begin with Waka that he has dug up the faults of our fathers to the light — my friend the Werupu this was begun for the land. it was against the soldiers we fought and not Waka. it was he who wished to fight us thinking he would exterminate us. this is all that I have to say to you. go my letter to my sister the Werupu

from her friend
Te Heira

To the Werupu
at Oriwa Hokianga

What Heira is saying, in effect, is that it was the right of every man to fight for British rule or against it, as he saw fit, but Nene was fighting his own people, with British military support, to settle old grievances.

Such was the political and social situation at Hokianga when in November 1851 the survey-ship HMS *Pandora,* with Commander Drury, entered the harbour. This vessel, and HMS

Acheron, undertook the first comprehensive surveys of the New Zealand coast since Captain Cook, and *Pandora,* in charting the Hokianga, followed Herd, who, twenty-four years earlier had done a quite serviceable survey from the Heads to the Narrows. Now *Pandora,* with the most modern techniques of the time at her disposal, produced a very good chart of the harbour from the bar to the upper limit of the tidal waters. And while this was in progress, some of the officers spent their time socialising and exploring upstream from the Narrows. John Jolliffe, the Surgeon, has left a vivid account of their adventures. Their first anchorage there, he tells us, was 'opposite the residence of Mr. Russell', where some of them went on shore to visit him and to 'walk through his sweetly pretty garden which is the [sic] by far the prettiest I have ever seen out of England it is a perfect garden of Eden in the Wilderness, one would hardly believe how vigourously [sic] the roses & other English plants & shrubs grow in this fine country'.[10]

By this time, John Webster had left Rangiora on a journey which took him to the USA, the Pacific and Australia, and also to Scotland, and from there he did not return to Hokianga until 1855.[11] Marriner, who, by the way, had at one time been McDonnell's storeman, seems to have acted as Postmaster following St Aubyn's defection, and Harcourt Aubrey held the position from 1851 to 1856.[12] Perhaps Collector of customs too, since, as we know, the *Pandora* chart of 1851 shows both those offices at Rangiora.

John's brother, William Webster, was still running his water-driven sawmill over at the Wairere River, close to Mangungu, and the *Pandora* officers, attracted by descriptions of the Wairere valley, strewn with its great rocks, proceeded there. They found William 'a very respectable young Scotchman residing at the village', cleaning up his neglected garden and finishing the building of his house. He was also finding time to build a large organ, of all things, in this howling wilderness of rocks and forest, which was intended for the Harmonic Society at Auckland. He was cutting and polishing the ivory for the keys himself, and the whole work was about half completed.

William then, in startling contrast to his organ activities, evinced an interest in what he called the 'Vegetable catapillar', and introduced the *Pandora*'s people to this revolting insect. Fascinated by the beastie, Jolliffe expounded on its anatomical and biological peculiarities over more than five pages of his journal. This, no doubt, was the obese caterpillar that lurks in the ground after the kumara have been dug, and bites off the roots of any plants grown subsequently.

Visiting McDonnell at Horeke, Jolliffe observed that he had not prospered, and was in 'much reduced circumstances'. Mrs McDonnell was very ill, and their two eldest daughters were in England, 'but a whole swarm of small fry were at home'. No wonder the poor lady was ill. Altogether, the McDonnell image of 1851 bespeaks a sad reduction both in industry and morale. The name of his establishment appears in those times to have been rendered 'Hauraki', and in fact, the Waihou, the river at whose mouth it is located, is shown on the *Pandora* chart as the 'Hauraki River'.

Morton-Jones, a fellow officer with Jolliffe on the *Pandora,* comments further on the McDonnells' sad condition:

> They appeared to be living very miserably, the house delapidated, the gardens, overgrown with weeds, a perfect wilderness, everything bearing the aspect of decay, and fallen greatness. He is a very pleasant, plausible person. Told us the history of his coming to New Zealand, and rattled on about himself as long as we choosed to listen to him: [His house, burned in 1842, he valued] 'at the lowest estimate' (as he told us, looking up to the ceiling thinking how high he could with any degree of conscience say) £8000 [was] totally destroyed. Had he conducted his affairs in a business-like and upright manner, he could in a very few years have secured an ample fortune.[13]

A function on board the *Pandora* on 15 November was recorded by Jolliffe and is interesting as a commentary on the developing bicultural nature of Hokianga society. The strangeness of the situation perhaps excuses the surgeon's faintly patronising objectivity. His account merits quotation in full, nevertheless:

> November 15th. Saturday. Mr. Hobbs [Wesleyan missionary] and his family, Mr. Russell & his family and Mr. & Mrs. Webster [William] came on board to tiffin (or I suppose it was dinner to them) in all about twenty in number Mrs. Webster was half caste & Mr.

> Russells children are all half caste the rest were English or European extraction; but altogether they formed as primitive and curious a group as I have seen for a long time, we did our utmost to amuse them all but particularly the young ladies which was no easy matter for they were all so shy, bashful or modest that it was with the greatest difficulty we could squeeze out of them a very meek 'yes' or 'no' so we had all the talk to ourselves I have no doubt but they would turn out decent sort of girls if they were stirred up a little and a little more life and animation drilled into them, they are much to be pitied as they seldom see any persons but their own family and those settlers who are living close at hand so that it is not to be wondered at that they should appear home spun and be diffident in the society of a lot of strangers.
>
> I am afraid our party was a little 'mixed' for we afterwards discovered that Mrs. Webster before her marriage was *servant* to Mrs. Hobbs, but of course it was nothing to us we were not to know the parentage and particular breed of each one of our guests indeed it does not do to ask impertinent questions of 'who and what people are' in this part of the world for they spring up in the Colonies like mushrooms and very often like those fungi out of any thing but *pure* earth so it is best to treat people as you find them deserving, regardless of their rank.

A predictable although not altogether uncharitable comment from a product of Victorian Naval society, who was clearly not interested in the social significance of the phenomenon he was observing.

The next day being Sunday, 'divine service' was celebrated on board, after which Jolliffe again went ashore and wandered around Russell's lovely garden, eating loquats and cherries. Russell's place, he mused, 'seemed to agree well with most English fruits even the apple trees bear far better than in most other gardens in this part of the country'. This, however, was no doubt due to Russell's devotion to his garden — something he later passed on to his future son-in-law, John Webster. In his partnership with Dr Campbell, Russell appears as a 'middle-man' rather than an active contractor in the timber business, and as Jolliffe's sketch of the place suggests, he put a great deal of time into developing his comparatively small land-holding at Kohukohu. Here was his home, but his timber interests were elsewhere. And according to Webster[14] he had 'got a road out through the bush for a number of miles at a great expense'. There can be little doubt that this road headed in a north-westerly direction from Russell's property along the ridge towards Rakautapu, in the general direction of Whangape and, in the long view, Kaitaia. That is, along the route followed by the Government-built Rakautapu road in the 1880s. Owing to the rugged topography there was nowhere else to go, but it is unlikely that Russell's contribution was more than the cutting of the bush along the route, which would have been all that was necessary along the ridge-top. Webster writes of coming upon this 'road' on a pigeon-shooting expedition:

> ... it is about 20 feet wide we walked gently along this fine shady vista of trees in some parts the road was magnificent palms & lofty fern trees ornamenting either side with the dark gloomy forest in the background at one spot was a tree that had been cut by the natives before the iron hatchet had been introduced it had been felled by the stone tomahawk we came to the top of a high hill when we had a splendid view of the river in all its windings ... after we had travelled on the road for about 7 miles ... we gained the summit of the hills [where] we had panoramic views of the country which was splendid to look at from our position.

Both Morton-Jones and Jolliffe have left sketches of Kohukohu and both thereby contributed positive evidence on contentious local matters; Jones, since he showed the two famous Kohukohu cannons on Russell's front lawn, and Jolliffe by showing the stone bridge across the creek in the bay, thus establishing the presence of both before 1851.

Having enjoyed Russell's hospitality, the *Pandora* people planned a three-day expedition to the Mangamuka, to include the ascent of the mountain Maungataniwha, at the head of the river.[15] It is apparent from a number of accounts that Mangamuka was a very prosperous settlement, second only perhaps to Pakanae, but unlike Pakanae it was very much under the influence of the Wesleyan missionaries — more so than any other major Hokianga settlement. Jolliffe noted that this was so to the extent that the people's traditional and uninhibited songs and dances were no longer performed, and the songs at the children's level had been replaced by English-style nursery rhymes in Maori. However, the graphics of existing tattooing were indelible, and fine examples of thigh and buttock designs were observed on the older men — and more unusually, the women. The women were also cruelly marked with scars on the breasts and thighs — evidence of self-inflicted wounds, the required means of expressing grief and mourning.

Maungataniwha was finally scaled in pouring rain, but standing at the summit shivering and wet the party could see nothing but the trees around them. Consoling themselves for this unrewarding experience with some 'spiritual comfort' from pocket-flasks, they set up their barometer and from this estimated the height of the mountain to be 2000 feet — only, in fact, about 100 feet more than it is now known to be. Returning, they dined on roast wild duck, doused with melted butter, which suggests the presence of cows at Mangamuka. And so, leaving at six o'clock on the Wednesday morning to return to Russell's place, they found on their arrival that while their expedition had been seeing the sights in the rain the *Pandora* had gone about its business, and was now twenty miles or so away, down near the Heads. By pulling down there against the tide, the unfortunate boat's crew got the disgruntled officers back to their ship around midnight — after eighteen hours of hard rowing that probably left little undamaged skin on their hands. Which inspired Jolliffe to remark gloomily, on account of this and the rain, that the whole affair had been most unsatisfactory.

A party then went socialising up to Captain Young's, at Koutu, on the Friday, but apparently thoroughly soured by the Maungataniwha experience, and still disenchanted by Hokianga society, Jolliffe was not impressed with Young's two grown-up daughters, 'with very red hair and painfully shy and reserved. We totally failed in "bringing them out" though we made ourselves as agreeable as we could, what can be more horrible than a stuffy girl to talk to!' An insensitive man to talk to, perhaps. However, on the ship at Pakanae he seems to have had better luck with 'a whole host of natives' including young ladies, who visited on board a few days later. And predictably, the young ladies were showered with presents. But a Maori girl called Julia, whom he met on shore after this festive occasion, impressed him even more, since he devoted nearly a page of his diary to her. She was 'very fair for a Maori, and really good looking and a remarkably fine girl for her age which could not have been much more than sixteen. But,' he concluded sadly, 'although young in years she was old in the ways of the world and I am sorry to say was as frail as she was fair.' He does not disclose how he discovered this, but he clearly preferred her to the red-headed Young girls. And he did confess to having been hugged by a pretty girl, sharing her cloak while sheltering from a shower. So perhaps he can be forgiven for his previous ungallant comments on his Horeke and Koutu encounters.

The survey of the whole of tidal Hokianga had been completed by 1 December 1851, having occupied only a fortnight — a remarkably efficient operation, surely. Only the bar remained to be sounded, but because of heavy seas breaking dangerously there, the Captain decided to leave this until a better opportunity presented itself. Jolliffe comments that there were 'no less than twenty four Rivers and streams which pour their waters into the Hokianga. Some of these are mere fresh water rivulets, others are rivers of considerable size.' He also observed what he considered to be signs of a much greater former population:

> The whole of the land in this district appears exceedingly rich and everywhere shows evidences of having at no very remote period been more thickly populated than it is at present, the native villages at present are very thinly scattered and at very considerable distances from each other, and the villages themselves are small, few containing more than a hundred inhabitants; the greater part of the low ground and the hills invariably are all most thickly covered with almost impenetrable forests of fine timber trees particularly the 'Kauri' and other Pines; here and there are cleared patches of land well planted by the natives with corn, potatoes, taro, onions and many other useful vegetables, the neat fences and

> bright green colour of the fields & gardens in these spots contrast most pleasingly with the more dusky and sombre hue of the surrounding forests.

What Jolliffe took as evidence of a greater former population, could, however, have been an indication of frequent shifts of population, due, perhaps, to the impoverishment of the land by intensive gardening over long periods.

17. Post-War Stagnation

Statistics as to the early population of Hokianga, other than Clendon's census, are largely speculative and the Maori element of it in different estimates was not necessarily computed using the same boundaries. Such a discrepancy appears on comparing the Reverend J. Hamlin's figures for about 1840[1] and Yarborough's for 1810.[2] Yarborough estimates the number of fighting men there to have been 2540, or a total population, calculated by multiplying this figure by three, of 7620. Hamlin, using the same method, arrives at a total figure of 3600. There is a large discrepancy here, but this surely cannot all be attributed to variations in the boundaries of 'Hokianga'. A reasonable inference, therefore, is that in post-European times the Maori population declined, as indeed it was known to have done elsewhere. The census of 1878 shows the number of Ngapuhi in Hokianga to be 2096, and Rarawa 668, a total of 2764 — lower, but roughly comparable with Hamlin's figure of 1840, bearing in mind the earlier rough method used. But again, the trend appears to be downward, and the figures perhaps support Jolliffe's opinion that the Maori population of the district was declining substantially.

The Europeans being much more visible and their numbers being much smaller, estimates of them are likely to be more accurate, and these indicate a very slow increase. Markham, it will be recalled, believed the European population in 1834 to be about seventy, and by 1843, according to Dieffenbach, it had risen to 200.[3] These 'found ample employment as long as fine spars and cheap labour were obtainable. But all this has now greatly changed.' Cheap labour, in fact, was not obtainable in 1843, since Maori had quickly discovered that they were being robbed by the early barter system, and demanded a fair return for their labour. However, regardless of all this, population estimates suffer from a want of information as to the methods used. Were the children of European fathers and Maori mothers regarded as Maori or European? Probably they were generally classified as Maori. They certainly were in Clendon's 1846 census, which determines the European numbers as 104. This, however, was taken at a time after a mass exodus had occurred. But in the official census of 1878,[4] before farm settlement or large-scale saw-milling influenced the figures, Europeans numbered 419, and included many Hokianga-born half and quarter-Maori young people. These, in the old families, were classified as Europeans, so that natural increases may have accounted for a substantial proportion of the rise in population in about forty years.

From any viewpoint, then, there had been little progress in Hokianga over this period, and the years between 1850 and 1860, and even to 1870, are largely bereft of both interest and incident. While the community relied for its survival almost completely on non-renewable resources in limited supply — only timber and kauri gum at this stage — its economic collapse, or at least decline, must always have been a possibility.

Progressively, the process of transporting timber out of the bush and on to vessels for export was getting increasingly unprofitable. The timber industry had been centred on the Mangamuka, the Orira and the Waima rivers, this being due to the proximity of large quantities of kauri to the banks of those tidal streams down which logs could be floated to the shipping-points at Horeke and Kohukohu. But the handy trees had by now been taken and the added expense in getting out those further from the tide was considerable. It had to be done by man-power, using sloping ground where it was favourable and block and tackle where it was not. And, of course, the bush-owners were selling a bulk product — generally the least profitable sort of trading. The market for spars had collapsed and there was little milling or pitsawing for export. Logs or baulk timber sold in 1853 for about one penny (about one cent) per superficial foot, while such sawn timber as was exported realised over one shilling (ten cents) per foot.[5] Yet over twenty years elapsed before any major milling enterprise was started at Hokianga. So the production of timber and the returns from it diminished until the late 1860s, when marketing and bush-working techniques were apparently improved, mainly by J. Webster, and later by Yarborough and Andrewes, and timber prices rose.

There had been a timber boom at Hokianga immediately after 1840. By September 1841 a population of 2500 at Auckland had been housed by timber obtained from the upper harbour. But this was the peak, at a time when the combined European population of the Bay of Islands, Kaipara and Hokianga was under 500. At Kaipara, at the same time, there were immense reserves of kauri, almost untouched and easy of access, but later, in the years 1854-60 inclusive, 32,438 superficial feet were exported from there, and only 13,798 from Hokianga.[6] And Hokianga's production never approached that of Kaipara from then onwards. Kaipara timber was also easier of access, and steam and bullock-power were soon to replace man-power.

Action at Hokianga on the industrial front, then, was minimal in the late 1840s and the 1850s, and during this period McDonnell was also having a harrowing time watching his land claims, which prior to 1840 had attained very ambitious proportions, diminish to quite modest figures. This was achieved largely by masterly inactivity on the part of successive Governors, Claim Courts and public servants. Only Busby suffered more, but his wounds, due to his mulish stubbornness, were self-inflicted. Even by the time of the first hearings by the Old Land Claims Commissioners in the early 1840s, it was clear that McDonnell's claims to land at Kaipara had no validity, and at Hokianga he had been reduced to two claims, his homestead at Horeke and the land at Motukaraka which he had 'sold' to the New Zealand Company in London in 1839, but which the Company had subsequently abandoned.

The Motukaraka claim was for eighty square miles, or about 51,000 acres. By one of several definitions it extended from Rangiora to and six miles up the Tapuae River, then called the Tora Mira. Thence by a line to the head of the Waihoehoe Creek and down the creek to its mouth at Rangiora. Including Motukaraka Island, at the mouth of the Tapuae. The statement in the claim that this had been a valid purchase from Makoare Taonui, Patuone, Whatia, Te Whaiti and others, was admitted by them at the Court of Claims, and Commissioner Richmond therefore recommended for McDonnell the allowable maximum grant at that time, 2560 acres (4 square miles). And strangely, in respect of his other claim, another 2560 at Horeke, although 2560 acres, except under exceptional circumstances, was legally the greatest area that could be granted to any one claimant by that Commission — and there was nothing exceptional about McDonnell apart from his rapacity.

In exchange for the Motukaraka land McDonnell gave the vendors 'double and single barrel guns, powder, shot, blankets, slops — and a great variety of other goods to the amount of upwards of £200'. The precise figure seems to have been, in fact, £134-15-00 at Sydney prices, but by the formula used by the Commission, the claimant was allowed to multiply this figure by three, which was supposed to represent the value of the goods in New Zealand. A rule very favourable to the purchaser it seems, and in applying it the goods became worth £404-5-00 at Hokianga. Then, by assessing the value of the land at nine pence per acre (seventy-five cents) in 1831, when McDonnell acquired it, the Commissioner, by this highly speculative process, concluded that McDonnell had paid for 109,780 acres. But the 2560 acre rule applied, and that was all he got at Motukaraka. And worse was to come.[7]

This, it might be expected, should have been the end of the matter, since Governor Fitz Roy confirmed the Motukaraka award, but not, for an undisclosed reason, the Horeke one. The grant was not signed, however, until Grey assumed office. He then did so pursuant to Fitz Roy's order, on 1 February 1846, but he, too, sidestepped Horeke. Then, a few years later one Hastings Atkyns cut a large amount of spars off the land and loaded £2000 worth of them for export on the *Honduras.* McDonnell then protested to Major Bridge, Resident Magistrate at Russell. From there Bridge administered scanty justice to Hokianga, and at long range he warned Atkyns off, giving Makoare Taonui permission to protect McDonnell's property from being plundered. He also refused to authorise the removal of the spars. But the 2560 acres granted to McDonnell had not been defined or surveyed off from the total claim (eighty square miles), so there was no evidence that the spars had come from his portion of the land. Off went Atkyns with the *Honduras,* well pleased.

In 1850 another crisis arose. Papahurihia, claiming that he had permission to do so from the Governor, cut 400 spars off the land. Protesting again, McDonnell asked for the 2560 acre Motukaraka grant to be made over to his children. But this raised further issues, since the investigation into McDonnell's proposal brought out the local Maori, who disputed the validity of the original sale to him. They contended that the vendors on the Deed, Taonui and company, had authority to sell only 200 acres of the land and that was all these locals would concede from then onwards. They said that they had not come forward before out of fear of Makoare Taonui, who was now dead. Their claim to the land was that they were the original owners, but having been defeated in a battle, had retired to Waima. Driven out from there also, they went to Utakura. The Mahurehure hapu of Ngapuhi then wanted to take over Motukaraka, but the evicted chief, Tuterangipouri, appealed to the paramount chief of the River, Muriwai, who installed them safely back on their land at Motukaraka. They then built a canoe called Nga Pukikairiri and presented it to Muriwai for his action in re-instating Tuterangipouri and his people on their land. Their claim, then, was that they had, in Maori terms, been legally restored to their land, and that Muriwai had accepted their recompense for this.

So, another enquiry ensued, conducted by Clendon, then Resident Magistrate at Russell, who recommended that the Crown grant McDonnell land elsewhere. A survey of Motukaraka was then ordered, so that a fair exchange could be made, but this was not done and the matter again lapsed. At this stage Commissioner McLean was instructed to report on the matter, but never did, and in desperation McDonnell in 1856 petitioned both Houses of Parliament. But the Legislative Council reported that in its view Grey's 2560 acre grant should stand, and retaining the confusion intact, the House of Representatives reported in favour of the 200 acres only. It is interesting that Nene intervened at this point in the matter of McDonnell's Horeke land, having been reconciled with him for some reason of his own, and offered to 'remove' Wharepapa as a claimant there. But he may have been against Wharepapa rather than for McDonnell — in any case his offer does not seem to have been taken up, and in fact, his influence in Hokianga now seemed to have declined.

At this stage, both the politicians and the public servants appear to have been thoroughly bemused by the matter; or had an aversion to it; or wished it would go away. Whichever the case, they seemed incapable of producing a solution. But the Land Claims Commissioner did try. Grey's Motukaraka grant of 1846 was apparently deemed to have lapsed owing to the area dispute, so in 1857 Commissioner F.D. Bell recommended: a) That Richmond's two 2560 acre recommendations be renewed, or b) that McDonnell's case be specially heard under recent empowering legislation. Nothing seems to have come of this proposal, but in 1860 Bell reported again. He advised that McDonnell had agreed that:

1) He should surrender Grey's 2560 acre grant of 1846.
2) He be granted 300 acres at Horeke.
3) He be granted the islet of Motukaraka, approximately 35 acres.
4) In satisfaction of all claims he be granted 1500 acres for himself, and 1500 for his children at places approved by him (Bell).

McDonnell having accepted this offer, he reconveyed his 2560 acre grant by Deed to the Crown, but since he was now financially embarrassed, most of his own new grant of 1500 acres went to creditors in payment for debts. But there is little to be gained in discussing the ultimate complicated distribution of the granted land. True to form, he appears throughout these difficulties to have directed appropriate tirades of abuse at all those concerned who did not agree with him. A shocked and incredulous F.D. Bell wrote in his report, 'He came here and used language which has never been applied to me before in my life.' Nevertheless, having grudgingly accepted land at Whangarei following Bell's report, McDonnell realised on it at once. He then retired to Auckland and died in 1864, with little to show for over thirty years of crafty dealing in New Zealand.

Before 1857, McDonnell had built a house on the Narrows, near Rangiora, where his daughter Anna lived until she removed to Sydney with her husband, Edward Spofforth. And a report by John Curnin dated 1885 advised the Surveyor General that St Aubyn, the Postmaster and Customs Agent, who had been at Rangiora since 1845, rented his land from McDonnell. And that upon his departure from there, Hastings Atkyns, who seems to have been a timber merchant, and an agent for almost anyone who needed an agent, resided at Rangiora after St Aubyn. It is interesting, too, that the report states that Christopher Harris, who has so many descendants on the River today, lived on Motukaraka Point in a cove in the Tapuae River opposite Motukaraka Island, in charge of McDonnell's timber-dock. There the nucleus of the family can be found centred on the marae and the church. Harris had purchased the Point from the Crown, which had surveyed and sold it separately following McDonnell's surrender of his 2560 acres, although the whole of the area had become Crown Land at that time. But later in the century the remainder of the Motukaraka Block was surveyed for settlement and at that time parts were reserved for the Maori.

In the midst of the Motukaraka furore, John Webster returned from his world tour, and in 1855, aged thirty-seven, he married G.F. Russell's half Maori daughter. In the same year Russell himself died, leaving his Kohukohu property to his partner J.L. Campbell, and, through his daughter, to Webster.[8] Adjoining the fifty-three acres of the Kohukohu land, to the south of it, there had been added, as we have noted, a further ten acres purchased from Marriner, which was later to become perhaps one of the most valuable industrial sites in the North. Before 1851 Russell had constructed his stone bridge across this bay, but although it is still there, it is buried under filling except for the arch through which the creek passes. Old photographs show its full length, which is considerable, perhaps thirty or forty yards. And above, on the ridge, Webster continued the beautifying of the homestead property that had been started by his father-in-law.

As a business partner Campbell appears to have been superseded by Webster's brother, A.S. Webster — a partnership that was apparently not short of funds. John had either employed his time very profitably during his absence, or had received a substantial injection of foreign capital, perhaps from his family, since the brothers now clearly had contacts overseas. They owned their own ships and purchased much timber-land along the River. They had offices in Australia and shipped timber in squared logs and baulks to England, the East and Australia. William Webster's mill at Wairere was unprofitable, however, and struggled on until it closed in 1869.[9] The returns for squared and baulk timber also appear to have fluctuated wildly. In 1853, 841,553 superficial feet were exported from the harbour and realized £4510-10-0, or about 1.3 pence per foot, while three years later the 1,146,000 feet sent out returned only £2357-0-0, or about 0.5 pence per foot.[10]

Such business as there was in Hokianga remained in the upper harbour, and in the 1850s there was little change in the distribution of the European population. The lower harbour, between Koutu Point and the sea came to be known generally as The Heads and remained a great deal more Maori dominated. Rangatira, Moetara's brother, now presided at Pakanae and across the harbour there was still little effective communication between Maori and Pakeha. Among the Maori people generally it could be said that the Queen's law did not 'run', and as we have briefly noted, Governor Grey was uneasy about this.

The concern over the absence of English law in the Maori districts was reflected in the enactment of the Native Circuit Courts Act, 1858. This led on 28 February 1859 to an Order in Council establishing a Native District comprising the Bay of Islands and Hokianga,[11] and it was pursuant to this that the Governor's meeting was held at Rawene (Herd's Point) in November 1861. Here the decision was made to station a magistrate at Hokianga. Following this, in January 1862, the Hundred of Hokianga was established by another Order in Council under the provisions of the Act, to which J.R. Clendon was appointed as Magistrate in April 1862. The last magistrate appointed at Hokianga had been St Aubyn, who relinquished the position in 1845, when it was abolished after an existence of only five years. Thereafter, magisterial authority, if any, was wielded from the Bay of Islands firstly by J.R. Clendon, then J. Patience, C. Bridge, G.P. Hume, again Clendon, then R.C. Barstow — all military men, except for Clendon and Barstow.

The sort of community that Clendon was to preside over is nicely depicted in a letter by F.E. Maning in the newspaper *New Zealander* of August 1864:[12]

> The state of this district, and the positions which the natives and European inhabitants hold towards each other, are peculiar ... *every* settler, every householder, in this district except one have been here from twenty-eight to forty years except such as has been *born* here ... *there is not one European female in the whole district* but one, who is not a settler's wife, *all* the settlers being married to native women or women of Maori descent, and their sons are grown up men, about fifty in number, many of whom are the acknowledged chiefs of their respective sections, and looked up to as such by all the younger natives up to thirty years of age, their cousins, in fact ...

Although Maning's meaning may be a trifle obscure, it is plain that he is describing a community such as existed in no other part of New Zealand, and whose inter-racial character continues to this day, although the intermingling becomes less obvious as the generations pass.

It is at this point that Rawene, previously a place occupied casually from time to time by Europeans as convenience dictated, assumed a sudden importance. The centre of gravity of the Hokianga community shifted a little when, in the summer of 1862, Clendon and his family took up residence as Magistrate at Rawene. Perhaps, then, 1862 qualifies as the founding date of the town. Clendon's first wife had died at Kororareka in 1855 — it was a common fate of pioneer wives to die comparatively young in those times — and in 1856 he had married Jane, born on 28 July 1838, the daughter of Dennis Cochrane and his late wife, Takatowai te Whata. Clendon was then 56.[13] Jane, a very able and talented woman, had previously been nursemaid to McDonnell's younger children.

In 1859, the surveyor William Clarke had been instructed to do a survey of occupations at Rawene, and his plan S.O. No. 878 (Auckland) illustrates this. Purchased for the New Zealand Company by Captain Herd in 1827, the point was abandoned in 1839 after a visit by its representative, William Wakefield. His nephew, E.J. Wakefield, remarked sourly some years later on McDonnell's alleged sales of land to the Company. Referring partly to Motukaraka, he wrote, 'He is reputed, moreover, to have deceived the Company as to the lands which he had sold them in England; the whole property in New Zealand being mortgaged to a house in Sydney, who had for many years supplied him with goods for carrying on the timber-trade at Hokianga.'[14]

Clarke's plan shows occupations on the point by Moses Tawhai and Arama Karaka Pi, chiefs of the Mahurehure, at Taheke. When interviewed in 1858 by Commissioner Bell they had not refuted the sale of the point to the Company by Muriwai thirty years before, and were satisfied with Bell's offer of a grant to each of them of an acre there. Apparently at the time of the purchase it was generally conceded that Muriwai was all-powerful on both sides of the harbour down to about Whirinaki, and, as we have seen, his family, through Makoare Taonui, later dominated the Motukaraka side in his time. However, in the period of which we write the Rawene district came within Mahurehure tribal territory, but clearly, Tawhai and Pi acknowledged the sale by Muriwai. This being so, Bell had little difficulty in gaining possession of the point as Crown Land, on the evidence of the Maori title having been extinguished by

Muriwai's Deed of Sale to the New Zealand Company.

Papahurihia of Omanaia was also in possession of a small settlement on the south side of the peninsula, but apparently this did not seriously affect the issue, since the Mahurehure chiefs had conceded the Crown's rights. Rawene then officially became Crown Land on Bell's determination of the position in 1858. Wi Hopihana Pohua (William Hobson Pohua) had made a half-hearted and unsuccessful attempt to substantiate a claim there, but John White, Francis' son, told him frostily that 'his own father Muriwai was the man who sold Herd's Point' and had, of course, accepted goods in full settlement.[15]

There is no doubt that McDonough's purchase of White's house and his sojourn at Rawene as Resident Magistrate and Postmaster from 1841 to 1843 had for a brief period given the place official status. But his successor St Aubyn's lease of land from McDonnell at Rangiora, and his residence there, snatched away this fleeting grandeur, which only returned with Clendon, nearly twenty years later.

Dennis Cochrane, late of Mangamuka, and later still of Matakaraka, across the mouth of the Waima from Rawene, had in 1849 obtained an Occupation Licence there from the Government for a 'run'.[16] Matakaraka had reverted to the Crown as 'scrip land' by that time, but in 1869 Buller called on Cochrane 'Before going up the Waima',[17] when he would have been eighty-eight, so by then he had no doubt retired to Rawene.

18. The Rise of Rawene

With the decreasing number of settlers actively engaged in the timber industry in the upper harbour, the decline in the effectiveness of the Wesleyan mission there[1] and the departure of McDonnell, a partial vacuum now existed at Horeke and Mangungu. Having left Hokianga in 1858, McDonnell, unpredictable as ever, took his departure from this life in 1864 at Onehunga, Auckland, in a manner befitting an officer and a gentleman, by a fatal fall from his horse.

For a year or two following the strange ceremony at Horeke convened by Hobson on his quest for signatures to the Treaty, the place had enjoyed a brief official status as the seat of Government agents such as Postmaster, Customs official and Magistrate, but by the 1860s all this glory had faded into the past. McDonnell's house had been destroyed by fire in 1842, deliberately, for insurance, if we can believe the uncharitable opinion of Morton-Jones, of the *Pandora,*[2] and Horeke was reduced to the status of a mere staging-post for travellers between the Bay of Islands and Hokianga. With McDonnell gone and with the death of Russell at Kohukohu in 1855, other personalities emerged to dominate such activities as there were on the River, and with Cochrane's shift to the Waima and Clendon's magisterial appointment, the Hokianga 'power-base' was moving downstream to Rawene, leaving only the Websters with any sort of influence up-harbour. Although Rawene was yet only a barren point, Government had plans for it, and now James Clendon, John Webster and Frederick Maning, through their professional, financial and literary and vocal aptitudes were the only contenders for political ascendancy in Hokianga. And Rawene's claims to municipal pre-eminence, supported hitherto only by the fleeting presence of a Resident Magistrate, and some Land Claims Court sittings in 1843, were now about to be restored.

Maning, described by Markham as a 'double faced sneaking thief' as we recall, seems to have done nothing until this point to live up to or to live down this description. But in the 1860s he became politically active and appeared then as a not very scrupulous sort of person and a denigrator of the Maori people, from whom he had chosen his wife, whose blood his children shared with his own. He had had a family from Moengaroa of three girls, Maria, Susan and Mary, and one boy, named Hauraki after his uncle, who died in 1845 following the fight at Waikare, in the Bay of Islands.[3] Greatly affected by his death, Moengaroa herself died in 1847.

Morton-Jones describes a visit to Maning in 1851:

> His is indeed an extraordinary history: he is a gentleman by birth and education, possessing some property in Ireland, which brings him in about £200 a year. he is also connected with the large firm "Manning Brothers" at Hobart Town.... he soon became a great favourite with the natives: fell in love with a very pretty Maori girl: and so mixed himself up with them, and conformed to their habits and manner of living, that he is now, in but few respects, little better or more civilised than themselves. He built a very good house at "Onoke": does a little in the timber trade, but cares very little for any thing beyond the necessaries of life.

But by 1865 all this had changed. Maning by then was the successful author of two books, under the pseudonym Pakeha Maori: *The History of the War in the North* and *Old New Zealand.* Perhaps their success gave him a yearning for a more exalted life-style.

Since he was a man of independent means, Maning does not appear, after his Kohukohu venture, to have been commercially active for some time. He had taken up residence at Onoke, near Whirinaki, in 1837, but in 1850 he apparently returned to the timber business in a small way. In 1865 he made a brief and bitter sally into politics,[4] campaigning actively against Hugh Carleton, the Reverend Henry Williams' son-in-law, for the Bay of Islands seat. In the process he vilified Carleton, and also Shepherd — the old Whangaroa missionary — and Clendon in the most intemperate and acrimonious terms: 'Carleton has been at Whangaroa drinking with the sawyers', and 'My impression of the Shepherds is that they are a cowardly lot ... especially the old man.' And referring to Clendon, 'I think I would try a knobby stick on him.' But after all this, in November, he was instead appointed a Judge of the Native Land Court, and eighteen months later we find him writing a letter in fulsome terms to Carleton.[5] Later again, however, in a letter to John Webster, he wrote of Carleton,[6] 'it has always been clearly transparent that any civility he showed to you and I was merely and utterly for selfish reasons, and all the time the old sinner was hugging his egotistical self and believing he was handling us for his own purposes'. And so on. In Maning's correspondence he is intensely preoccupied with the unquestionable rightness of his own views. No dispassionate evaluation has ever been made of his Court judgements, but the consistently derogatory opinions on Maori that appear in his writings cast some doubt on his impartiality. His letters seem to suggest, too, that underlying his animosity is a feeling that the Maori had little time for him.

In his 1864 correspondence[7] with his brother at Hobart, Maning refers to the fighting already occurring in the Waikato against the disillusioned Maori there: '... even though peace may be made with the Southern natives, this part of the country not yet engaged in the war is nevertheless like a powder mine, & the slightest attempt by the Govt. to enforce the British law or jurisdiction here would set it off'. Whether this judgement was sound or based on his own stated hatred of Sir George Grey and his policies is difficult to determine. But that his attitude to the Governor was influenced by his own problems he made amply clear in this correspondence. 'I fear that as long as Sir George Grey is in the country there is no chance at all of me getting anything to do under Govt. though many men without half my ability to be useful, indeed every one of whom anything at all can be made in dealing with natives are enlisted by the Governor & receive high salaries.' Nevertheless, he got his appointment to the Native Land Court, which may confound his complaints in one respect. And later in this letter, 'Sir George both fears and dislikes me, & the natives here have no confidence in me sufficient to let me do them any good.' But he plainly states that he is interested in becoming Minister of Native Affairs, and this, no doubt, inspired him to oppose Hugh Carleton, a Grey man, for the Bay of Islands seat. So Grey's appointment of Maning to the Land Court could well have been a crafty way of keeping him out of Parliament.

Clendon seems by now to have been an institution in his own right. Already a Magistrate under the Native Circuit Courts Act, a measure calculated to give Maori some sort of autonomy in law, and so perhaps allay their suspicion of British law as applied to them, he had a proven record of twenty years or more of public service. He was married to Cochrane's talented part-Maori daughter Jane, and appears to have dispensed justice to the Maori in informal surroundings and in an equally informal way, usually in conformity with the acute Maori sense of justice.

But Clendon had his difficulties too. An unsigned and undated report, apparently written in the 1860s, describes problems involved in a road constructed in 1866 by the Rarawa chief Wiremu Tana Papahia, between Hokianga and Whangape, pursuant to the Government's policy of 'opening up native districts by roads'.[8] This is interesting in itself, since there is an existing old road of sorts from Paponga towards Whangape still known as the Whangape Track. It could in fact have been an extension of Russell's 'road', which in 1851, according to Jolliffe, extended for at least seven miles from Kohukohu, to, and perhaps beyond, the 'summit of the hills [where] we had a panoramic view of the country'. This summit was without doubt Rakautapu, nearly 800 feet above sea-level, on the present Rakautapu road, which almost certainly followed Russell's. The identifiable parts of the Whangape Track still in use beyond there are Humphrey's Road, and, at the north end, Buchanan's road. Between these the old formed track can still be seen. This was probably Papahia's work, and the earliest formed road of any significance on that side of the harbour.

The construction of this track cost the Government the modest sum of £40, and was carried out by Papahia and his people under the general supervision of Magistrate James Clendon, whose son, also James, was, according to the report, the Clerk of the Court, and dealt with the finance of the project. Not a very onerous task. In this capacity he advised Papahia by letter in September 1866 that his £40 had come to hand, but when he applied for the money Papahia was told by James senior, who probably knew no better, that it was still in Auckland. The truth, however, was that James junior, being short of cash himself, had received and made temporary use of it. After some manoeuvring the matter was negotiated by James senior, who gave Papahia his son's newly-built house at Rawene in settlement, 'which' the report concluded sourly, 'was of little use to him [Papahia] or his people who made the road'.

Maori contempt for British law in Hokianga arose without doubt from the fact that the only law effectively imposed on them was concerned with punishing their infractions of it, and no benefits of the law seemed to extend to the Maori people. So the task facing Clendon as a Resident Magistrate of the Native Circuit Court was to dispense the sort of justice acceptable to the Maori people, which for five years or so he appears to have done.

An example of the lawlessness then prevalent at Hokianga is to be found in an incident related by A.C. Yarborough.[9]

> About the year 1864, the Kaitutae proceeded across the river to Whirinaki, on the south side of Hokianga, where there was a dispute about some land in the valley. Parleying having proved abortive, the parties camped on each side of an open space, across which a line was drawn, with an intimation from Te Wake that if any of the opposite faction crossed the line he would be shot. Presently a man named Nuku did cross it, as has since been asserted, with the intention of obtaining water. Several of the Kaitutae fired and Nuku was killed. The Kaitutae retired, and there were several days spent in firing at each other across the Hokiange river, near Mr. Manning's residence at Onoke, which is at that place over a mile wide, so that no harm was done. The Government thought it necessary to saddle the offence of the killing of Nuku on someone, and Te Wake was singled out. It would have been hopeless to have taken him captive without the assistance of a strong force, but he was persuaded to give himself up, and was eventually lodged in Mount Eden gaol. The story of his escape from that institution, told in his own language, is excessively interesting. It includes the scaling of the wall of the gaol with the assistance of two other prisoners, who attempted to escape with him ... and his journey through a friendly country across Kaipara Heads and back to his home, where he was safe.

From Clendon we get little of the denigration of Maori such as from Maning and Webster, and later from Resident Magistrate von Sturmer. 'The old Maori gentleman is dead or dying out', is the lament of the first two, and von Sturmer echoes that view. But they fail to appreciate that men of their ilk all over New Zealand had killed off the Maori gentleman, by depriving him of his self respect and authority. But Clendon does appear to have been a man of different calibre. He had taken up his appointment in Hokianga in 1861-2, where at that time there was neither a home for his family nor a courthouse from which to operate. At Rawene only a few squatters were present, one of whom was Bryers, and with him the Clendons apparently lived for a time. Here, at Herd's Point-cum-Rawene there were at the time few if any more European residents than Morton-Jones observed in 1851:[10] '... two or three sawyers with very ruinous residences at present hold quiet possession'. But there were Maori too, as we know.

While the foregoing events were occurring, the social and racial attitudes of the dominant Europeans were taking form and these soon led to a recognisable social structure on European lines, based on financial and professional status, despite the mixed racial nature of all the families. Morton-Jones believed he had detected a sensitivity about this on a visit to Russell, of whom he wrote, 'It almost appears a subject of regret that he should have formed any connection with the natives by a marriage.' However, any comment Russell may have made could have been in deference to his visitor's prejudices,[11] since at no time did his marriage seem to have an adverse effect on his social, financial or domestic affairs.

In the late 1850s the Government had, as we have seen, initiated action to lay out a township on Herd's Point, on the land which it had resumed as Crown property, and in 1864 the surveyor W.G. Clarke was sent up to do this work. Clendon had clearly been aware of the Government's intention in this regard before he arrived at Hokianga, having applied to the Native Minister for an acre of land at Rawene to build on. He subsequently got this, but not until 1866, when he commenced building the house which still stands, and is now owned by the Historic Places Trust.[12] In the meantime Clarke had surveyed and set out the 'Township of Rawene', which extended from the end of the point to the Tahere pa, a little to the south of the present hospital. It was designed with several streets running north and south, some parts of which were never formed, with a dozen or so running across the point, intersecting them, which have also not all been formed. From the end of the point, south to Marmon Street, there were over 240 lots, mostly of a quarter acre, and southward again from there to the pa were some 100 more, varying in area from one to three acres. Substantially the same as the original Township of Rawene, this today is known officially as the Town of Rawene and the Suburbs of Rawene.

The establishment of this town may be seen to reflect the Government's intention to promote law and order and to found an orderly community at Hokianga with the introduction of some of the trappings of civilisation. Sir George Grey's meeting at Rawene in 1861 and Clendon's appointment had initiated this process, which arose out of the Native Circuit Courts Act and the Native Districts Regulation Act of 1858. This legislation also gave rise to a proposal by the Governor to establish *runanga,* or Maori councils, of which twenty were proposed by him throughout the country.[13] Only three District *Runanga* were in fact appointed. That centred on Waimate, in the Bay of Islands, comprised three Hundreds, or divisions, Waimate, Kororareka and Hokianga, and was bounded in the north by a line commencing at the North Head of False Hokianga, or Herekino, to the summit of Maungataniwha, thence by a line to the South Head of Whangaroa, thence along the coast (including the islands) to the North Head of Tutukaka Harbour, thence to Maunganui Bluff on the west coast south of Hokianga Heads, and thence to the point of commencement.[14]

This *Runanga* sat first at Waimate on 26 March 1862 under the presidency of George Clarke, a former missionary who had earlier been appointed by the Government to the position of Protector of Aborigines. He was a man devoted to the interests of the Maori people and was thus unpopular among many of the European settlers. The function of the *runanga* was to advise the Governor on the promulgation of regulations to be applied in Maori Districts, which were to have the force of law. But the scheme failed: perhaps at Waimate partly because of the heavy influence of Pakehas on the *runanga,* and certainly because of its ineffectiveness. There also appeared to be a want of impartiality among the Maori members. But its final demise in 1865 was certainly due to the outbreak of war in the Waikato and the uncertainty about the attitude of the northern Maoris to this situation. In 1869 the Reverend Buller[15] did, however, attend some sort of informal Maori *runanga* at Taheke, presided over by Hone Mohi Tawhai, which probably owed its existence to the defunct Waimate body.

The official *Runanga* at Waimate sat for four sessions, in 1862-5, but its influence was negligible. Its members were elected for four years and its executive consisted of a Civil Commissioner and fifteen chiefs for the District *Runanga* — five for the hundred of Hokianga, four for Kororareka and six for Waimate, the last being a strangely disproportionate number. Staff appointments were three magistrates, three wardens and twenty-six *karere,* or messengers, divided among the hundreds. At the inaugural meeting the Government-appointed members were:

The President:
Mr George Clarke
Members:
Tamati Waka Nene
Maihi Paraone Kawiti
Arama Karaka Pi
Aperahama Taonui
Rangatira Moetara
Wiremu Hau
Hemi Marupo
Hira te Awa
Kingi Wiremu Tareha

On the next day these members recommended further appointments to the Governor, who duly approved them. They were:

Hare Hongi Hika
Wiremu Taua
Ruhe
Piripi Korongohi

Members appointed at subsequent meetings were:

Tana Papahia
Henry Clendon
John Webster
Henry Williams (Rev.)

James Davis
John King
Mr Barstow

In the last group the Anglican Church Missionary Society is seen to be well represented. Tamati Waka Nene, a Hokianga chief who had at that time lived more or less in exile at Kororareka for twenty years, may have represented that place, while Arama Karaka Pi, Aperahama Taonui, Rangatira Moetara and Tana Papahia would have been Hokianga representatives. The Maori members in the last two groups were nominated by the various hapu, or sub-tribes. But grass-roots Maori opinion was plainly modified by the European members and the pro-European Maori. However, the matters dealt with were mostly minor breaches of peace and order.

Although the Northern Maori did not openly come out in support of the Waikato tribes involved in the war there, the conflict did indeed affect matters at Hokianga. As Maning wrote in his Hobart letters: 'The natives have been disheartened & demoralised by the war from suspecting & fearing that when we conquer the south we may make some excuse to attack them here & this has caused them to be dispirited & to do almost nothing for the last two years, [1862-4] for we have been at war or threatening it for that time.' What disturbed Maning and other trading Europeans in this situation was the growing indebtedness of the Maori to them.

So Hokianga drifted through the troubled 1860s. In 1869 Buller noted an air of despondency and disillusionment both at Waimate and Hokianga. At Waimate, 'there were more than a thousand natives living near to it, whereas now they did not number above two hundred'. And, 'There were from two to three thousand natives scattered over the wide district of Hokianga, but not many could [now] be found living together in any one place.'

It seems that at this time only the Websters at Kohukohu were operating on any significant scale in the timber business. They were apparently well organised and financed and were said to have employed as many as 700 Maori in the bush at a time, and also to have recruited Europeans and Canadians.[16] Gum-digging was at that time a very sporadic occupation. In 1853 two tons were exported from the Hokianga and in 1854 107

Soldiers at Waima during the Dog-tax War. *(Alexander Turnbull Library)*

Maori prisoners, Dog-tax War; Hone Toia is standing. *(Alexander Turnbull Library)*

Kauri logs in the Koutu booms, Hokianga. *(Auckland Institute & Museum)*

Weighing green flax at Bolton's Mill, Waiwhatawhata. *(Auckland Institute & Museum)*

Walker and Reid's flax mill. *(Auckland Public Library)*

Bullock team hauling kauri logs from the bush. *(Auckland Public Library)*

Kohukohu, circa 1900. *(Northern Advocate)*

A Maori raupo whare, circa 1870. *(Auckland Public Library)*

tons, but in 1855 exports dropped back to two tons. They rose again to 295 tons in 1856, fell once more to 125 tons in 1866, collapsed to eight tons in 1872 and in the next year, when at one stage the price dropped to £18 per ton, the lowest for ten years, then to nothing.[17] But by the end of the century the industry attained major importance in the economy.

By 1862 the Government had unravelled the tangled skein of its Hokianga land acquisitions in exchange for scrip. As we know, Bell had ruefully reported, following the completion of the surveys of these scrip-lands, that the Crown owned only 15,446 acres. This, in view of the scrip issued, should have been very considerably more. In fact a report of 1857 estimated that Hokianga land purchased by Europeans and later exchanged for scrip amounted to about 75,000 acres.[18] So the Government was about 60,000 acres short. This would scarcely have encouraged it to expend capital on roading to open up a meagre 15,000-odd acres of dubious quality for settlement. And although it did encourage development in other areas, and indeed fought an expensive war to open up land in the Waikato and Taranaki, it ignored Hokianga until the 1880s, having by then purchased very substantial additional areas there, exceeding 190,000 acres.[19]

19. The Beginnings of Orderly Administration

The year 1870 opened with an event of some significance at Hokianga, which initiated a social and administrative change there. This was the appointment of a Resident Magistrate with the power of summary jurisdiction over both races, made under the provisions of the Resident Magistrates Act of 1867. It repealed the Native Districts Circuit Courts Act under which Clendon had been appointed, and established the Bay of Islands District for the purposes of its own functions. Hokianga was included in this district and there on 26 February 1870 Spencer von Sturmer was appointed Resident Magistrate, based at Herd's Point, now officially Rawene, although the name Herd's Point died hard among some Europeans. With the passing of the Resident Magistrates Act Clendon retired, after five years at Hokianga.[1]

Clendon had been a very experienced and successful magistrate for most of the period since the assumption of British sovereignty and appears to have had a good rapport with the Maori people and success with Maori-European disputes. When Resident Magistrate at Russell in 1858 he had visited Hokianga and dealt with sixty-seven of these, but difficult problems had since been occurring there. Notable among these in 1862, when the Waimate *runanga* was supposed to be functioning, was a matter of contention about land claimed both by the upper Managakahia chief Tirarau, and Matiu, of the Otaua locality on the Punakitere River. This had generated bloody battles between the contenders but Tirarau refused to refer the matter to the *runanga*. Arama Karaka Pi, who was actually a member of it, introduced further complexity by joining the fray on Matiu's behalf, mainly because he felt obliged to do so, his own father having been killed fighting Tirarau's people twenty years earlier.[2] In such matters, British law had no room for Maori traditional values and remedies, and it was many years before their differing views were reconciled.

Clendon had nevertheless been successful later in arranging

arbitration in a confrontation over disputed land between the Rarawa chief Te Tai of the Whakarapa (now Panguru) district and the Hikutu Makarena of Whirinaki, across the harbour. Makarena having built a pa on the land, both sides were poised for battle when Clendon intervened and succeeded in having the matter arbitrated by the *runanga.*[3] It was at this stage that he had been appointed Resident Magistrate at Hokianga under the Native Circuit Courts legislation. Much of this sort of trouble seems to have been generated by rivalry between the Rarawa people and the Hikutu on the other side of the River, but the ineffectiveness of the *runanga,* or the Government's views on it, caused it to be closed down after the 1865 session. The building at Waimate thereafter became a courthouse, and there and at Rawene Resident Magistrates dispensed justice, Clendon to the Maori people at Rawene until 1867, and von Sturmer to both races after 1870. When the Resident Magistrates Act was under consideration there had been much talk about the same law applying to both Maori and Pakeha, and some of the chiefs favoured this. But although the new Act did apply to both races, it still contained special provisions relative to Maori custom, and it was not until 1893 that this Act was repealed and Maori became subject to the same law as European.

Another event in April 1870 was celebrated gladly by the Bay and Hokianga settlers, since it reflected their views on their safety, prosperity and social pre-eminence. The Maori population seem to have regarded the State visit to the North of the Governor, Sir George Ferguson Bowen, with curiosity, caution and some hope. Bowen had been appointed two years previously to succeed Sir George Grey[4] and on this tour he first visited Waimate, the old ecclesiastical centre of the North, and long the focus of gentility there. The time was well chosen, since it was toward the end of the wars to the south at Taranaki, Taupo, the Bay of Plenty, the Urewera and the East Coast, and the consistent Maori defeats at these places must have been uppermost in the minds of the Northern people. While the tribes there had remained neutral during the wars, there had been much discontent among them and sufficient unrest to justify close watchfulness by the Government. With the persistence of the sort of disorder we have examined, law and order at Hokianga was plainly an urgent matter to be dealt with and much time and oratory was expended by the chiefs on this matter at the meetings with the Governor that followed. The troublesome Arama Karaka Pi did not appear, having recently died. He had been a very influential chief and the *hahunga,* or exhumation and cleaning of his bones for their final disposal was then being organised.

At Bowen's Waimate meeting the main theme of the Ngapuhi representations seemed to be their eagerness to be granted confiscated Maori land in the Waikato by the Government. The obligatory loyal address to the Governor having been delivered by the Reverend Clarke, and the socially eminent having shaken the Governor's hand, the Maori speakers plunged without hesitation into this topic. The first speaker, Wi Hau, suggested that if the Governor had not come to talk about this, Ngapuhi were wasting their time here. The Waikato land was needed so that Ngapuhi could stand on their own ground and negotiate a peace settlement between the Waikato tribes and the Government. Tango Hikuwai said, 'We expect an answer now from your Excellency upon the subject. Our desire is that peace should be made with the Waikatos, and that you should place a portion of the Waikato land in our hands, that we may have something wherewith to appear before the Waikatos to request them to give up their Kingship and be like us. If we have nothing in our hands we cannot present ourselves before them.' But the Government and its supporters in the late wars were intent on confiscating huge areas of Maori land in the south for settlement, which, incidentally, would benefit influential individuals who had waited eagerly for this. Ngapuhi, or indeed any other sort of peacemakers, had no place in these activities. So the Governor said very little in a lengthy speech on this matter, which, when untangled, amounted to a firm, if oblique refusal of the proffered Ngapuhi assistance.

The Northern attitude to the Maori defeats in the south, particularly among Ngapuhi, with whom a great number of ex-Waikato slaves had lived, married and been assimilated, must indeed have been a matter of concern to the Government. As early as 1861 it had been busy compiling statistics on the names, hapu and residences of the Ngatiuru, Ngatirehia, Ngatiwai, Kapotai, Rarawa and Ngapuhi chiefs, of Whangaroa, the east coast and inland Bay of Islands and Hokianga.[5] And even back in 1860, C.O. Davis had informed the Government that gunpowder was being made at Tautoro, south of Kaikohe. But it seems that the Northern people feared that the Government, having disposed of the 'rebels' in the south, might turn on them, as Maning had suggested. Hence the conciliatory speeches of most of the chiefs during Bowen's visit, which were relieved only by Kingi Hori Hira, who asked pointedly, 'After the ten years you have now been slaying men, when will you cease and save the remnant?'

Otherwise, apart from protestations of peaceful intentions, complaints about insufficient Maori representation in Parliament, and a request to have restored to Maori here the right to purchase arms and ammunition, which had been revoked during the wars, little of importance was discussed and less achieved during the vice-regal progression. This was a show of pomp and power following the Government's military victories in the south and as such it appeared to be effective. At Taheke the Governor was received by Mohi Tawhai and the Hokianga tycoons J. and W. Webster, von Sturmer and Maning, and was entertained at Eru Hiri's house with a luncheon served by Hariata Rongo, daughter of Hongi Hika and widow of both Hone Heke and, after his death, Arama Karaka Pi. Then on to the Hokianga Harbour down the Waima River, to join the Government steamer *Luna* at Rawene. And so to Maning's house at Onoke. Many chiefs, including Rangatira Moetara, Wi Tana Papahia, Papahurihia and Wi Hopihana came aboard for the ride, while the *Luna* cruised the harbour from the Heads to 'Mr. J. Webster's timber station at Kohukohu.... On the beach there were several thousand tons squared and ready for exportation. A large foreign export trade is carried on.' The Governor and a party went ashore here then proceeded down-river, anchoring off the Catholic mission station at Purakau. Continuing downstream, they passed the 'new flax-mill of Messrs. Walker and Reid' at Waiarohia, which the party later inspected. This had been in operation about six months. Then, in the evening, to 'a most agreeable ball at the commodious residence of Judge Maning'.

A gathering there next day was attended by influential chiefs of the harbour, but only about a hundred Maori people were there all told. The report adduced various reasons for this, but a likely one may have been a negative Maori feeling toward a Government that had been fighting the southern people for twenty-five years, and had certainly done nothing for those in the North. Various Maori speakers anxiously assured the

Governor of their loyalty and devotion to the Queen and to law and order, and Tawhai was careful to remind him that the Hokianga people fought against Heke in 1845. All expressed a welcome to Europeans and their industries, while some deplored the sale of alcohol and the establishment of 'public houses'. The new magistrate, Spencer von Sturmer, also got a welcome. There was no doubt that the defeats in the south had engendered at least an appearance of devotion here to law and order.

Having listened to and replied in diplomatic terms to all questions and complaints, with assistance from aides at awkward moments, the Governor and his party left the harbour for Ahipara, having attended to much important business — particularly the ball at Maning's place. Bowen was an unimpressive man and largely an ineffectual Governor, devoted to good living and race-horses — not the last of that ilk — who, commenting on the Maori people, is recorded as patronisingly approving efforts being made to preserve the 'surviving remnant of a most interesting race'.[6]

The disapproval of many of the chiefs of the sale of liquor at Hokianga had probably been influenced by the Methodist missionaries, yet strangely enough the Horeke hotel, among the first to be licensed in New Zealand, was only a mile or two from the mission station at Mangungu. But this and the Taheke Terminal Hotel, at the head of the navigable part of the Waima River, licensed at about the same time, were legitimately travellers' hotels. Both were at points where those journeying overland from the Bay and southerly districts took to Hokianga's main road — the harbour. Clendon, after his retirement from the magistracy, took out a wholesale licence to sell beer and spirits, and also a licence as a Wine and Spirit Merchant. These were current yearly from 1869 to 1872 and the address for his business is given indiscriminately as Hokianga, Herd's Point and Rawene.[7] Bush or restricted licences had also been issued to John Bryers of Herd's Point in 1869 and to Charles Bryers at Omapere, between Opononi and the Heads.[8] By this time there was no shortage of alcoholic solace at Rawene, since Clendon and Bryers were assisted in its provision by George Hardiman, son of Robert Hardiman, who in 1839 had bought 50 acres of land from Huhu Papahia and others, near Waireia. George now had Hardiman's Hotel on the end of the point at Rawene, where the building still survives.[9] George had married Mary Maning.

Apart from the law, then, the sale of liquor was probably Rawene's most profitable, if not its first industry.

The Native Land Court had been established in 1862 for the specific purpose of giving Crown Grant titles to Maori for their land so that they could dispose of it to the Government or to individual Europeans more readily, and without dispute over their right to do so. This gave rise to a tremendous spate of land sales, as it was intended to do, amounting at this time to about three quarters of a million acres a year.[10] And it was sales to the Government under the Immigration and Public Works Act of 1870 that belatedly opened up Hokianga land for settlement — something that the chiefs had, in fact, approved at Bowen's meetings.

An enterprise or rather a proposal in this period having a Hokianga interest, although it was located at Ngawha, near Kaikohe, involved the discovery of mercury there. Maning mentions this in a letter to Webster of 4 October 1872: '... there is going to be a wonderful quicksilver mine at Ohaeawai [the original name for the present Ngawha locality] it is said there is kerosene and other minerals also.'[11] But the Hokianga connection concerns John White, old William's nephew and Francis's son, by this time notable as an interpreter, a magistrate and a Maori scholar. In 1873 he entered into an agreement for lease for 100 years at a rental of £25 per annum of the mercury-bearing land at Ngawha, with Wiremu Hongi, Hirini Taiwhanga, Renata Pure, Waikato Whakaita, Umu Whakaita, Whai Te Hoka, Matenga Taiwhanga, Hira Wahapu, Rukia Koao and Teira Raumati, all of the Uriohua hapu of Ngapuhi. Apparently this agreement expired only in 1973, unless it was previously revoked. In the Maori language lease the mercury (quicksilver) is rendered 'Kuiki Hiria'.[12]

An event on the River at this time which was to have a profound effect on the economy there was the advent of the two men whose names came to be synonymous with Hokianga. These were Alfred Cooke Yarborough and Alfred Spry Andrewes. John Webster, by now apparently a wealthy man, and certainly the most influential on the River, had decided by 1872 to move to a pleasanter and more accessible locality. He chose Opononi, which he had earlier purchased from Captain William Young, and for which, as a result, he had got a Crown Grant for forty-one acres in 1862.[13] To this he later added some 600 acres, and in 1874 he sold his Kohukohu home to Yarborough and his timber and trading business there to the partnership of Andrewes and Yarborough, and moved to Opononi.[14] Yarborough, a well-educated Englishman, came to New Zealand in 1872, aged twenty-five. He had been in partnership with Joseph McMullen Dargaville, who founded the town of that name on the Kaipara Harbour. They had established a flax mill on the coast between the Hokianga and Whangape harbours — an unsuccessful venture that broke up the partnership, although flax milling at the time was a growing industry in the North. Both men, however, turned out to be commercial nabobs in their own right.[15]

Yarborough then entered into a partnership with Andrewes, who was another Englishman, son of a Lincoln's Inn barrister. Andrewes came to New Zealand in 1869 at the age of seventeen. He went to work for Dargaville and four years later opened a store at Hokianga Heads, where he no doubt made Yarborough's acquaintance.[16] Together they opened stores at Omapere, Rawene, Kohukohu and Horeke, thus serving the Maori population along the whole length of the harbour, and with this expansion and their later move to Kohukohu they commenced a partnership that lasted nearly twenty-five years. They remained general traders and timber merchants for some time, since sawmilling had still not come to Hokianga on a significant scale.

Having moved to Opononi, then variously referred to as 'Opunune' or 'Panoni', Webster proceeded to make it the show-place of Hokianga, as he and Russell had done for Kohukohu, and at the same time he ran a prosperous mercantile business. So the lower harbour, previously a Maori-dominated area, began to develop in Pakeha ways. Indeed, in his house, which is still standing and in fairly good order, Webster entertained lavishly for many years as the population increased due to sawmilling and settlement on the Crown lands. And, 'Frowning out on the river are embrasures, and the four guns (formerly of Captain McDonnell's battery at the Horeke), kept for saluting purposes when the Governors of the colony visited Mr. Webster.'[17] Truly Mr Webster had clambered to the highest pinnacle of New Zealand social eminence. That The Heads had begun to attract Europeans is reflected too in a minute of the Auckland Provincial Council of 1 November 1870, which deals with a petition 'from certain settlers at Hokianga' asking for a ferry service between Herd's Point and Hokianga Heads.

Overseas shipping for 1870 is not impressive, however. There were four arrivals and eleven departures, which suggests that there must have been seven loading in the harbour late in 1869. But even in 1878 there were no arrivals and four departures.[18] Clearly the internal coastal trade was taking most of Hokianga's production. Apparently a good deal of the Webster-Yarborough baulk timber was being used within New Zealand, since it was not until the 1880s that Kaipara so decisively outstripped Hokianga in timber production.[19]

Letters written by Maning to Webster in this period do him no credit. Commenting on hearings at his Maori Land Courts, he confesses to being 'deaf and dizzy with listening to the brutes trying to rob each other and swearing lies without limit'. If this was so then Maori had indeed been quick to appreciate the advantages inherent in Pakeha business ethics. The many intemperate and cynical remarks of this sort in Maning's correspondence scarcely seem consistent with discreet and impartial judgements, particularly when he describes the Maori mind to Webster as 'acute only in mischief — opposed instinctively to all improvement and progress'. Even Clendon's court decisions are vilified in Maning's letters to Webster.[20] An objective review of Maning's life and legal career is clearly overdue.

But all this was about to change. The agonies suffered by Maning in the administration of his Land Court came to an end when he retired, first to Onoke in 1876 and then to Auckland. And Webster found himself, although still active and prosperous, more of a senior citizen, although one with considerable political influence. In 1872-3 the Government had already purchased land for settlement at Waimamaku, inland from Opononi, and other extensive purchases were proceeding.[21] Returns from the kauri-gum industry improved, flax fibre was being produced, and a strong sawmilling industry was about to develop in Hokianga. And to exercise some control over this activity, local government was on the way with the passing of the Counties Act in 1876. Hitherto, such government that trickled through to Hokianga had been dispensed by the Auckland Provincial Council, and occasionally Central Government, but the constitution that had given birth to this sort of remote control had self-destructed, due to squabbles between Central and Provincial Governments.

Since its inception as a Crown Colony of Great Britain

several systems had been employed to govern New Zealand. The first was by a Governor with the advice of a Legislative Council. To this was soon grafted a structure of two provinces, New Ulster and New Munster, each having a separate government. These had some autonomy but were dominated by the Central Government, and indeed, to a great extent by Sir George Grey. Both expired under his governorship, mainly because they failed to function, and they were replaced under the Constitution Act of 1852 by the General Assembly, elected by a wide franchise, and six Provincial Governments, each with a Superintendent, which were financed partly by the general revenue.

The provinces were self-governing but were also inclined to encroach on the exclusive privileges of the General Assembly, which, in fact, had over-riding powers over the ordinances of the provinces. The exclusive rights of the General Assembly included the purchase of Maori land and the administration of Crown Lands, and on these and other issues the provinces battled with the assembly for twenty years. The system's virtue was its ability, due to the local Provincial Governments, to better attend to local issues at a time when communications with Wellington were poor. Its failings were many, but principally involved the essentially different methods used by the various provinces to deal with the same administrative matters, which caused all sorts of confusion in the country as a whole. Also, some were financially viable and others were not.

The upshot of all this was that by legislation the General Assembly abolished the provinces in 1876, when they had increased in number to ten, and a unified set of legislation and regulations was applied throughout the whole country. But to provide for the continuing necessity for local government, the Counties Act was also enacted. This created, among other things, sixty-three counties, one of which was Hokianga, hitherto governed, if at all, from Auckland. However, profiting from their experiences with the provincial governments, the legislators saw to it that the Act gave the counties little chance of thwarting or embarrassing the General Assembly.

Hokianga had been living for over forty years on a sort of subsistence economy, with only a handful of people such as McDonnell, Russell, Webster and a few smart operators doing much better than earn their daily bread, but some order and corporate industry was now on the way.

20. The County and the Mills

Local government came to Hokianga pursuant to the Counties Act of 1876, when little doubt remained as to the status of Rawene as the River's future administrative centre. There, von Sturmer, the magistrate since 1870, was established on a Government-created town subdivision which supported bush-licences and two hotels. Clendon, who had died in 1872, had for four years held a wholesale licence there to sell beer and spirits, and had been a licensed Wine and Spirit Merchant.[1] A fitting foundation indeed on which to build a county establishment having the needs of its ratepayers at heart. In 1878, shortly after the birth of the county, Rawene's population had rocketed to fifty-nine, with thirty-two males and twenty-seven females, double that of Kohukohu,[2] although soon the sawmill there and the population growth it generated would restore the up-River town's prestige for many years.

The mid-1870s then were a time of fast growth for Rawene. Six cottages, pre-fabricated in Auckland, were erected in Parnell Street, the main street, believed to be for immigrants coming here in the *Cospatrick,* which was, however, burned at sea with great loss of life.[3] The Methodist church and the Masonic hotel date from this period, together with the courthouse,[4] which was to be shared by von Sturmer and Maning, who had hitherto used a small building at his home at Onoke.

As to legal liquor sources, in the mid-1870s in Hokianga the hotels or licensed sources operating were the Herd's Point Hotel, Rawene, run by Hardiman, and the Hokianga Hotel, Rawene, by J. Bryers. Downstream, presumably at Pakia, was The Heads, C. Bryers, which may have been the same hotel as the later-mentioned Traveller's Rest there, conducted by B.G. Howe. The Horeke Hotel, as we know, had long been established, and the Taheke Hotel also, but this was now run by Eruhiri, a Maori proprietor, who was no doubt doing very well out of the Punakitere gum-fields. Another Maori publican was Kereama Tauehe, who had a hotel at Whirinaki, on State

Highway No. 12, at the north side of the Whirinaki bridge. This licence is said to have been transferred in 1878 to the Masonic, at Rawene. Webster also had a wholesale licence at Opononi.[5]

The stage was thus set for the seal of officialdom to be stamped indelibly on Rawene. The boundaries of the County of Hokianga were proclaimed on 26 November 1876,[6] and comprised two ridings, Waihou, which was to return three members, and Waima with four.[7] Waihou was bounded 'towards the North by Mongonui [sic] County; towards the East by the Bay of Islands County to the middle of the main road between Bay of Islands and Hokianga; thence towards the South by the middle of the said road to the Taheke River, and by the middle of that river and the Waima River to the Hokianga Estuary, and by the south shore of that estuary to the ocean; and towards the west by the ocean'. Waima was bounded 'towards the North by the Waihou Riding; towards the East by the Bay of Islands County; towards the South by the Hobson County; and towards the West by the ocean'. The date of the first election was set at 22 December 1876,[8] and the first meeting on 9 January 1877 in the Resident Magistrate's Court at Herd's Point.[9]

The European and half-Maori population of this county one year later was determined by the census as 419 total — 242 males and 177 females — so that using earlier Maori population statistics as a comparison, they would have been outnumbered by the Maori by perhaps 10 to 1, or even more. Only half-blood Maori-Pakeha living as Europeans were included in these figures as Europeans. Neither does the 419 look very impressive, even against Clendon's 145 including half-Maori thirty-two years earlier — a figure which had been depleted to that level by the exodus to Auckland after Heke's War. Growth at Hokianga had been painfully slow, but the most surprising European figure in the 1878 census is that for Pakia, a growing settlement near Omapere, at the Heads, presumably where Andrewes had opened up his store in the early 70s. Here in 1878 the population was fifty-one, only eight less than Rawene, and more surprising, females outnumbered males there by seven. But there is now no sign of Pakia. It never threatened Rawene, which, by the early 1880s was beginning to assume some semblance of its present form. Most of the public buildings had been erected including a school, the Post Office and the County Hall and offices, and now well set up, the township settled down to its official duties.

In due course the magistrate, von Sturmer, attended to the collection of back rent from the early Pakeha squatters who had been on the Rawene land before its resumption by the Government — a painful process extending over some years. Two of these, Bryers and Cochrane, the son of Dennis, figured largely in the town's and the county's future activities. There was now a steamer service subsidised by the county, between the harbour and Onehunga, not notable for its regularity, which brought mail and whatever the people of the River required from the outside world. This was the *Rowena.* Mail was dealt with by Rawene's first postmaster, Thomas Millar, old James Clendon's son-in-law, appointed on 1 December 1875.[10]

But to match Rawene's triumphant progress, Kohukohu was also about to take off in a new direction, albeit under the stern supervision of officialdom across the river. The date of the building of the sawmill at Kohukohu appears to be reliably documented in Brett's Auckland Almanac of 1879,[11] but when the first mill at or near Rangiora was built remains a mystery. A mill there probably antedated that at Kohukohu, since in a report of March 1885 by John Curnin to the Surveyor General, he states that, 'The Motukaraka Block ... adjoins the Kohukohu block where Webster's sawmill is erected.'[12] That is, at or near Rangiora. When this mill was built Curnin does not say, but the Webster brothers had been associated with Rangiora, on the Motukaraka Block, where the mill was apparently located, since the mid-Forties. There was, as we know, a water-driven mill operated by them with little success at Wairere, across the harbour, but this ceased production in 1869, when it could well have then been shifted to Rangiora.

We have, however, a considerable body of information on the Kohukohu mill, built in the bay there on the additional ten acres Russell had purchased from Marriner, and now leased to the Mill company by Yarborough. In 1879 this company, the Sydney firm of Greenfield and Stewart, built the mill, recognising the advantages of milling timber at its source.[13] Nowhere in the harbour was there a better situation. This was always the largest mill in the River, with an ultimate capacity of 6,000,000 feet, which, however, it never achieved. Logs could be floated from the Mangamuka, Orira and Waihou Rivers right to the intake of the Kohukohu mill and the sawn timber then loaded on to vessels for export at the same point. But trees were now at a distance and could no longer be found close to the river-banks and man-handled into the rivers. So bullock power had been introduced to haul the logs out on rough graded tracks, and later the 'corduroy roads' were introduced — graded tracks with six-inch to nine-inch logs laid transversely across them, about two feet apart. This greatly reduced friction on the logs, lightening the load on the bullocks and speeding up their otherwise very slow progress.

At Whangape too, a Melbourne firm intended to build and operate mills. It proposed to spend £60,000 on these and on dams and the purchase of steamers. In 1874 it had, in fact, leased forests there but on encountering legal difficulties, the proposal foundered.[14] Nearly thirty years were to elapse before the Mitchelson Timber Company did, in fact, build and operate a mill at Whangape.[15]

Land purchases by the Government at Hokianga had been proceeding apace and this was clearly a factor influencing its policy in establishing local government there. As we know, nearly 200,000 acres had been acquired in this district prior to 1877,[16] which included some very large blocks, such as one in excess of 25,000 acres in the Waoku, east of Waipoua Forest, 35,000 at Waipoua itself and 27,000 at Waimamaku. This was totally unroaded, as an engineering report of 1880 demonstrates.[17]

> Roads are the great necessity of the country; and a main line running up the east side of the peninsula [north of Auckland] has been under survey and construction, at the expense of the Government, for the last two or three years. But on the west side, from Dargaville north there is no road, only a most wretched track to Hokianga. There are several thousand acres of both open and forest Crown lands between Kaihu and Maunganui Bluff, very suitable for settlers, and which would be taken up if it could only be got at. This area is but the fringe of a solid block of 400,000 acres of Crown lands which stretches away inland through the forest, over a plateau-country, to near Kaikohe. It is proposed to explore a road-line through it, and, if funds are available to open a bridle-track. Until this is done no settlement can take place; for in its present state it will to the settler for ever

remain an impenetrable, unknown land.

A road has been surveyed and graded up the Kaihu Valley to this land, and tenders are now invited for its formation. It is continued through the forest behind Maunganui Bluff, thence by the beach to Hokianga.

Again, from opposite Herd's Point, Hokianga, [at Motukaraka] a road has been surveyed through the forest for thirty miles to Victoria Valley, seven or eight miles of which have been made at each end, and other contracts are now let in extension of the work thus begun at either end. On this being accomplished a good bridle-track will be opened from Awanui to Dargaville, Wairoa River, Kaipara Harbour. Settlers can then see the land, and will have a way to and from it. In the course of the next two or three years, the monotony of the long stretches of uninhabited country on this line will be relieved by the homesteads and clearings of the settlers.

These bridle-tracks are all made on carefully graded lines, which will be eventually the main road-lines, and can be easily widened out for dray traffic. Wherever they run through the bush it is felled at least half a chain, generally a chain wide.

A meagre achievement indeed in the forty years since Hobson's treaty-signing foray into Hokianga, and the promise and benefits it foretold.

But the new County Council had not been backward in levying rates for the construction of roads, much, it seems to the annoyance of Maning, who in a pre-election letter to Webster of October 1876 recommended 'a sensible Council ... that wont do anything ... that is I think all we want at present'.[18] Nevertheless, road and bridge-building on the south and east side of the harbour was undertaken almost at once on routes that are now followed by main and State highways, and on others.[19]

The Government's road-building and settlement policies of the 70s and 80s certainly had strategic objectives. In 1871 John Webster, then a magistrate, had reported to Donald McLean, the Defence Minister, that relations in the North between Maori and Pakeha were poor,[20] despite the assurances given to the Governor there a year earlier. He also believed that, 'The opening of the country by roads and the introduction of settlers is of vital importance to the *safety* as well as progress of the north & money is better spent roadmaking than in fighting.' The threat of war had not receded entirely even here in the North. At that time Webster had even favoured encouraging Ngapuhi to assist the Government in its wars with the Maori to the south, which 'would have weakened our foes both north and south'.[21] So he plainly regarded his Ngapuhi relatives as 'foes'. Webster, Maning and von Sturmer — the upper-crust of Hokianga — all display the pervading Pakeha insensitivity to the plight of the Maori. They, and people like them throughout the country, had deprived the Maori of his land, his authority, his dignity and his way of life and had given him nothing in return, and now professed to be puzzled as to why his behaviour and his attitude to the Pakeha had deteriorated so badly. To them, the Maori was only a source of cheap labour to make their enterprises profitable. If it was withheld, this was an affront.

The settlers' distrust of Sir George Grey undoubtedly arose out of the rapport, if guarded, that he had with the Maori people, and his short tenure of office as Prime Minister, 1877-9, was clearly influenced by this. Land-owning settlers bitterly resented 'soft' attitudes to Maori. At the beginning of the 1880s Hokianga still had a Pakeha and half-Maori population of only about 500, of which perhaps fifty per cent would have been part-Maori.

As to the Motukaraka Block, thanks to the dubious activities of Papahurihia and Mr Hastings Atkyns and of McDonnell himself, the easily accessible timber was all gone from it, but this troublesome piece of land continued to generate problems. Curnin's report of 1885 states that in about 1883, 'some half-castes claimed some 40 acres at Parawanui', the best part of the block, facing the entrance to the Waima River. Also, 'When the telephone wire was to be stretched across the narrows, some old women sat upon the pole and would not allow its erection on their land, as they called it, and they withdrew only on being menaced with arrest for impeding a public work.' Parawanui was a critical piece of land, since from there it was proposed to construct the six-foot track through Broadwood to Kaitaia, and to connect it to Rawene by ferry. These nameless 'half-castes' had, according to Curnin, 'smuggled' this claim through the Native Land Court 'in an indecent hasty manner through the culpable connivance of a half cast who was then acting as Clerk of the Court'. However, Curnin had struggled manfully against this outrage, and, as can well be appreciated, the Crown got the whole of Motukaraka.

Tamati Waaka Nene played a helpful role in Government land purchases as a sort of 'hatchet-man' for the responsible officers. He appeared throughout the era of intensive northern transactions as a persuader for the Government, and in the case of Motukaraka, for McDonnell. A paper on his activities over this period could make interesting reading. Even as late as twenty years ago an old Maori gentleman commented bitterly to the author about Nene's pro-Pakeha influence.

All the foregoing activity, the land purchases, the birth of the county and the roading gave rise to a very significant change in the economy of Hokianga. Although flax and the non-renewable resources such as timber and kauri gum continued to be exploited until they were practically exhausted, the Government was proceeding with plans for developing the land into farms, clearly with the intention of reducing the dominating influence of Maori in the district. Webster's correspondence with McLean, the Native Minister, had recommended this in 1871, although much of Hokianga generally was not very promising farm material. But Motukaraka and Kohukohu, Punakitere and the rather more attractive Waimamaku Valley were selected to initiate this plan. The last two certainly contained some very good land, but some of the later areas opened up comprised not at all attractive clay hills.

A man who figured very largely in Hokianga activities at this stage was John Lundon, an Irishman[22] and a supporter of Sir George Grey, loathed by the Webster, Maning, von Sturmer coterie on both counts. Rabid conservatives all, with a ferocious hatred of Grey and his liberal policies, which they were convinced threatened their livelihood, they ascribed all sorts of villainies to Lundon, who was, indeed, a colourful character, if one of dubious repute. He moved in exalted circles, was involved in anything that looked as if it would return a quick profit, and he earned a reputation for undesirable if not unscrupulous cleverness. A very visible, audible and gregarious personality, he clearly revelled in all public activities. In 1843 at the age of thirteen he had arrived at Auckland with his father Patrick Lundon and family, but at a quite early age went off with the first Australian gold-rush to Bendigo. Astute enough to conclude that only lucky gold-miners made fortunes, he returned to New Zealand, and acquiring vessels, he sent off large shipments of food and supplies to the goldfields — a certain winning ploy.

These activities apparently made much money for him, with some of which he built the Harp of Erin hotel on the Great South Road at Auckland, at the intersection which still bears the hotel's name. He was then only twenty-seven. He later became embroiled in the Waikato Wars, and until the 1870s served spasmodically as an officer in various units he raised for the war. In between times he made an incursion into the North, to Awanui, near Kaitaia, where he farmed on a large scale, but in 1869 we find him at Thames, in partnership with Whitaker, a solicitor and notorious entrepreneur, lately a Superintendent of the Auckland Provincial Council and a former member of the Legislative Council and a Prime Minister. A man as capable as Lundon of doing well for himself with little concern for the means employed. At Thames, as miners and land speculators, they took a gold-mining lease from one Wiremu Kingi and others, on land which had already been leased by the Kingi faction to James de Hirsch. Or that was what de Hirsch claimed, with some justification it seems. In some circumstances this is known as claim-jumping, and the battle over it surged back and forth for some three years, even involving a special Act of Parliament in 1869 and a Commission, which found against Lundon and Whitaker in 1872, upsetting a judgement of 1870 by Fenton, Chief Judge of the Native Land Court. However, as the owner of the celebrated Imperial Crown mine, and the lessee of the whole of Grahamstown, that is most of the business section of Thames, Lundon no doubt prospered there.

In 1874 (1876 according to his obituary) Lundon again turned his attention to the North, successfully tendering for a contract to supply railway sleepers to the Government to the value of £80,000, 'and proceeded to Hokianga to fulfill that undertaking', as his obituary tells us. But it does not add that he got at least some of these sleepers off Government land, probably the unsurveyed part of Motukaraka. This gave rise to a question in the Auckland Provincial Council:[23] 'What action the Government intend to take relative to the Petition of certain Settlers of Hokianga with respect to the cutting of Timber by J. and P. Lundon without permission on Government Land.' (Since this minute is dated 13 May 1874, the date of the contract quoted in the obituary is incorrect.) The reply was: 'Upon receiving intimation that the Messrs. Lundon were cutting timber on Government Lands at Hokianga a person was at once despatched to the place and the timber cut was seized and branded.' However, upon the representation of Lundon's old mate Whitaker that the timber was urgently required for Colonial Railway Works, the Government permitted Lundon to remove the timber, on condition that its value be assessed and paid. The questioner, still unhappy, then wanted a detailed report by the persons assessing the value and amount of the timber. A year later on 18 May, he wanted to know what the value of the timber was and if the Lundons had paid it. The answer to the first question was a suspiciously paltry £50-10-0, but there was no reply to the second question. Apparently few people worried too much about what was going on on unsupervised Government land at Hokianga.

It is possible that some of this timber went into Lundon's second Harp of Erin hotel, which remains as a dwelling to this day on the end of the point at Rawene. This was also known as Hardiman's Hotel, and since Hardiman had occupied it as early as 1870, the obvious additions to the building as well as its new name were probably made later by Lundon. With all his successes behind him, Lundon was elected in 1879 as the Member of Parliament for the Bay of Islands, figuring largely thereafter in the roading and settlement of the North, but still loathed by the 'upper crust' in Hokianga.

Von Sturmer suffered, or professed to suffer, from poor health, which he appeared to bear with some fortitude, frequently protesting to Webster that it was only their friendship that sustained him in his trials. In spite of all this, plus his frustrated expectations of a transfer from Hokianga, borne over many years, the Government kept him there from 1870 until 1886, when he was transferred to the Wairarapa as Resident Magistrate. Apparently he carried out his duties on the River competently and conscientiously, which may have accounted for his long tenure there. However, his hostility to successive governments may also have had something to do with it. He shared with Maning and Webster their distastefully expressed prejudices against 'the natives', which were endemic among their class at that time.[24] This hostility on the Pakeha side and lethargy on the Maori had been induced largely by the Maori dominance in Hokianga and the recent wars in the Waikato, Taranaki and the Bay of Plenty districts, which, as wars inevitably do, had engendered mindless and fearful reactions. But von Sturmer, who was also Customs Agent, did not, in fact, seem to have much more than minor offences to deal with, as his 1879 Report states.[25] This was fortunate, since for his very large district, poorly roaded if at all in places, he seems much of the time to have had no more than one Pakeha and one Maori constable.

The first constable recorded at Rawene was a Maori named Rahu, in 1877, who overlapped by a year Constable William Couglan, appointed 10 December 1877. Rahu resigned in January 1879. Next was Resident Native Constable Hone Mete (John Smith). Charles Hogg succeeded Couglan, who was transferred to Kawakawa in 1883. Constable Edwin Charles Hughes was then appointed as a second constable and served at Rawene until June 1889, throughout and beyond von Sturmer's service. H.W. Bishop was the Magistrate's Clerk. Mete, by the way, distinguished himself later, as we shall see, as one of the 'rebels' in the Dog Tax War.[26]

Until now, settlement at Hokianga had been confined largely to the land acquired by the pre-1840 'pakeha-maori', since Hokianga, mostly rugged and almost roadless, was not the most attractive place for Government-financed settlement schemes. At Okaihau, some 5000 acres of relatively level volcanic land called Mawhe, around Lake Omapere, had been acquired by the Government in 1858, and ten years later 2000 acres of this were set aside for wheat growing. A Dr Stratford having been sent to Canada to recruit farmers for this purpose, the settlers he selected finally took up their land at Okaihau in 1868.[27] But there was little communication between these people and those at Hokianga, since the Bay was a farming community considerably more developed and populated, and the people there had little common interest with the bicultural kauri workers and gumdiggers of Hokianga. Each community looked in a different direction — the Bay people to Russell and down the east coast to Auckland, while Hokianga's access to the outside world was via the west coast to Onehunga and thence to Auckland. Nevertheless, although Hokianga's Government-sponsored settlement was delayed until the 1880s, from that time it supported both kauri milling and its growing farming industry, and for a time enjoyed greater prosperity than the Bay.

21. Industry and Settlement

The events in which John Lundon was involved at Auckland, Coromandel, Hokianga and elsewhere were a prelude to a more or less permanent residence in Hokianga of some eight years. Having gone there in 1874, apparently with his father Patrick and some of the family to undertake the controversial sleeper contract, he remained to conduct his Harp of Erin hotel and other enterprises until 1882. A Liberal, compulsively devoted to public activities, his participation and influence in local affairs infuriated Hokianga's self-appointed Conservative hierarchy. First and last he was a politician, and we find von Sturmer referring to him distastefully as one of Sir George Grey's 'principle advisers', noting that on one occasion in 1875 Sir George had summoned him from Hokianga for advice.[1]

Before 1876 Lundon had been a member of the Auckland Provincial Council, which could have been of some help to him in winning the sleeper contract, and after 1879, as we know, he held the Bay of Islands seat for a time in the Grey interest. Defeated by the son of the veteran missionary, Hobbs, in 1881, he unsuccessfully contested the Franklin seat in the next year,[2] and although bereft of elective office, continued to be active in practical politics. While in office he had been a friend of the influential Waima chief Hone Mohi Tawhai — a sinister association in von Sturmer's view — but Lundon apparently forfeited this privilege upon his loss of the Bay of Islands seat.

Those of his family at Hokianga appear to have lived at Motukaraka and Rawene. Von Sturmer refers to 'the Misses Lundon', his two sisters, and to Miss Lundon, then in Wellington with her brother, starting a ladies' committee to collect funds for the Irish Land League — not a popular cause among New Zealand's ruling gentlemen in those times. He also refers to the presence of 'Young Lundon ... the late County Engineer', then a Registered Surveyor. This was apparently Lundon's nephew, Robert, who in 1880 had been appointed Hokianga County Engineer at a salary of £400 per year, true to von Sturmer's uncharitable prophecy that 'some creature of Lundon's will be selected I suppose'. And he adds pleasantly, in the manner of a papal denunciation, 'The Lundons are all devils.'[3] Included, presumably, are Theresa, aged seventeen, Helena, thirteen, and John, aged eleven — Lundons who appear on the 1879 Rawene school roll. The Lundons also perpetuated their name in Hokianga, since Hiria, a Maori woman born in 1858, married a John Lundon, according to the Harris family history, *Te Whanau Harris,* and tradition has it that Hiria's children were half-brothers and sister to our John's Auckland family.

Von Sturmer records Lundon's objection to the location of the Herd's Point terminal of the new Auckland to Kaitaia road in front of his Harp of Erin hotel, from where it would be joined with Motukaraka by a ferry.[4] But Lundon was himself very active later in promoting both roading and settlement in Hokianga. Shortly, however, the first phase of his Northern activities ended, when in 1883 he left New Zealand to take up a position in Samoa with the South Sea Islands Produce Company. He then acted there as the Government's representative in negotiations for the annexation of Samoa by New Zealand, which on this occasion was forestalled by German occupation at Apia. If distrusted at Hokianga, Lundon clearly had the confidence of the Administration in Wellington, since he was to have been New Zealand's representative in Samoa had the annexation proposal succeeded. One of his more spectacular actions before abandoning Hokianga had been to sue about 120 Maori people in von Sturmer's Court for debts he claimed were due to him. Having returned to New Zealand to consult with the Government on the unemployment problem then afflicting this country, he proposed the roading and settlement schemes that so profoundly affected Hokianga in the 1880s.[5]

Civilisation was belatedly penetrating the *terra incognita* at the River at this time. Sea communications with Auckland, hitherto haphazard, were provided by a weekly Government-subsidised service from the harbour to Onehunga with the steamer *Oreti,* and by coach and boat, travellers could get to Auckland from the Bay of Islands. Telephone communications had arrived too, with lines from Rawene to Taheke and the Heads, and also northward over the harbour at the Narrows, in spite of the opposition from the old women there that we have noted. And probably due to the 'kuiki hiria' find at Ngawha, near Kaikohe, interest had been aroused by the possibility of gold at Hokianga, which had attracted Government prospectors. These, however, according to von Sturmer, employed a great deal of their time getting drunk at Rawene, where ample provision for this was available. But no gold. On a more constructive note we find that a new parson was also in residence, guaranteed a salary of £200 by the residents, and bearing the unlikely name of Cockayne Cockyne Frith MA, of St John's College, Oxford. Cockayne must indeed have been in dire straits to end up in Hokianga at half the salary of the County Engineer. More surprisingly, a doctor was later acquired at the same price. And by 1885 Kohukohu had been surveyed and a Government township laid out there.[6]

Wine making, an occupation that has failed to survive as a major industry in Hokianga, was initiated at Kohukohu by Heinrich Breidecker in 1884. He grew two acres of Isabella grapes on what, to his consternation, turned out to be Crown land, immediately south of Marriner Street. Happily he was later confirmed in his occupation, and in the opinion of the Okaihau Agricultural and Horticultural Association, Breidecker produced 'excellent wine' there. Indeed, he later won prizes for hock at the Dunedin Exhibition. In good years he took as much as £400 from his Isabella patch from which he could expect to make 1200 gallons of wine annually. Another grower named Lester terraced the steep face behind the Kohukohu township and planted vines and an orchard there, but his venture did not prosper.[7] At the turn of the century only Breidecker's vineyard survived as a going concern in the harbour, and the fruit-growing industry had migrated across the river to Ivydale. All this activity was apparently encouraged by a report submitted to the Government in 1880 by a London expert, George Galbraith. He wrote to the Agent General there:

> Sir — with reference to the matter of a special settlement in the North of Auckland, for the culture of the vine, which I had the honour of bringing under your notice on Friday last, I now, in accordance with your desire, beg to submit, for the consideration of the New Zealand Government, reasons for encouraging a suitable settlement.

This is not a new idea. The *New Zealand Herald* of

> 21st July 1879 ... says:— 'The Waste Lands Board, at the instance of the Government, have reserved from sale a block of 26,000 acres in the Hokianga District, it being the object of Sir George Grey to establish there a settlement of skilled vine-growers, in order to regularly test the capacity of the colony for wine-production. It is of exceeding importance to ascertain as soon as possible what we are really able to do in this way.... The locality for the experiment has been well chosen, the climate of the northern districts of New Zealand being, of course, the most favourable.'
>
> ... It is submitted that the proper introduction of the vine-culture would be a much more important factor in the general prosperity of the colony than the establishment of an agricultural settlement ... inasmuch as a successful settlement of vine-growers would give a new and powerful factor towards the product of the general prosperity, whereas an agricultural settlement would relatively be merely a unit.
>
> ... The lands in the north, at Hokianga, being in the meantime of little commercial value, it is submitted that the colony could not better deal with them than by holding out for the occupation of a portion of them, as proposed, the most liberal inducements, in the shape of free passages, employment of labourers, and land at a nominal price.[8]

Galbraith then recommended the formation of a company to promote such a settlement at Hokianga. However, the proposal expired with the Grey Administration, and with it went any hope of large-scale viticulture here.

Sawmilling was now the industry that was to support the majority of the growing population of the harbour, although its early activities were by no means without problems. In 1881, Greenfield and Stewart's Kohukohu mill had been taken over by the Hokianga Sawmill Company, promoted by Yarborough and Andrewes,[9] but on 29 April 1882, when only three years old, it was 'gone to Eternal smoke', according to von Sturmer, who also informs us that the damage amounted to £800 to £1000. This was the first of a series of disastrous fires at

Kohukohu that ultimately reduced it from a sizable, prosperous township to the roadside village it is today. By June the mill was nonetheless in full work again and in 1883 was employing thirty men, with some sixty to eighty more supplying logs to it from the bush. Yarborough had by this time tapped the timber resources of Whirinaki, which had remained unexploited for so long. He had put about twenty Nova Scotian bushmen in there on a royalty basis, and in his customary charitable fashion von Sturmer expressed the devout wish that they would perhaps help 'with drink and other things to clear off some of the noble savages'.[10] He also notes that the mill had purchased all the kauri on the Mangamuka from the Maori owners 'for a mere trifle'.

However, the Hokianga Sawmilling Company was, it seems, much under-capitalised and attempts were made to obtain timber bush from Maori land-owners by payment in shares. But by 1885 this problem had attained crisis proportions. Apparently a viable undertaking, only the want of capital threatened the mill's closure, an event that inevitably occurred in 1886.[11] The Yarborough-Andrewes enterprise then reverted to its baulk-timber dealing and its extensive general trading on the River. However, in 1888 the Kauri Timber Company was formed at Melbourne with a capital of £1,250,000, and profiting from the mid-Eighties depression and the consequent low state of the timber industry in New Zealand, bought up twenty-eight important mills and bushes in this country, together with 1,563,000,000 feet of standing timber and 303,000 acres of freehold and leasehold timberland. All the mills were in full working order, with dams, tramways, animals, etc.[12] So, in 1889, the Kohukohu mill passed to the Kauri Timber Company, which ran it for twenty years.

While all this was taking place the Government's extensive roading and land purchase programmes were proceeding and Hokianga land was becoming available for settlement. 'A goodly number of people are here land-hunting, I think "Land Hunger" will soon commence', von Sturmer wrote. And oddly, he also observed that 'the natives have left Pakanae and Toi Settlement at Wairohia, and gone to live at Waimamaku'. Adding, in his waspish manner, 'so may they remain for the future'. As to why this exodus from the erstwhile Maori 'capital' of Hokianga occurred, he offers no useful comment. Maori-Pakeha relations being poor at that time, the move may have been away from the growing Pakeha inroads and influence at the Heads. In July

1886 he notes further disquiet: 'At Waihou, Aporo Pangari & Hohaia Patuone have declared themselves Te Whiti adherents, [Te Whiti, the Taranaki "rebel" activist] and hold meetings, but they are at present simply laughed at by the natives — but still these things spread, so something may come of it.' These two were very influential chiefs.

Yarborough, with his timber and other enterprises sagging under the weight of depression, produced a publication calculated to promote emigration to New Zealand — specifically to Hokianga, and more specifically to Motukaraka, about two miles downstream from his own establishment at Kohukohu.[13] He left New Zealand from Lyttelton in April 1885 to pursue this objective in England, where his handbook was published.[14] Nostalgia must inevitably affect the reader on inspection of the 1885 prices of provisions, which are converted here into decimal terms: onions 2¼ cents to 4½ cents per kilo, bananas 5½ cents to 10 cents, oranges 22 cents to 28 cents, etc. Hokianga wages he quotes at:

Labourers	80 cents per day
Carpenters	$1.00 to $1.40 per day
Bullock-driver	$6.00 per week
Sawyer	$1.10 per day
Sawmill hands	70 cents to $1.00 per day
Bush cook	$4.00 to $5.00 per week plus food & lodgings
Bush hands	$3.00 to $4.00 per week plus food & lodgings
Blacksmiths	$1.00 to $1.20 per day.

$4.80 to $8.40 for six days of ten to twelve hours seems a little inadequate, even for 1885.

The upset price of Crown Lands at auction at Hokianga, Yarborough says, averaged $1.00 per acre. However, for settlers who did not have the cash, the deferred payment system could be used. In applying this the price of rural land was assessed at not less than $2.00 per acre ($5.00 per hectare), repayments being due half-yearly in equal instalments over a period of ten years. Those using this system had to cultivate not less than 1/20 part of the land in the first year, 1/10 in the second, and within six years must have cultivated 1/5 and effected improvements to the value of $2.00 per acre (0.4 hectare). This, says

Yarborough, was the most popular method of purchase, and it was probably the basis upon which most early Hokianga and Northern settlers obtained their land. Very poor land was easier to acquire, under the Homestead Act, whereby the purchaser paid the price of the survey and got his title after completing five years' occupation, and carrying out certain improvements. But Yarborough considered that, owing to the poverty of such land, the result for the settler could only be ruin.

Lease of Crown Lands with perpetual right of renewal, at five per cent of the capital value per annum, was also a popular method of acquisition, land valued at $5.00 per hectare being leased at 25 cents per hectare per year. The lessee had the option of purchase at any time within eleven years of the commencement of the lease or renewing it on the expiry of its term, for twenty-one years, the land being revalued three years before the expiry. Certain conditions applied as to the improvement of the property during the original lease period for both purchasers and lessees. Yarborough quotes the *Crown Lands Guide:*

> There are 306,000 acres of crown lands in Hokianga, soil generally fair, but the best lands are at present (1884) inaccessible for want of roads. (Since then a large amount of money has been expended in making roads.) The completion of the road in course of construction from Hokianga to Takahue will open a large extent of country for settlement, and the part situated in Mangonui Owai Valley, [Broadwood] is famed for its excellent soil. (Two roads have now been constructed leading direct into this valley.) The water communication throughout the district is extensive, the soil varies much, though the Waoku plateau is all volcanic.

There were other ways to acquire Crown Lands, all, like the above, necessitating labour rather than capital, and among these were Special Village Settlements, of which a number were promoted at Hokianga in the 1880s, some by John Lundon. These were Motukaraka and Kohukohu, 1544 acres, Punakitere, 1934 acres, Waimamaku, 951 acres, Takahue, 1032 acres and Herekino 3737 acres,[15] and they usually involved a group of not less than twenty-five people taking up the block of land.

It was developed in accordance with the group's requirements into rural, urban and suburban lots. The payment for the land was then arranged by the group in the terms required by the Government. These were the essential conditions, another being that the group named their own settlements. Understandably, Yarborough recommended particularly what was obviously the Motukaraka Block, that closest to his own establishment.

To service these settlements road construction proceeded. The Herd's Point to Takahue and Kaitaia road was probably the most important of these, since in spite of the Rawene to Motukaraka water-gap, this was part of a main road from Auckland to Kaitaia. It also opened up over 20,000 acres of Crown Land. By 1890 the early six-foot tracks at the Motukaraka and Kaitaia ends had been widened to take wheeled traffic, and the road through the Waiotemarama gorge, between Waimamaku and Pakanae, was under construction as a six-foot to nine-foot track. And in the Waimamaku and Punakitere village settlement blocks considerable roading had been completed. Roads into the Motukaraka, Takahue and Herekino village settlements were also in hand.[16] At the same time, the County Council was constructing roads in the interests of its ratepayers, and into the gumfield at Punakitere. At this stage the strange name 'Niu Terini' (New Zealand) arises again, this time applied to the 7000-acre block of land centred on Moehau, the Maori village in the Waima River which is even now referred to by older people as 'New Zealand'.

Maning, one of the oldest of the settlers, did not live to see these developments. Sour and embittered, he became estranged from his family, and particularly from his son Hauraki, described as a 'handsome philanderer', whom he finally rejected. His strong-minded daughters Maria and Mary then incurred his displeasure, and finally, in 1880, after a break with his crippled daughter, Susan, he left Onoke to live in Auckland. Susan died shortly after this. There is no doubt that Maria, later Bishop Cowie's housekeeper, was indeed a woman of strong views. Commenting on the religious convictions of Pakeha generally, she has been credited with the profound dictum that while they unctuously declared their reverence for the Father, Son and Holy Spirit, the Holy Trinity to which they were truly devoted was Firewater, Firearms and Fornicating. And with this one remark she outgunned her father's many years of verbal sniping at his

Maori relatives. Two years after his departure, Maning learned that he had cancer and went to England for treatment, but he died there on 25 July 1883. His body was returned to New Zealand, where it was buried in the Symonds Street Cemetery on 8 December.[17] He was without doubt a man of very considerable intellectual potential, but an intolerant, uncharitable and opinionated one. Paranoia seems to have blighted his later life. He had sold Onoke to one Burt, on mortgage, and to add to his problems Burt was not paying.[18]

Maning's daughter Mary was married to George Hardiman, erstwhile owner of the Herd's Point Hotel, later the Harp of Erin. He was apparently Maning's executor, since von Sturmer, in a letter to Webster, writes: 'Mrs. Hardiman returned by the Steamer and brought deeds for Geo Hardiman to sign — She has borrowed £600 from Abbot (moneylender) of which she has lent £500 to Shan and spent the other £100 that means £700 of the £2000 clean gone what would poor old Maning say to seeing his money flying away at this rate.' A sad if not unusual scramble at the winding up of a man or woman's life and work.[19]

Von Sturmer himself, during his sixteen-year tenure of office here never ceased to yearn for a transfer, complaining bitterly about his unrewarding life at Hokianga and the misery 'the natives' inflicted on him. But he was not obliged to bear his trials much longer, since a merciful providence influenced his employers to transfer him to Masterton, whence he departed in October 1886. Apparently even that did not please him, as he complained to Webster, 'I am far from being elated at the idea of my removal.... It will cost me some hundreds of pounds for Masterton has a population of over 4,000 and I will have to live decent.' But it is difficult not to have some sympathy for von Sturmer. Only such rugged uncompromising Pakeha personalities as Russell, White, McDonnell, Clendon, Lundon, Webster, Yarborough and their ilk lived comfortably with the very basic conditions under which social, commercial and professional activities were conducted in Hokianga. As to their women, as is consistent with nineteenth-century culture, we hear little of their problems. Von Sturmer was indeed a tender plant in a hostile environment, but we are indebted to him for the details of daily life on the River contained in his sometimes touching correspondence with Webster.

Hokianga seems now to have been left without a Resident

Magistrate, these duties apparently being assumed by H.W. Bishop, then a RM for the District of the Bay of Islands. He is shown as RM for Mangonui and Hokianga in Wise's New Zealand Post Office Directory, from 1887 to 1890.[20]

Another personality who came to Hokianga with high hopes and departed leaving little to celebrate his passing was an Italian named Federli, who would now, perhaps, be described as an 'entrepreneur'. He settled at Umawera, at the head of the harbour, and of him Yarborough wrote in 1885:

> Mr. Federli, an Italian gentleman, has given a great deal of his time to the rearing of silk-worms and the culture of sub-tropical fruits, and has now settled down with some friends at Hokianga, with the intention of throwing his whole attention into the subject. It is quite clear, from his experiments, that so far as climate and other natural conditions are concerned, the north-west of New Zealand is exceedingly well adapted for the industry, but it will be necessary to grow the white mulberry to an extensive degree before this industry can be greatly developed. Mr. Federli and his friends are exceedingly well satisfied with their choice of land, and are, I understand, doing well. It will be a great advantage to future settlers to be able to have their advice regarding the culture of sub-tropical fruits, and more especially of the mulberry, olive and orange, and to observe the results obtained by this party of pioneers. A short treatise, compiled by Mr. Federli, containing practical hints as to the growing of the mulberry and the rearing of the silk worm can be obtained in New Zealand ...[21]

Von Sturmer, having no axe to grind, was by no means as optimistic as Yarborough when Federli and his schemes erupted onto the Hokianga scene. He confided to Webster, 'The Federli party are on the land 2 single men, Sharland, and Fletcher, and Mr & Mrs Federli and two little children, I am afraid Federli is a visionary, and will not do much, had he got his original scheme off, of the Italians, he might have succeeded.' A year later, Federli, financially embarrassed, went off to Wellington to find a remedy for this condition, at which the now disillusioned Yarborough commented sourly that if he succeeded, Hokianga would neither see or hear of him again. He did return, but not with an enhanced reputation, since he inspired von Sturmer to comment, 'Federli is here he is not going home now, but wants to get up an agricultural school for him to be manager and to get £100 per annum for pupils; he is a schemer and nothing else....' Federli appears almost as another de Thierry, intending as he did to sponsor an Italian community in Hokianga, at Umawera. His enterprises were not successful, but all was apparently not lost, since he seems to have promoted a 'Sanatorium' at Opononi, which was later incorporated in the hotel there. But economically speaking, Federli, like de Thierry, sunk leaving scarcely a ripple.[22]

Hokianga was now approaching the peak of its potential. Roading and settlement were proceeding apace, gumdigging in South Hokianga and the Bay of Islands had expanded into a major industry, and sawmilling was recovering from its depressed condition owing to the injection of foreign capital by the Kauri Timber Company. Kohukohu's first hotel had been opened in 1882, and according to von Sturmer took the astronomical sum of £10 for beer alone on its first day. And in spite of the closure of the mill in 1886, it survived, due no doubt, to some extent, to the new settlement at Motukaraka where, by that year, the land, subdivided into small farms, had nearly all been taken up.[23] And so Hokianga came to the Nineties, with its three present centres of population and commerce firmly in place.

22. New Settlers and Gumdiggers

A report of 1893 presented to Parliament stated that the area of gumfields north of Auckland at that time was 724,000 acres, consisting of 380,000 acres of Crown Land, 270,000 acres of Maori land and 74,000 other.[1] The Crown fields are usually shown on Government maps as KGR (Kauri-gum Reserve), indicating land reserved for this purpose. In the report this interesting comment on the industry is also given:

> We have evidence that in or about 1836 some kauri-gum was shipped from Hokianga to England; but this led to nothing, owing to the ignorance prevailing in England about the qualities of kauri-gum. Previous to the year 1845 a small consignment was shipped from Parengarenga to America. In the years 1847 to 1849 further attempts were made to introduce the article into the English market, and we are told of a consignment of 20 tons which was pronounced by experts in England to be worthless, and was thrown into the Thames. In 1847 and 1848 and even up to 1853, gum was bought in New Zealand at £5 a ton; but shortly after that time, at all events by the year 1856, the export trade was fully established....

Apparently a profitable use for kauri gum had been discovered in the United States by the mid-1830s, since it was being purchased then by Americans at one penny (one cent approx.) per pound, but the buyers were not disclosing the use they were putting it to. Then at Hokianga in 1848 it was reported that the gum was added to 'Oil of Wood' (turpentine?) to mix with paint. By that time its use as a suitable resin in the manufacture of slow-drying varnish appears to have become generally known, and exports rose from 829 tons in 1853 to over 4000 tons in 1870, averaging about £40 per ton. At the peak of the trade in 1900 it was fetching over £200 per ton, and some 11,000 tons were exported. Gumdigging was by then a major industry, with techniques fully established. Gum spears — long quarter-inch steel rods on a spade handle — were used to locate the gum underground after the surface gum was exhausted and even swamps were being mined.[2]

How much of this came from the North, or particularly from Hokianga, it is impossible to say, since gum was to be found in many places north of Auckland, and also at Coromandel. By 1885, 2000 diggers were at work on these gumfields.

The most extensive fields at Hokianga were on the south side of the harbour, where the adjacent Punakitere and Mangatoa fields totalled 11,850 acres. Very large fields further inland were at Lake Omapere and east of Kaikohe but there is little evidence to indicate the output of any particular area since it seems that much of the Hokianga gum may have been exported eastward through the Bay of Islands. However, in May 1883 von Sturmer reported that 'an immense number of natives are digging gum up there [at the Taheke field]'. There were lesser kauri-gum reserves at Omahuta, near Mangamuka, at Warawara, on the coast north of the Heads, and a small one at Waipoua, south of the Heads.[3]

From 1890 onwards, gum-digging flourished in Hokianga and elsewhere, and was attracting Europeans — particularly those who had taken up land here and needed money to develop it. Indeed, some of these ultimately preferred gumdigging, and abandoned their land. But New Zealand diggers soon had competition from Dalmatians, then called Austrians. These, with their single-minded application to the work and their co-operative group system of operation, were seriously in competition with indigenous European and Maori diggers. Reacting to this, the Government passed the Kauri Gum Industry Act which excluded non-British diggers from certain kauri-gum reserves and imposed a licence-fee on aliens.[4] But the industrious Dalmatians laboured on and survived.

The industry in the 1880s provided much needed work for the Hokianga Maori people, and in the next decade for the Dalmatians, but in both these periods it was also an almost essential source of income to some of the impecunious settlers on the small farms which were being allotted to assisted settlers under the provisions of the Government's new land settlement policy. There was a serious depression in the 1880s and early

1890s, but gum prices then recovered and production increased. Gum was mined from Crown Land, Maori and private European land and was paid for by buyers at so much per pound, the buyers being either merchants or the owners of the fields. Owners usually required a licence-fee from the diggers.

Unemployment in Auckland in the mid-1880s brought men on to the Hokianga gumfields in two ways. Directly, and by way of settlement of government land there. These settlers generally had little or no capital and needed outside work both to support their families and to improve their land. John Lundon, as we know, had been commissioned by the Government to advise on means of dealing with the unemployment situation, which at that time was critical, and moved von Sturmer, writing to Webster on this, to comment 'I hear that the amount of misery and poverty (real) in Auckland is simply appalling.'

Lundon's solution was to put men on the land in the North, and he held meetings in Auckland and locally to promote this objective. Predictably, von Sturmer pronounced his proposal 'a most disgraceful scheme and will end in serious loss to the Govt'.[5] However, the Government approved Lundon's 'Auckland Special Settlement' on land near Tutamoe, east of the Waipoua forest, to which the only reasonable access then was from Omapere on the Hokianga, thence up the Waimamaku River by the Wekaweka Valley.[6] At the same time much other land was being subdivided under this scheme into fifty-acre farms for government-sponsored settlement. On these blocks, the first of such settlers, known as Lundon's Specials, arrived to take up their land toward the end of 1886. Von Sturmer, commenting on the 'land-rush' to Hokianga at that time, noted that, 'All the land put up for settlement at Taheke (Punakitere) is taken up, and nearly all opposite the point.' The land 'opposite the point' being the Motukaraka Block, originally McDonnell's, from the struggle for the ownership of which few contenders other than the Government had emerged unscarred. 'Pakehas are here in shoals all land hunters they come both via Russell and Onehunga and a few over by Kaipara — above 20 of Lundons specials came in "Oreti" today they seem hard working men but regular "Micks" — They will help Marriner & Co as gumdiggers.' Others followed them.[7]

There were two settlements in the Waimamaku Valley. Upstream was the 'Canterbury Settlement' at the present village of Waimamaku, and the later downstream block was at Waiotemarama. Punakitere and Motukaraka were soon taken up, the first due, no doubt, to the work available on the adjacent gumfields, and at Motukaraka after 1890, the Kohukohu sawmills provided work. And as an additional attraction, a modicum of urban facilities were available at the township. However, at Punakitere by 1889, only forty-one of the original seventy-two sections taken up were still occupied — deserted for the gumfields, maybe. Another settlement at Herekino, now in Mangonui County, fared as badly. There and at Takahue, near Broadwood, only about half of the first settlers were still in possession in 1889, but Motukaraka and Waimamaku were a good deal more successful. The Government settlements at this stage totalled over 9000 acres.

At the same time Crown land was being taken up by independent settlers, mainly on the north side of the harbour, where a small village called Mangonuiowai (now Broadwood), soon appeared, and eventually serviced the large area opened up for settlement between Kohukohu and the Awaroa River to the west.[8]

Of Government settlements, Waimamaku probably suffered most from poor access, due to the high ridge lying between it and the harbour, at Pakia (now Omapere). Because of this its supplies were sometimes landed from vessels anchored in the open roadstead at Kawerua, on the west coast south of the Hokianga Heads, where there was some protection from reefs. From here there was reasonable access along the coast and up the Waimamaku River. Kawerua was a small settlement itself, being on the old original route to Hokianga from Kaipara, and it also served the Waipoua gumfield. A hotel was opened there about the end of the century, and the building still exists, in use now as a university hostel. No doubt the Waipoua gumfield provided extra money for some of the Waimamaku settlers, and, of course, for the Kawerua publican.[9]

The economy of Hokianga now took off in a different direction, although for many years farming there was at subsistence level. With few exceptions the blocks were in heavy bush, so that many years passed and much labour was expended before farming as a commercial activity emerged. Roading was still a problem. In 1890 much of the Herd's Point to Kaitaia (Motukaraka to Kaitaia via Broadwood) road was still only a six-foot bridle-track, but since it opened up 20,000 acres of Crown Land it was in the process of being widened to fourteen feet for wheeled traffic, although this was not completed for another five years. In 1890 too, a remedy for the Waimamaku access problem was undertaken by the Government, when construction began on a road through the Waiotemarama gorge to Pakanae, the over-riding virtue of which, it might be suspected, was that it gave access to a further 5000 acres of Crown Land. In 1896 it was completed, but only as a bridle-track, and required a further expenditure of £1000 to make it into a cart-road.

The Government's most ambitious undertaking in hand in 1890 was the Kaihu to Punakitere (Waima) road, which passed through 100,000 acres of Crown Land and incidentally provided access to Lundon's 'Auckland Special Settlement'. By 1896 this work, thirty-two miles in length, was completed as a fourteen-foot cart-road. 'At the north end, for want of good timber, I have had to construct nearly all the culverts of stone', the engineer reported. These 'stone flushes', that is, stone-paved water-courses across the road surface at low points, may still be seen today by anyone energetic enough to walk through the now closed 'Waoku Road', some fifteen miles or so of which have long been abandoned. The Waimamaku (Canterbury Settlement) road was at this time extended up the Wekaweka Valley to the Auckland Settlement, where it joined the Kaihu to Waima road. Thus a direct link was formed between Dargaville and the Waimamaku-Opononi district, which made redundant the old track from Kaihu to the north of the Maunganui Bluff, where the traveller then had to take to the beach. By 1889, roads within the Motukaraka, Punakitere, Waimamaku, Takahue and Herekino Village Settlements had also been made.[10]

Owing to all this, by 1895 the European population of the county had risen to 1889 — 1142 males and 747 females — a sad and frustrating imbalance. These figures included half-Maori people living as Europeans.[11] This minor population explosion, together with the re-opening of the sawmill at Kohukohu by the Kauri Timber Company in 1891, and the government-sponsored and other settlements on both sides of the harbour and inland, were, of course, of great benefit to the merchants, Yarborough, Andrewes, Webster and others. These years saw them transformed from small country traders into the commercial tycoons of the River. Photographs of the 1880s and

1890s show substantial buildings at Kohukohu, some two-storeyed. There were stores, offices, a hotel, a large mill establishment, a town wharf and a mill wharf. The town had a school, a church and other public buildings. Cottages and substantial houses sheltered the population, and large ocean-going vessels lay anchored or moored off the town. Rawene, a small administrative residential village only, had little industry until the sawmill opened there after the turn of the century.

Opononi, where in 1872 Webster had established himself, and where now he was the 'squire' of the River and the leading merchant on the lower harbour, was by the 1890s the showplace of the Hokianga. 'Our Special Correspondent', writing in the *Auckland Weekly News* of 16 April 1892, is ecstatic on this subject:

> Opononi, the homestead of Mr. John Webster is the most beautiful place on the Hokianga River. The station was selected with great judgement, as it is bound, as settlement goes on, to be the outlet of all the country in the rear of it, and especially the Pakanae and Auckland (Waimamaku) and Canterbury settlements [*sic* — Waimamaku was the Canterbury Settlement] and the territory southwards. It is, in fact, the key to the backblocks. At his private wharf vessels lie in safety, in 18 feet of water at low tide, while from the deck one could throw a biscuit ashore. Adjacent to the wharf are his gum store and general store for the settlers' and native trade. It is a fine two-storeyed building, and the most substantially built and best fitted up that I have seen north of Auckland....

The Webster business also engaged in fish curing and preserving, and fruit growing at Pakanae while the Opononi establishment included a farm of some 700 acres on which were 800 sheep feeding on 'Buffalo grass and ratstail' — an unseemly diet in modern terms. At the headquarters:

> The homestead itself is belted in by about 100 acres of plantations, on a point formerly known as Cape Horn, owing to its breezy qualities, but now within the line of these plantations is created a Hokiangan Paradise — a place which might be coveted by Lotus-eaters,

> A land
> In which it always seemeth afternoon.
>
> It has been created by the enterprise, skill, and refined taste of its owner. There are few places on the Hokianga River with which Mr. John Webster's name is not associated, and when he departed from Kohukohu for Opononi, he left the former place as lovely a paradise as could be found in the whole North, till the timber mill replaced the fruit groves, and the whirr of machinery the song of birds.... The two-storeyed mansion of Opononi fronts the harbour, and there, embowered in flowers, fruits and foliage, the septuagenarian philosopher looks out from 'the loopholes of retreat' on the busy world beyond, in which in days gone by he has borne his part and borne it well. Frowning out on the river are embrasures, and the four guns (formerly of Captain McDonnell's battery at the Horeke), kept for saluting purposes when the Governors of the Colony visited Mr. Webster.... The hybiscus, koromiko, tree ferns and Queensland palms, are all around, while a specimen of pisonia, a cutting from the only one known, in Whangape, flourishes apace. The mansion is flanked by bits of native bush, and orchards. In the latter are to be seen growing in perfection grapes, apples, peaches, oranges, bananas, lemons, dates, almonds, and other semi-tropical fruits. One of the date trees is from Moses' well, the seed of which was procured by Mr. Webster while travelling in the East.

Credit for the erstwhile beauty of the Kohukohu place was not all due to Webster, however — Jolliffe's description of it in 1851, when Russell owned it, leaves no doubt as to its beauty in his time.

The correspondent notes too that at the request of S.P. Smith, then the Surveyor General and Editor of the Journal of the Polynesian Society, Webster had prepared for the Journal a paper on the early history of the Northern Maori people, which unfortunately does not seem to have survived. Having digested all these wonders our correspondent took a ride to the Heads to watch the Northern Steamship Company's *Glenelg* take the bar. Here he met the pilot, Martin, whose father's life had been saved sixty-five years earlier as we will recall, by his mother, Kate, the daughter of Te Manene, the tohunga who controlled the wind and waves at the Heads.

At Opononi Webster had truly set himself up in a princely fashion, even to the saluting guns for Governors who came visiting. By this time, too, Andrewes, Yarborough's partner at Kohukohu, was also in business here. The original hotel was first built as a house and gum-trading store in the 1870s for the Andrewes Trading Company, and it appears to have been licensed as a hotel in the 1880s by Andrewes, with few modifications, and remained that way until it burned down in 1959.[12] The old hotel was also a monument to the optimistic Federli, the departed creator of the 'sanatorium' that it housed. This institution, whatever its function may have been, was still existing, if only in name, in 1902, since it is advertised in the New Zealand Encyclopaedia of that date as operating in conjunction with the hotel. But like its originator and his ambitious proposals, it was soon to be only a memory.

John Lundon, in the meantime, having promoted settlement and roading in the North, made an incursion in 1892 into the tricky business of Government land purchases. This involved Maori land at Kaitaia, and it appears to have been his swan-song in the area of public affairs, since, in 1899, his obituary states, 'About seven years ago Mr. Lundon retired into private life', at the age of sixty-three. A wise move, perhaps, since the highly questionable Kaitaia affair concluded a spectacular career in public and private affairs, which, although it was generally effective and beneficial, was punctuated with incidents of dubious righteousness. The Kaitaia episode was one of these, and so dubious was it that for the second time in his career a report on Lundon's activities was initiated by Parliament.[13]

The preamble to this enquiry states, 'Petitioners Herewini te Toko, H.T.W. Papahia and Wi Rikihana complain that Mr. John Lundon has wrongfully detained part of the purchase-money for the Kaitaia Block, and pray for re-dress.' Toko, Papahia and Rikihana were Hokianga people with an interest in the 5200 acre block, which may have arisen from Hongi Hika's early conquests in the Kaitaia district. Interestingly, the form of the petition was drafted for the complainants by John Webster, an implacable enemy of Lundon's, and at the subsequent enquiry convened by the House, whence the report emanated, very considerable lying occurred. But at this distance it is difficult to say who lied. The choice is among Lundon the respondent, Robert Cochrane the interpreter and finally the Maori vendors, each of whose evidence, however, rather convincingly corroborated the others'.

The sequence of events, disclosed in evidence before the committee of enquiry, commenced with Cadman, the Native Minister, agreeing, strangely enough, to Lundon purchasing the block for the Government for 7/6d (75c) per acre, thus bypassing a function of the Government Land Purchase officers. Lundon was to get £50 ($100) for his trouble, but he perceived an opportunity to add to this. So, in his negotiations with the owners at Flood's hotel, in Rawene, he reduced the price to 4/- (40c) per acre, but later, on account of his 'great love' for them, he raised it to 4/6d (45c), apparently stating that the Government would pay no more. And the owners agreed. However, Millar, the Postmaster at Rawene, had already received from the Government the purchase-money at the rate of 7/6d (75c) per acre, and Lundon's problem at that stage was how to extract from it his 3/- (30c) cut.

This problem was only overcome by his risky reliance on the supposition that the vendors, bemused by the Government procedures, and the various documents they were obliged to sign, and also perhaps by the hospitality at Flood's hotel, would lose their way at an early stage of the transaction. And so it apparently proved to be, since at Lundon's request Millar paid the money to each vendor in two cheques, totalling 4/6d and 3/- per acre. Each then gave the 3/- cheque to Lundon, who claimed that at the same time they had signed a document appointing him their agent. This gave some sort of visible if doubtful legality to Lundon's acceptance of the cheques as commission, but at the subsequent enquiry the vendors conceded that they had signed a paper, but with no knowledge of its import. Lundon claimed that the paper was, in fact, an agreement that he was entitled to any amount over 4/6d that he could get from the purchaser (the Government). He produced this document at the enquiry, and it bore out his claims; but it was suggested that the wording might have been inserted after the signing. In any case, all the vendors denied having knowingly agreed to such a proposal, and were quite unaware that the

Government had been willing to pay 7/6d per acre. They also swore that the interpreter, Robert Cochrane, did not explain the purport of the document to them. But the upshot of all this was that Lundon went off £780 ($1560) to the good, plus his commission from the Government.

Unfortunately for him, however, a woman who was entitled to a share of the purchase-money by succession to a deceased vendor, had not attended the crafty ceremony at Rawene, and having applied direct to the Government, got the full 7/6d per acre. Lundon's Rawene vendors, becoming aware of this, made enquiries of the Minister, Cadman, from whom, understandably, they gained no satisfaction, and therefore petitioned the House of Representatives. This led to the interesting transaction getting an airing. It seems that before the negotiations, the owners of the land had actually been willing to sell at 2/6d (25c) per acre, and were overjoyed at Lundon's offer of 4/6d. However, this did not diminish their resolve to get the full 7/6d when his chicanery was disclosed. And rightly so.

Since the Government had authorised the expenditure of 7/6d per acre and had paid that much, it seems to have taken the view that it had not been swindled, but that the Maori vendors may have been. Since the Government was in its own opinion not implicated, the vendors' recourse now, as the report suggested, was to take legal action against Lundon to recover the balance to which they were entitled. No evidence has been found that they succeeded in this, or even made the attempt, which indeed would have involved them in great expense. The committee of enquiry had reported with lofty disdain, that, 'if the petitioners considered Mr. Lundon had not acted in accordance with any agreement entered into or made with him, they should have applied to the law Courts before applying to Parliament; and as there are sufficient grounds to warrant that belief which, if their allegations be true, render them considerable sufferers thereby.... The Committee would also suggest that the Government be asked to carefully note the apparently peculiar conduct of the officials in the performance of their duties in connection with the above transaction.'

But whether or not the Maori vendors agreed that Lundon should do so or not, he certainly pocketed his £780. And if the Maori people concerned were not entitled to it, the Government was. But politics overcame scruples in the matter, and a resolution in the terms of the report was passed by the House on party lines.

We hear little of Lundon after this time, other than his obituary.[14] He died at his Auckland home at Franklin Road, Ponsonby, on 7 February 1899. Apart from any family he may have had at Hokianga, he was survived by two sisters, one brother, a son — J. Lundon, a solicitor — and six daughters. One brother, David, pre-deceased him. Owing to his public services (and his style), it is difficult to think of Lundon as a villain — he just could not resist any opportunity to make money.

It is interesting to recall the redoubtable John Marmon at this stage. We left him behind many years back, but he survived until 1880.[15] Living at Rawhia, up the harbour opposite Horeke, he identified more with his Maori relatives than with Europeans, but he seems to have acquired a sort of hard-nosed respectability which, in his own accounts he never claimed for himself. He died at the age of eighty-one on 3 September 1880 at his home, and was buried on the hilltop adjacent to it — in a vertical grave, some myths claim. Another apocryphal though persistent tale concerns his old enemy, Mrs McBreen, who had always vowed that she would dance on his grave, but who reconsidered this resolve since she would need to climb the very steep hill to get at it. To avoid this, the story goes, she danced on his coffin as it lay in his house. It is said that the Parish Priest, sometime later, had his body exhumed and buried at Purakau.

Ironically, considering that this was a man who freely admitted to countless fornications with a multitude of identified and anonymous females, he had only one child, by his wife, Hauauru. This was a daughter, Mere, who married a Pakeha named Himi (Jimmy?) and had Hariata, who married Heperi, founding a family well-known and respected in Hokianga today. But without such characters as Marmon, Cochrane, McDonnell, Markham, White, de Thierry and Lundon, the history of Hokianga would indeed have been a considerably less rewarding subject for examination. And for them, therefore, we should be duly grateful.

23. The Final Pattern Emerges

Prior to the 1880s the pattern of industry at Hokianga had been simple. A handful of minor tycoons exploited the expendable resources and the labour there, but in the development of stable industry based on land-use, the North was far behind the rest of New Zealand. The Government had achieved this sort of development in the Waikato, Wanganui and Taranaki districts after the defeat of the Maori people in wars, by the punitive confiscation of their lands there for settlement by the Pakeha. This had two effects. One was to initiate a farming industry in those places, and the other, a strategic one, followed from the first. It eliminated strong Maori-dominated areas which might threaten the European settlements of Auckland, New Plymouth and Wellington, and exclude substantial European settlement. There being no pretext for such confiscation in the North, the policy of Government land purchases from Maori owners had, as we know, been intensified since the southern wars of the 1860s. In the 1880s then, embarrassed also by serious unemployment in Auckland, the Government was in a position to pursue a land settlement policy in Hokianga similar to that undertaken earlier in the south, but on land purchased on terms very advantageous to itself, from a depressed Maori population.

Nonetheless, because of the time, labour and expenditure needed to develop a Hokianga farming industry, the exploitation of the non-renewable resources, kauri timber and kauri gum, and to a lesser extent flax, persisted into the twentieth century as the dominant industries. In the kauri gum industry there was great poverty and distress among the diggers during and after the First World War, but it remained viable to some extent, although diminishing in significance, until the depression of the 1930s. And the milling of kauri and other native timber followed much the same pattern. In fact, 'gum-towns' still existed in the 1930s, a notable one of these being on State Highway 10 at Aranga, south of the Waipoua forest. The 'town' consisted of two rows of dwellings facing each other across a sort of common pathway. All were to the same pattern. Each house-site was surrounded on all four sides by a narrow, deep ditch, from which sods were carefully taken to build, within the ditch enclosure, earth walls about two feet high. These were the base of the house, and superimposed on them the house-frame of tea-tree or other poles was erected, to support a tent-roof and walls and a fly made of gum-sacks sewn together. Women sometimes presided over these lowly households, and here the diggers lived and worked, laboriously scraping and washing the gum they had retrieved from the Aranga gumfield. And across the highway facing the 'town' was the large gum and general store.

The hours were long, and the work dirty, hard and often wet, since much gum was gained from swamps. It was also not very rewarding, since in 1892 it was recorded that the average annual production per man was 1¼ tons, which, at £56 per ton would give the digger an annual income of £70, or $140.[1] And his amusements were few, being confined largely to getting drunk, attending to such local women as were available and running horse-races. At $140 per year presumably none of these activities could be enjoyed to excess. But this average income would include some part-time diggers, so that the return for full-time work — and for the lucky ones — was no doubt a little greater than the average.

Life on the gumfields then was indeed primitive, and on some of the newly-acquired small farms equally so. There the pioneer housewife often lived in isolation, sometimes tending her family in a nikau-thatched shanty, and cooking outside. Or if she were more fortunate she had a split-paling shack with an earth floor, the whole of one end of which would be occupied by a corrugated iron or paling chimney, for the open fire over which she cooked. It was a harsh and testing experience, the alternative to which in many cases was poverty in Auckland. More comfortable were the workers at the trading centres such as Opononi and at Kohukohu, where the mill-workers at least had fairly reasonable accommodation and social contact. And at Rawene the officials, traders, publicans and their employees were probably the best provided for of all. But Hokianga remained, as it does now to a large extent, a mixed-race community, since it was still from the Maori people that many of the wives came.

In the early 1890s Kohukohu, and possibly Rangiora,

remained the only saw-mills in Hokianga, this apparently being due to the pre-eminence in the North of Kaipara as the centre of the timber export trade.[2] And it was not until the demand increased with the lifting of the economic depression and increasing population in New Zealand at the end of the century, that the timber business boomed at Hokianga. The industry leaned heavily on water-transport, and here, on the River itself, the term Roadless North certainly applied. Roads of a sort radiated from the harbour inland, but the River remained the principal means of communication and transport throughout its length, until well into the 1930s.

Since most of the foregoing activity was lower down the harbour we have not yet dealt with settlement and development in the Waihou Valley, at the head of the harbour. The orientation of this area was ambivalent, the upper part of the valley being centred around the village of Okaihau, which itself was a Bay of Islands outpost. The land here was first taken up in the 1870s, but the lower valley looked toward Hokianga, and its little centre was at Rangiahua, the erstwhile Pukeaitia. Emphasising this situation, the boundary between the Hokianga and Bay of Islands counties was half-way up the valley.

Rangiahua, like many early settlements, owed its existence to its location at the head of the navigable tidal water. Here were the timber-booms behind which logs from the valley forests were held before being rafted down to the Kohukohu sawmill. The hotel there was built and owned by the Ogle family, cheek by jowl with the only general store in the locality other than Horeke. But in 1963 it was burned down and not rebuilt, and the store expired with it. Improved roading had made both redundant, and the hotel licence was transferred to the present hotel at Mangamuka Bridge. But the Ogle and Whitaker families, the early Rangiahua settlers, still survive there. A quaint tradition concerning the hotel and our Jacky Marmon also survives. It seems that this turbulent old sinner had his own reserved seat there in the public bar — a chair sacred to himself in a corner — and great personal danger attended anyone with the effrontery to seat himself on it, since Jacky's temper had not improved with the advance of age.

The large Government block in the Rangiahua valley was settled in the 1880s and 90s, and extended downstream from Okaihau to de Thierry's old property at the intersection of the present State Highway and the Horeke road. It was subdivided into blocks from 50 to 200 acres, and a road down the valley from Okaihau served them.[3] This was to become part of the main road north, now State Highway No. 1, and a vital link on it was the bridge over the Waihou River at Rangiahua. This, the first bridge here, was built by the Hokianga County in 1886 under the supervision of its engineering consultants, Boylan and Lundon — Lundon apparently being our John's nephew, formerly the County Engineer.[4]

Nearby, an interesting personality settled on de Thierry's former land, whose family is still remembered by older settlers. This very versatile gentleman, named Coxhead, was a small farmer, gardener, bootmaker, woodturner and photographer, and in his house and outbuildings evidence could be seen until quite recently of all these activities. An unusual feature of the house was a quite primitive outside stairway, the only way by which its upper storey could be reached. Very inconvenient on dark, rainy nights, surely.

Communication by road from Auckland was still a problem. In 1890 this inspired a petition from Northern settlers to the Minister of Public Works humbly praying that he would secure the completion of the Main Road north from Devonport as a most urgent requirement.[5] However, this fulsome plea shared the fate of most such documents, and its ineffectiveness was evident as late as the 1920s, when the term Roadless North was still in general use. Earlier, an interesting booklet prepared in 1913, publicising the North and its display in the Auckland Exhibition of that year, had coyly evaded discussion of roads, preferring to draw attention to the excellent railway and shipping services. But brightly, on the unrewarding topic of roads, it soothes the reader with the dubious assurance that, 'Year by year they have improved.'[6] Unhappily, however, the 1917 issue of the booklet reported no such improvements, and in the 1920s the passage of a car from Auckland through to Kaitaia was hailed as a triumph of human endurance and mechanical genius.

But in 1898 roading suddenly plunged to very low priority among the county's problems, since its recent attempts to enforce its dog-tax by-law came near to precipitating a second war in the North, and as a result peaceful Rawene became temporarily a centre of military activity. The display of might here arose from some provocative action by Hauhau sympathisers among the

Hokianga Maori people, and particularly the Mahurehure of Waima, in procuring and concealing firearms and ammunition. In due course this unrest led to thirteen of these being arrested for refusing to pay the dog-tax, an annual county charge of 2/6d (25c) per dog, which many Maori felt was aimed specifically at them. Hauhauism was a cult that in the 1860s had originated with the prophet Te Ua, and had since spread somewhat thinly from Taranaki throughout the North Island. The name derived from the exclamation 'Hau' repeated by its disciples at the end of their chants, but the cult-name was in fact Pai Marire. The objective of this movement, which was both religious and political, was to evict all Pakeha from New Zealand.

Richard Seddon, the Prime Minister at the time, at first displayed little sympathy with the Council and its civil disobedience problem, asserting, surely not without supporting knowledge, that some Hokianga settlers had recently been making money from supplying the dissident Maori with arms. This elicited a plaintive letter to him from the Council indignantly calling for proof of this, which they must have been aware they were unlikely to get.[7] Since the letter is indicative of the social problems of this very mixed community at the time, it is given here in full:

> (10 June 1898)
> The Honourable, The Premier.
> Dear Sir,
>
> We venture to address you in regard to the late native rising at Waima because, as representatives of the ratepayers here and as permanent and bona fide settlers in this district, we have perhaps a more accurate knowledge of the feelings of both the settlers and the natives than others may possess.
>
> Referring to your telegram of ultmo [sic] in reply to ours of the ultmo [sic] we have delayed to reply because it appeared to contain a charge against the settlers, that while they sought Government protection in the time of trouble, they did not hesitate to supply the rebels with the means of effective resistance so long as they found it to their profit to do so, by selling and carting arms and ammunition. This charge appeared of such a serious nature that we

have waited in the hope that Government would fix it upon some one individual or group of individuals. As a month has now elapsed, and no steps appear to have been taken to show that any settler in Hokianga supplied rifles and ammunition to the natives in question, we ask that either the stigma placed on the residents of this county be withdrawn or that the offences be sheeted home to the guilty parties.

In reference to the so called *sudden* rising of the Waima natives, we beg to submit that either this or some other analogous form of resistance to the law had long ago been determined upon by these natives, and that as a matter of fact they neither are now nor have been for several years prepared to submit to the law. It may perhaps be scarcely of service to refer at any length to what has passed but we must be permitted to point out that two years ago these same natives caused fear and disquietude in the district, when some of them were disarmed by having 14 guns taken from them but none of them punished. On that occasion we were agreed that all fear of trouble was at end since then the head native official and the inspector of police were either aware that there was a likelihood of further disturbance or they were ignorant of it. If the former proposition is true, they deserve censure for not having brought the matter so forcibly before the attention of the Government as to induce them to take steps to make any native disturbance impossible. If the latter is the fact our contention for reform in the management of natives in the north, which we propose to submit will be strengthened. There is a third alternative which supports itself, that the natives are under no sort of special supervision at all which we think is unsatisfactory in view of the number of risings which have taken place in recent years.

We beg to call your attention to the fact that 12 years ago there were stationed in the county one resident magistrate, who constantly settled maori troubles before they became dangerous, one magistrates clerk who was also a native interpreter and one constable. In place of these now we have the protection of one constable who has control over nearly 2000 Europeans and 2000 natives, in a district measuring some forty miles by forty miles.

In conclusion we submit that we have no sort of belief that because after a large expenditure the natives have been brought to trial leaving 40 or 50 of their fellows amongst whom are some of the worst characters, and many sympathisers and after some shotguns and a rifle or two have been seized therefore all difficulties have been disposed of and all danger at an end.

We do not believe this but we think it more than likely that in the course of the next few years there will be more serious troubles. We are of the opinion that the Government should be brought more in touch with the natives than they appear to be at present. We are also of the opinion that the Police Force should be increased in the district that the Administration of the law should be more efficient and that more equal justice should be shown to Europeans and Natives.

We have the Honour to be Sir
Yours Faithfully

Chairman Hokianga County Council
Councillors
Clerk and JPs

How profoundly the roles of Maori and Pakeha had been reversed in fifty years is clearly demonstrated in this somewhat querulous epistle. It should be noted, incidentally, that the letter exists only as a typed copy — the original was not found.

The first of the sequence of events giving rise to the military action following the 'uprising' described in the letter, occurred on 28 April, when Constable McGilp, of Rawene, went to Waima to investigate information that trouble was afoot. There he found the leader, Hone Toia, and a considerable body of men under arms, stubbornly confirming their refusal to pay the tax. Furthermore, they announced that they would go armed to Rawene to dispute the issue. McGilp at once rang Rawene from the Waima Post Office and advised the evacuation of women and children from the town.

This alarming message was transmitted by telephone to Yarborough at Kohukohu, who agreed that it would be unwise to resist any attack on the town, and sent boats over to undertake the evacuation as advised by McGilp. Meanwhile, old J.R. Clendon's son James, now a magistrate, had gone over from Russell to Waima, where he found the Hauhau Maori truculent, but in his view they were not, in fact, threatening Rawene. So back went the evacuees. But later threats from Hone Toia altered Clendon's earlier assessment of the position, causing him to go to Kohukohu to consult with Yarborough and a committee of settlers. There, a decision was made to appeal to the Government for military assistance, which at first drew the unsympathetic comment from the Premier that we have noted. The whole population of Rawene was now brought over to Kohukohu, and a group of volunteers, including Yarborough and two constables, returned to find Rawene deserted by the Maori people also, except for a few from Waima who were opposed to Toia and his people.

Rumours abounded as to the activities and intentions of the 'rebels', and at this stage the *Glenelg* arrived from Onehunga with an inspector and five constables, who set up a cannon at the wharf. Sure enough, a Hauhau party did appear, brandishing their weapons, whereupon the volunteers fled at once to the *Glenelg,* leaving their deserted cannon looking sadly and silently up the main road. But the Reverend Gittos and Bob Cochrane, son of old Dennis, remained, and Bob, at some risk to himself, talked the Toia people out of any rash action. The *Glenelg* then returned to Kohukohu leaving Cochrane, who refused to be intimidated, and the Hauhau returned to Waima that night.

Then, in response to the cries for help, and despite the Premier's cynical views, the Government steamer *Hinemoa* arrived on 2 May, four days after the alarm was raised, with ninety men under Colonel Newell. She was followed by the *Gairlock* with thirty soldiers and a machine-gun, and two days later HMS *Torch* turned up with a detachment of sailors. Thus equipped, this warlike ensemble of seven constables, 120 men and their officers, a machine-gun and a squad of sailors, together with the small fleet of vessels, prepared for battle with the 'rebels'.[8]

In the meantime, Hone Heke Rankin, the member of parliament for the Northern Maori electorate, was riding for

Waima from the Bay of Islands to intervene, while at the same time seventy of Hone Toia's men lay in ambush awaiting the military force at the saddle between Omanaia and Waima. However, the troops, now advancing on Waima, were permitted to proceed unmolested, and in due course arrived at the deserted school there, where they camped. Toia's base was some miles away on the Waima River, and there Hone Heke arrived after a gruelling ride from Kawakawa and at once consulted with the dissident leaders. This Hone Heke, by the way, was the great-grandson of the original Hone Heke's brother, Tuhirangi. On the day after his arrival at the Toia camp he attended a meeting of about 250 men, women and children, the *Herald* reporter and the neutral chiefs Hapakuku, Rangatira Moetara, Retetai, Pene Taui and Hirini Te Wake. All visitors were received courteously and the meeting proceeded with decorum. Here, Hone Toia, a man of much dignity, six feet eight inches in height, spoke impressively to the gathering, and Hone Heke explained his presence and his intention to prevent the trouble escalating into a major conflict.

A general discussion then took place, resulting in a decision by the 'rebels' to submit, and accordingly Colonel Newell marched his troops to the camp and took under arrest Hone Toia, Romana, Makara, Rakena Pahi and also Hone Mete, who, as we may recall, had many years earlier been a Maori constable at Rawene. So ended the Dog-tax Rebellion.[9] Arms were later seized and further arrests were made, and no doubt further resentment was engendered. Maoridom in New Zealand had again learned in a bitter way the futility of opposing an all-powerful government supported by a professional army to give weight to its arguments. This settlement did not, of course, remove the resentment of Pakeha dominance and government that underlay the actions of Hone Toia and his followers. Nor did it satisfy the belligerent among the Pakeha. The *Weekly News* report reflects both views:[10]

> GRIEVANCES AGAINST THE PAKEHAS
>
> Some of the young men are sullen, and appear dissatisfied at the result, and one of them arrested said, prior to being taken prisoner, 'The pakehas have oppressed us for a long time. First they took our lands, and then the Treaty of Waitangi was signed. They

broke their word and taxed us and have oppressed us ever since. If we are to be trodden on and killed with persecution let us take up arms and resist bad laws and die fighting.' The young men are said to have been more enthusiastic than the others. They would not listen to the older Maoris' advice, and broke completely away from parental control, when they joined Hone Toia's band.

The *Weekly News* was clearly not concerned with causes, and showed somewhat more interest in the Pakeha view of the result:

> RESIDENTS DISSATISFIED
>
> Many of the residents of Rawene, Waima and Kohukohu expressed dissatisfaction at only a portion, and not all, of the malcontents having been made prisoners, and because only a few arms have been secured. They state that there are still many rifles and cartloads of ammunition secreted. Tonight they have waited on Colonel Newell and Inspector Hickson, and emphasised the gravity of the position, and the danger of a similar rising taking place after the departure of the troops, as soon as the disaffected Maoris have time to gather together. Many old residents who are well acquainted with the Maoris, state against this that the Maoris are subdued, and will not again venture to rise and take up arms against the Queen, and defy the law.

From June through to August there followed impassioned telegraphic appeals by Hone Heke Rankin to the County Council to adjourn the trials of Hone Toia and his associates on the various charges, 'to give time to Natives for settlement of mind'.[11] These did eventually result in a letter from the Hokianga County Council to the Minister of Justice reflecting a very sensible and placatory attitude to the situation, in view of the origin and outcome of the unhappy incident.[12]

> County Office Rawene Hokianga
> Sept 10th 1898
> The Hon The Minister of Justice
> Wellington.

Sir

I am instructed by the Hokianga County Council to communicate with you in reference to the late Native trouble here in the matter of Dog Tax. I have seen a draft of the letter to you from Mr. Honi Heke M.H.R. and other influential Ngapuhi Chiefs, stating that those Natives who caused the disturbance have now submitted to the law, and are going to pay the Dog and other Taxes. The Council have every reason to believe this is true, and that those Natives will give no further trouble, and also that they are settling down to their former peaceful habits of life, and are cultivating their ground for crops.

I may here say that this peaceful state of affairs gives great satisfaction to the inhabitants, and also to the Council, who have to deal with local taxation, as it is most unpleasant to live at variance with the Native people. And one and all here welcome the return to that cordial feeling which existed previous to the late disturbance. This being so, the Council would respectfully ask you to remit to those Dog Tax defaulters the heavy Charges imposed on them by the S.M. Court in the shape of fines mileage and to charge only such sum as will cover the actual costs, a schedule of which is attached.

I am in a position to verify the contention of Mr. Heke, that the Natives are not in a position to pay this large amount in addition to what they have to find for the Supreme Court Judgement against them, and taking all the circumstances into consideration the Council think it would be a graceful act on the part of the Government to treat those people with leniency and consideration.

I should also like to point out that the Settlers here, and the North generally are under a very large obligation to the friendly Chiefs above mentioned but more particularly so to Mr. Heke, who has devoted much time and patience to reasoning those people into a peaceful frame of mind, and but for his presence with them and his great influence, the trouble would still have been with us.

Trusting your Department will see its way to grant the concession here asked.

I have the honour to be Sir your obt. servant
William Burr
County Chairman Hokianga.

And the response from the Minister:

Department of Justice, Wellington.
14th. October, 1898.

Sir,

I have the honour to acknowledge the receipt of your letter of the 10th September last, with reference to an application made for a remission of the fines inflicted upon the Natives for recent breaches of the Dog Registration Act.

In reply, I am directed to state that the Natives have been informed that they must pay the *costs* incurred, but payment of the fines will not be enforced now, but if at the end of twelve months, there has been no further trouble, then His Excellency the Governor will be advised to remit the fines; but if any further trouble arises, then the fines will become payable.

I have the honour to be,
Sir,
Your most obedient servant,
(signature illegible)
Under-Secretary.

The Chairman of the
Hokianga County Council,
Rawene.

And this was the end of the last organised violent protest in the North by its Maori people, who had in such a short space of time suffered the ignominy of transformation from landlord to tenant by the activities of their erstwhile guests.

24. Climax and Anticlimax

All the industries that Hokianga was capable of supporting at that time having been established, there remained only the full exploitation of their potential, and at the end of the century this process was well in hand. Until then, only the two sawmills at Kohukohu and downstream at Rangiora had operated on the River, but there appears to be only scanty information on Rangiora, first heard of in the 1880s as a Webster enterprise. The Kohukohu mill, built in 1879 by the Australian company which was soon happy to sell to Yarborough and Andrewes, did not initially have a promising career. The new owners, too, were shortly in financial trouble, aggravated in 1882 by the mill fire that did so much damage. This was the first of many such disasters that progressively destroyed Kohukohu, which had a built-in vulnerability to fires, since at no time did it have even a minimally adequate water supply. The mill, closed owing to a want of finance in 1885, was re-opened in 1889 when the Kauri Timber Company acquired it.

The timber industry reached the peak of its performance in the early years of the twentieth century, but its profitability dwindled after the first decade, due to the heavy expenditure involved in transporting millable logs ever-increasing distances from within the bush to the rivers.

By this time three further mills existed at Hokianga: at Koutu, the scene of the Battle of the Plank many years earlier, and at Rawene and Waimamaku. Of these, only Waimamaku did not suffer from dependence on the river to bring down its logs. The mill, with an output of 2,500,000 superficial feet per year, was built in 1905 by the Kauri Timber Company near the source of millable trees, thus minimising this problem. But the delivery of the sawn timber the five miles or so to the harbour at Omapere, where the company had built a wharf, was an expensive operation. It involved surmounting the steep Pakia ridge, above Omapere, which was achieved by the construction of a tramway up the Waimamaku side of the ridge, and along this a power winch hauled the timber-trolleys to the summit.

At Rangiora it seems that the mill had operated for many years, but had recently been equipped with modern machinery. Its output was 4,000,000 feet comprising rimu and kahikatea as well as kauri. Across the harbour at Rawene, Messrs Dives and Ramsay's mill, built about 1904, was located at the mouth of the Waima River on a tongue of land on the foreshore, about half a mile from the point. It too cut several varieties of timber totalling 1,250,000 feet per year and was later taken over by the Union Box and Timber Company, which also operated a joinery factory at Rawene.

The Koutu mill, the largest of them all, was built in 1901 by the New Zealand Timber Company, but it did not have the greatest output. It produced 3,200,000 feet annually, little more than thirty-five per cent its capacity of 9,000,000 feet, and was later acquired by the Kauri Timber Company. In fact Kohukohu was the largest producer, turning out 5,000,000 feet, or nearly a third of the River's timber. The report of 1906 from which these figures are drawn, gives the number of men employed by the five mills as 158,[1] and, of course, many more were engaged in the bush to supply them. Their combined output in 1906 was 15,950,000 superficial feet, but if the Whangape mill, built in 1904 by the Michelson Timber Company is included, the total is increased by 4,000,000 feet. This company was obliged to purchase its own ships to export its timber owing to the objection of shipowners to the narrow entrance to the Whangape Harbour, and the bar there.

But Hokianga's production of timber, a large proportion of which was exported to Australia, was greatly exceeded by the Kaipara Harbour's 40,737,954 feet. And since New Zealand's total output of timber was 190,543,000 feet annually, the production of which employed about 5000 men at the mills and in the bush, it will be appreciated that Hokianga's contribution was not as great as may popularly have been supposed.

Another small mill producing mostly house timber for the local market, and railway sleepers, was operated by W.B. Stephens at Maunganui Bluff. Its output was 300,000 feet from trees supplied by neighbouring settlers. The Hokianga mills on the other hand took their logs mainly from Government and Maori lands, but some did come from settlers' properties. Of all these mills, only three — Kohukohu, Rangiora and Koutu

— survived into the First World War, and the last to close was Rangiora. This was perhaps the first to operate, and was still cutting timber spasmodically in the 1930s. However, due to the dwindling sources of native timbers in recent times, there has been a tendency for quite small sawmills to be set up to exploit remaining pockets of useable trees, and, of course, the exotic timber stands.

Although it has now been reduced to insignificance, Kohukohu at the turn of the century probably ranked third or fourth in size of the settlements north of Auckland. It was by far the most important industrial and commercial town in Hokianga. It had been pre-eminent in baulk-timber production since the early 1830s, but did not achieve the status of a town until the sawmill was set up there. Supported by this and the Yarborough and Andrewes enterprises, which also serviced the farm settlements at Motukaraka, inland, and around the upper harbour, growth and prosperity then attended Kohukohu. At its most prosperous, the town had a population of about 600, reasonably housed, with its Town Hall, Masonic Hall, school, churches, banks, newspapers and brass band. Photographs of the 1880s and 90s show a substantial town, comprising commercial buildings, some two-storeyed, and stores, offices, two wharves and the sawmill. Served by a regular weekly steamer service from Onehunga, it retained this form and its unrivalled commercial eminence on the harbour until its decline was initiated by the closing of the mill in 1909.[2]

It was the dairy industry that at this point rescued Kohukohu, and indeed, Hokianga, from economic oblivion, developing as it did slowly from its early subsistence level into a major producer. The areas allocated to the settlers under the Government Farm schemes had been about fifty acres, but when they were later raised to 100, surplus production became possible. The independent purchasers of the Government lands were at the same time developing larger areas. This encouraged dairying and led to the formation of the Hokianga Co-operative Dairy Company, which in 1908 took over a factory at Motukaraka recently built and operated by Dalgety and Company.[3]

Dairying and gumdigging thus kept Hokianga afloat while the timber industry was suffering its progressive dissolution, and ensured the commercial survival of the three urban centres at

Kohukohu, Rawene and Opononi.

At Rawene, the smallest of the sawmills on the River remained in operation well into the 1920s, owing mainly to the enterprise of its management in building tramways from the rivers into the inland forests. The most ambitious of these was laid from the tidal limit of the Punakitere River at Taheke, to Tautoro, a few miles south of Kaikohe. This tramway served a mill built on the River at Waima in 1906 by Ramsey, Runciman, Bawden and Gulliver, who set it up using a boiler and engine acquired from the Kauri Timber Company at Waimamaku. But two years later these people sold out to the Rawene firm. Rawene itself, being the county seat, survived on this and on the mills and other small industries — and its hospital. But between the two World Wars, Opononi and Kohukohu lapsed into depression.

Kohukohu gained much impetus towards its final demise from its successive fires. The mill fire of 1882 left the young town unaffected, but in 1900 Gabolensky's twelve-year-old hotel and Wallace supply store were burned, and fires of the early 1920s, 1937, 1954 and 1967 reduced it to its present status of Post Office, store and hotel. Providentially, the progress of this destruction kept pace with Kohukohu's diminishing importance, so that little replacement of the vanished buildings was necessary, except of course for the essential hotel. This was again destroyed by the fire of 1954, but quickly replaced, although not, unhappily, by a building as elegant and dignified as its predecessor. Then in 1958 the dairy factory at Motukaraka closed. Improved roading throughout the North had made amalgamation of factories an economic process, and so the town lost its last industry. While Opononi and Omapere are developing as popular residential places, Kohukohu clings to its past, and with its mellow, picturesque houses, legacies from those eventful days, it is a haven for quiet people in search of a quiet life.

Rawene is now the undisputed metropolis of Hokianga, and the harbour ferry terminal. No hope of a bridge here. And the hospital sits on the hill above, certainly the town's most important industry.

The Rawene we see today is much the same little town that thrived at the turn of the century. Most of the buildings remain, but their functions are sadly reduced. Not so, however, the hospital. That the expanding medical presence here has clearly influenced the habits of the citizens is demonstrated by this early letter from the Medical Officer of Health to Constable McGilp. With professional severity he informs the constable of his views on a distasteful aspect of local hygiene and demands that the nuisance be abated.[4]

Public Health Offices,
Rawene.
Hokianga, N.Z. December 15th. 1897.

Dear Sir,

I must draw your attention to the fact of the inhabitants of Rawene, and the Public Well, situate some distance round the River face, towards Mr. Cochranes.

The inhabitants wash their clothes etc., etc., at this Well, and after they have done this, they throw the water all around in close proximity to the said well.

This dirty water will in time percolate thro' the soil and again reach the fresh pure water in the Well, and so poison it.

This must be stopped entirely, and the inhabitants warned under the penalty of a fine, that they must at all times take their Dirty Water and throw it into the River, or to have a deep hole dug, distant from the well and having a declivity from the well, and there bury it. If Typhoid, Diptheria, or Low Fever break out, then they will have the fault at their own doors.

I am, Sir,
Yours truly,
George de Clive-Lowe. M.O.H.

What etc., etc., embraced was apparently so unsavoury as to be left to the imagination and judgement of Constable McGilp, who two days later was again directed by the M.O.H. to abate a similar nuisance at Kohukohu. There, in a drain on the premises of Mr. Hayles, 'The odour is extremely offensive and the drain in such a state, that with a sun, as hot as we are now experiencing it, beating down on it, the production and multiplication of disease germs is to be expected and looked for....'

Constable McGilp's life was certainly punctuated with much

incident. Even at this time he was no doubt faced with the early symptoms of the Dog Tax furore and following that he had to deal with a complaint raised late in 1898, which he had reason to believe he had settled two years previously. This piece of effrontery is so breathtaking as to merit quotation of the outraged complainant's letter in full:[5]

The Commissioner of Crown Lands
Auckland
Sir

I have the honour to bring before your notice the following case of serious trouble in this neighbourhood & pray that you will take immediate steps to have it removed.

A Mr. W.J. Flavell who about two years ago was turned out of Section 30, Bk. IX Mangamuka Survey District, by the Police, by order of the Commissioner of Crown Lands on account of complaints of settlers, has again (on the section being taken up by Mr. Beasley) taken possession of the same building, and is again committing the same offences for which he was turned off before, and is making himself a perfect nuisance to the neighbours generally. He is felling valuable timber on other people's sections, including my own, and selling it in defiance of the rightful owners. It is useless prosecuting him, as the few belongings he possesses are held in his wife's name. He took up a section conjointly with Mr. James Black lower down the Hua Hua Creek some two years ago but he has never resided on it. He was stopped by the Crown Lands Ranger from removing & selling the valuable timber on it, both puriri and kauri.

Although he does not own an inch of land in this Valley [the Huahua Valley, a few miles to the north-west of Motukaraka] he has lately bought several head of cattle & is running them on other settlers' property & on the public roads. He has pulled up a fence for which he was paid 6/- a day to erect for the convenience of the other settlers, and has made from the material a stockyard for his private use in the middle of the public road. The roads in this district, as is well known, are almost impassable and it is scandalous that this man should be allowed to run & graze cattle on them, destroying culverts & drains. I myself have 35 chains of frontage to this road which is my only outlet by road which is in some places after heavy rain a foot under water. A lot of drainage along the road has been done from the proceeds of 'thirds', which will soon be made useless by his heavy milking cattle & bull. — I repeat that a man without an inch of land in this valley should not be allowed to graze his cattle upon the public, damaging the roads and subjecting all the bona fide settlers to his trespassing & removal of valuable timber, and other acts of petty tyrany [sic] too numerous to mention. — I have the honour to be, Sir,

Your obt. Servt. C.N. Mardon.

The sad predicament of Mr Mardon and his neighbours and the enterprise of the bold Mr Flavell were no doubt duly dealt with by Constable McGilp, concurrently with his attention to the problems of the other 4000 people within his jurisdiction.

So events at Hokianga arrive at the point where they may be recalled by those still alive to tell of them. But perhaps reference to a little-known incident concerning the loss of a ship off the harbour may be of interest. This was the steamer *Ventnor,* 3961 tons, which, on 22 October 1902 left Wellington with among its cargo the bodies or bones of some 500 Chinese who had died in New Zealand since the gold-mining days in the South Island. Since these remains were intended for re-burial in China, nine aged Chinese were aboard as 'body attendants'. When supposedly five or six miles off Cape Egmont the vessel struck a rock which holed her to the extent that the pumps could not cope with the inflow of water. But strangely, Captain Ferry continued on his voyage up the coast, until, having travelled about 250 miles from the point where she struck, the *Ventnor* foundered on 28 October, ten miles off Hokianga Heads. Four boats had by then been launched. Next day two of these arrived at Omapere, in the harbour, and a third was picked up off the Whangape Harbour by a small steamer, the *Energy,* and brought into Hokianga. But the wreckage of the Captain's boat was cast ashore north of Hukatere, on Ninety Mile Beach, on 11

November. It had carried fifteen people, none of whom had survived, and it seems that five of the 'body attendants' were among them. The remaining twenty-four were looked after at Omapere until 5 November, when they left for Auckland.[6]

Two substantial vessels have since been lost at Hokianga.[7] The *Joseph Craig,* a barque of 751 tons, stranded at the Heads on 7 August 1914. She was under tow in a heavy sea when the line parted and she went ashore, becoming a total wreck. No lives were lost, since the crew abandoned the ship in boats and safely made the 300 yards to shore, but the *Joseph Craig* quickly broke up, and all that remained of her the next day was the forecastle head, still hanging by the anchor.

Then, on its regular run from Onehunga to Hokianga on 14 July 1928, the *Isabella de Fraine,* an auxiliary schooner of 110 tons, owned by A.G. Frankham Limited, foundered on crossing the bar. It seems that the mainsail gybed, causing her to go broadside on to the sea when she capsized, turned bottom up and sank with the loss of the whole crew of eight.

An important event in the development of Hokianga occurred in the year that the *Isabella de Fraine* was lost, when the road through the Waipoua Forest was opened. This was to become a world-famous scenic drive. It also eliminated the long, tortuous haul from Kaihu throuugh Donnelly's Crossing and Tutamoe to the head of the Mangakahia River, and thence northwards down the Wekaweka Valley to Waimamaku. This, the old main route from Dargaville to Hokianga has long been abandoned and State Highway 12 now passes through the Forest. And in the 1940s, Hokianga's final major communications problem, of some sixty years' standing, was laid to rest when the last major bottleneck in the highway system there was eliminated. Since the 1890s the road between Waimamaku and Pakanae, and thence to Rawene, had been through the rugged but impressive Waiotemarama Gorge. An intimidating challenge to nervous motorists, this route by-passed Opononi. Since it was steep and winding, prohibitively expensive to improve and quite unsuitable as a link in a main highway system, an alternative route was necessary. Therefore, as a road of sorts existed between Waimamaku and Omapere, or Pakia, this was brought up to highway standard, and from there extended along the foreshore to Opononi, and on to Pakanae. So ended the comparative isolation of Webster's erstwhile baronial establishment, now sadly bereft of its former splendour.

But two major parts of the county remain relatively isolated. They have never been a focus of Pakeha interest, as we have already observed, and are still almost wholly in Maori hands. These are Pawarenga, on the Whangape Harbour, and the Panguru (Whakarapa), Motuti and Mitimiti settlements, on the western side of the lower reaches of the Hokianga. The roads serving them end with them, and their remoteness, and the condition of these roads, contribute largely to this isolation — when you get to places like this, the only way out is the way you came in.

And so we leave Hokianga, much as it is to be found today, a land still beset by problems arising from its scanty resources, its rugged terrain and its remoteness from markets. The past here lies brooding, steeped in the majestic beauty of the mountain-girt harbour.

25. Kupe

Having dealt fully with European events and personalities, it now seems appropriate to conclude this narrative with an affirmation of the basic Maori belief at Hokianga of the importance of the ancestor Kupe, both to the people and to the harbour. Despite doubts that may be cast by scholars on this man's ancestry and traditional activities, ancient tales of these are firmly and ineradicably woven into the cloth of Hokianga lore.

The following extract from Sir George Grey's *Nga Tupuna Maori* (The Maori Ancestors) is interesting since it contains no reference to Hokianga, whereas the people there believe that their harbour is the 'Returning-place of Kupe', the place from which he returned to 'Hawaiki', wherever that may have been.[1] This is a southern account, telling of the matters leading to Kupe's association with Hokianga, described later in this chapter. Oddly, the names of the people and the canoes in the Grey account suggest the possibility that Waiharakeke could have been a New Zealand place-name. No such suggestion appears in the Hokianga account.

KUPE

> Waiharakeke (at Hawaiki) was the name of the river, on the bank of which stood the forest out of which was taken the tree to build the canoe Aotea. Toto cut the tree down and then split it in two; Mataatua was made of one slab and Aotea of the other. Matahourua (or Mataatua) was given to Kuramarotini, and Aotea was given to Rongorongo, the daughters of Toto.
>
> Matahourua was the canoe which went over the long face of the sea, and Reti was her commander.
>
> Kupe and Hoturapa went out to sea to fish. When the canoe had gained the fishing-ground Kupe let his line down, and no sooner had it touched the bottom than Kupe thought he would practise some deceit on his companion. Kupe said to Hotu, "O,

Hotu! my fishing-line is foul at the bottom; do dive and clear it."

Hotu said, "Let me have your line."

Kupe answered, "Oh, no! you cannot get it loose unless you dive."

Now, this was done by Kupe in deceit to kill Hotu, so that he (Kupe) might have the wife of Hotu, called Kuramarotini.

Hotu dived, and when he was down Kupe cut the cable of the canoe and pulled away. When Hotu came up he saw that Kupe had gone off in the canoe, and he called, "O, Kupe! bring the canoe to me;" but Kupe did not so much as look round, but pulled on. Hotu swam after him until exhausted, and then sank, and was drowned.

Kupe got on shore and took the wife of Hotu; but he was afraid lest evil should come to him, and, to escape vengeance, he and his party embarked in the canoe "Matahourua", and came away to these Islands (of New Zealand), but he did not see man.

Kupe crossed over to the South Island and pulled over the sea of Raukawa, and went on to the Kurateau (French Pass), where he met the Wheke-a-Muturangi (octopus of Muturangi). When it heard the canoe coming it rose to take it, but Kupe killed it.

Kupe did not remain in these Islands, but he went back across the sea to the other side. He left signs here, but his body returned across the sea to those Islands there.

When Kupe arrived again in Hawaiki he found Turi there, which was after four years of absence, and in the year of the death of Hawepotiki.

Doubts have been expressed by students of Maori tradition as to the integrity of the Kupe legends, or less drastically, as to their antiquity.[2] This is on the evidence of wide differences indicated by genealogical tables from various localities throughout the country, in the supposed time of his advent, or even his birth, in New Zealand. However, so entrenched are tales of Kupe's activities, and the belief in the symbolic signs of these in Hokianga, as to clearly establish his presence here at some time.

The most contentious matter concerning him is chronology, and involved in this are Nukutawhiti and Ruanui, who were supposed to be contemporary with Kupe, or at least near enough to him to have profited from his advice and to have used his canoe in their voyage to Hokianga from Hawaiki (see Chapter 1). And Nukutawhiti is undoubtedly a Ngapuhi ancestor. Assuming twenty-five years to a generation, we find that conflicting genealogies record Kupe as having flourished anything between twenty and forty-five generations back from AD 1900. Indeed, Nukutawhiti suffers from the same complaint, appearing anywhere between twenty-five and forty generations back.

Now we will look at the recitation by Aperahama Taonui of his Ngapuhi genealogy, and his story of the coming of Kupe. Having descended twenty-nine generations from Kupe, he arrives at a point between the undisputed ancestors, Puhimoanaariki and Rahiri, where he makes an interesting distinction between the names above this point and below it.[3] Here is Aperahama's account:

Translation of Extract of the History of the Migration of Nukutawhiti, by Aperahama Taonui. [1849]

This is the account of the ancestors of the Maori.

Kupe was the man who came to these lands in days of old. He came to search for Tuputupuwhenua; and after going all over this (North) Island (he did not find him in the South) he found him at Hokianga. It was a returning (Hokianga) of Kupe: hence Hokianga-o-Kupe, returning of Kupe, the name of that river.

Tuputupuwhenua and his wife Kui live in the ground. When men sleep, and see Tuputupuwhenua come up out of the ground, then the dreamer says that it is a sign of the land being forsaken; or, as it is interpreted by the word forsaken, all the people will be killed or die of sickness.

Now, when one builds a new house, when the house is finished the builder goes and pulls up some grass and offers it to the little insect which has a lump on its back, and is found in holes in the ground in summer. That insect is called Kui, and that grass is a sacred offering taken to that insect, as it is the original possessor of the land.

Kupe had a son called Matiu. He had Makaro; he had Maea; he had Maahu; he had Nukutawhiti.

Now Nuku and his brother-in-law, Ruanui, came from the other side of the sea in the canoe Mamari. Kupe had said that Tuputupuwhenua was at Hokianga; so that when Nuku arrived off the heads of Hokianga Tupu went down into the ground....

... Nukutawhiti had a son called Papatahuriiho, and Moerewarewa, a daughter. When Nuku died Moerewarewa cried for him, and this was her lament:—

> Clap, ye thunders, up above yonder,
> And flash, ye lightning, it is a calm,
> Tu is angry, Rongomai comes down.
>
> Repeat the incantation
> Over the spring Waipunatea,
> Ru, Ngana, Aparangi, and Kapitiwhano.

Papatahuriiho had a son Papatahuriake. The meaning of Papatahuriiho is the sky is inclined towards the earth; and the meaning of Papatahuriake is the earth is inclined towards the sky. Papatahuriake had a son Mouriuri; his son was Morakerake; his son was Morakitu; his son was Whiro; his son was Toe. The tribe of Toe were a numerous tribe, and the proverb for them is "The many of Toe, the thousands of Toe, killed by Rauoatu." Toe had Apa; he had Rauru. This man was the ancestor of those who know how to carve in wood, of the Ngatikahungunu Tribe. Rauru had Kanea. This man turned into a sea-god and went underground, and came out from under the earth a little west of the Kerikeri, at the Bay of Islands. Kanea had Tetokooterangi; he had Terangitaumumuhu; he had Terangitauwananga; he had Hekana; he had Poupa; he had Maroro; he had Teikatauirangi; he had Awa; he had second Awa; he had Awanui. This man was the ancestor Ngatiawa, who live at Taranaki, who owned and occupied this Hokianga District in ancient times. All men know this. Awanui had Rakei; he had Tamakitera. The descendants of this man, the Ngatitamakitera, are in the Thames, at Hauraki.

> Tamakitera had Puhimoanaariki. This man is the ancestor of the Ngapuhi, and hence the name of Puhi, or Ngapuhi, from this ancestor.
>
> At his name we end the Popoarengarenga, that being the end of the line of the names of our ancestors, which we repeat to take the tapu from the hands of any who have touched the dead, or when they come from attending the sick, or the burial of any one.
>
> The next name after Puhi is that where the tuatangata commences, and is not the sacred part of our genealogy.

This genealogy is one of Nukutawhiti's 'long' ones, which place him some twenty generations above Puhimoanaariki, whereas in the 'short' ones, Nuku is only about five generations above Puhi. However, it is quite certain that Taonui's *tatai,* or genealogical recitation, is of great significance at Hokianga, and therefore for Ngapuhi. Perhaps it is one of great antiquity, and because of this the names therein are likely to have been carefully remembered and preserved. It is also possible that some of the names recited could be of ritual or supernatural significance, rather than those of ancestors. And that there may have been two Kupe and two Nukutawhiti, separated in time, is another possibility that cannot be entirely dismissed. Or even that the identities of different men may have become confused with time. Any of these factors could have a bearing on the problem of the short and long genealogies.

Here, then, we leave both Kupe and Hokianga. There can be no doubt that on his advent he did, in fact, find the place sparsely populated, if at all. And that he lingered long enough, and with traditionally known activity, to have had the harbour named for his departure from it. There can have been no reason for the invention of such stories, and doubts concerning them can be reasonably entertained only about their place on the time-scale — a conception of no significance to the ancient Maori. Kupe was certainly at Hokianga, but when, where he came from and returned to, may well continue to be matters for conjecture.

Epilogue

It may be recalled that early in this narrative relations between Maori and Pakeha were observed to be as those between landlord and tenant, and that the Maori dominated life at Hokianga. This he continued to do until the wars in the south. He had been politically dominant because he held all the cards — his authority was supreme and he owned the things that the Pakeha wanted. Progressively this changed. The good cards were frittered away until the Pakeha finally gained possession of the things he had come for — first the timber, and then the land on which it grew — all in exchange for perishable and expendable goods, or for the money to purchase them. In the 1860s the Maori here still had potential power, in spite of the ascendancy of the Pakeha government, but he was intimidated by its military successes in the southern wars. The settlers' administration now had the means to enforce its will with little expectation of effective resistance, and the Pakeha thus gained courage. In consequence his attitude to the Maori changed from respect to pity, condescension and even contempt. Governor Fitz Roy had observed the awakening of this new relationship as far back as 1846. 'More settlers arrived in every ship. The natives were ... treated with less caution and less kindness than previously....' And further, 'they were perplexed ... by finding that people were becoming averse to their company.'

These people were the new breed of settler, who had never been dependent on Maori goodwill. In early Hokianga the scanty European population had been less affected by this trend. As welcome guests they had worked alongside their Maori neighbours, although they later exploited their labour. But finally, when Pakeha settlers filled the land, the Maori, out-manoeuvred, defeated and displaced, retired aimless to his segregated villages, without status and with his culture in ruins.

With this thought we have brought our Hokianga story to and beyond its high point, and it is appropriate in conclusion to quote a very perceptive prediction made in 1880 by Captain

W.R. Russell, Member of Parliament for Napier, during the debate on the Maori Prisoners Bill. Introduced to facilitate the imprisonment of Maori men involved in Te Whiti's protest at the Government's determination to take land in Taranaki, the Bill inspired Russell to comment, 'I may say, what I have often said before, that I have no feeling of animosity whatever against these people who are called rebel Natives in New Zealand. In days to come, when historians write the annals of this country, they will view the struggle which has taken place in this country from a very different standpoint from that which we can take who are mixed up in its turmoils and its disagreements. The men whom we look upon as rebels, and who some think are traitors, will, to my mind, occupy a brighter page of history than many whom we look upon as faithful and loyal Natives.'

Thus a people was overwhelmed by the essential rapacity and greed inherent in the syndrome we know as civilisation. The long road back to the mutual respect of those first days remains to be trodden, but where better can this journey begin than at Hokianga, where truly the ancient blood and the new are now irretrievably intermingled.

KA MUTU TE KORERO

Sources

Chapter 1

1) Smith, S.P., *Supplement to the Journals of the Polynesian Society,* Vol. 5. p. 38 *et seq.*
2) Yarborough, A.C., *Journals of the Polynesian Society,* Vol. 15.
3) Kamira, Himiona, *JPS,* Vol. 66.
4) Simmons, D., *The Great New Zealand Myth,* pp. 15-59.
5) Te Whetu, *JPS,* Vol. 2.
6) Kamira, *op. cit.*
   White, J., Maori Superstitions, Appendices to the *Journals of the House of Representatives,* 1861, E-No. 7, p. 6.
7) Kamira, *op. cit.*
   Tregear, E., *The Maori Comparative Dictionary,* 'Tuputupuwhenua'.
   Smith, S.P., *op. cit.,* p. 20.
8) Taonui, Aperahama, 'A Genealogical book of the Maori Ancestors', (Mss).
9) Tregear, E., *op. cit.,* 'Araiteuru'.
10) Smith, S.P., *Maori Wars of the Nineteenth Century,* pp. 98-9.
    Smith, S.P., Suppt. to the *JPS, op. cit,* p. 26.
11) *Ibid,* pp. 19-20.
12) Simmons, *op. cit.*
13) Minutes of a Meeting of Ngapuhi, Te Rarawa, Te Aupouri and Ngatikahu at Whakarapa (Panguru) in June 1924.

Chapter 2

1) Smith, S.P., Suppt. to the *JPS, op. cit.,* p.25.
   White, J., *op. cit,* p.27.
2) Graham, G., *JPS,* Vol. 49.
3) Minutes of a Meeting ... in June 1924, *op cit.*
4) Smith, S.P., Suppt. to the *JPS, op. cit.,* p. 38.
5) Graham, G., *JPS,* Vol. 48.
6) Smith, S.P., Suppt. to the *JPS, op. cit,* pp. 44-7.
7) *Ibid,* pp. 15 *et seq.*
8) *Ibid,* pp. 16-18.
9) Morore Kaupeka Piripi, Ko te timatanga mai o Ngatiwai, *History of Ngatiwai* (Extract).
10) Lee, Jack, *'I have named it the Bay of Islands ...',* p. 287.
11) Smith, S.P., Suppt. to the *JPS, op. cit.,* p. 29.

12) Edmonds, H., Personal communication to the author.
13) Lee, J., *op. cit.,* p. 287.
14) *Ibid.*
15) Taonui, Aperahama, *A Genealogical book ..., op. cit.*
16) Kawiti, W.B., *Waiomio Limestone Caves.*
Various personal communications to the author.

Chapter 3

1) Yarborough, A.C., 'Ngatiawa in the North', *JPS, op. cit.,* Vol. 15. 'Approximate strength of the Hokianga Hapu, c. 1810', *JPS,* Vol. 18.
2) Maori Land Court, Northern Minute Book No. 9, Punakitere No. 2 Block.
3) Taonui, A., *op. cit.,* p. 14.
4) Maxwell, C.F., 'Origin of the Tribal Name Ngatikuri, Whangape', *JPS,* Vol. 4.
5) Witehira, Paepae, Personal communication to the author.
6) Taonui, A., *op. cit.,* p. 41.
7) Smith, S.P., Suppt. to the *JPS, op. cit.,* p. 58.
8) Smith, S.P., 'Maori Wars', *op. cit.,* p. 120.
9) Minutes of the Te Rawhiti Block Committee.
10) Smith, S.P., Suppt. to the *JPS, op. cit.,* p. 94.
11) *Ibid,* p. 94.
12) Tarakawa Takaanui, *JPS,* Vol. 3, p. 70.
13) Smith, S.P., 'Maori Wars', *op. cit.,* pp. 52-4.
14) Simmons, D.R., Personal communication to the author.

Chapter 4

1) Lee, J., *op. cit.,* p. 26 *et seq.*
2) Elder, J.R., *Marsden's Lieutenants,* pp. 51-2.
3) Barton, R.J., *Earliest New Zealand,* pp. 115, 220.
4) Elder, J.R., *Letters and Journals of Samuel Marsden,* pp. 181-201.
5) *Ibid,* p. 237.
6) McCrae, A., *Journal kept in New Zealand in 1820,* pp. 19-25.
7) Cruise, A., *Journal of a Ten Months Residence in New Zealand,* pp. 87-8.
8) *Ibid,* pp. 88-91.
9) McCrae, A., *op. cit.,* p. 26.
10) Cruise, R.A., *op. cit.,* p. 235.
11) Smith, S.P., 'Maori Wars', *op. cit.,* pp. 96-126.
12) Barton, R.J., *op. cit.,* pp. 114-15.
13) Sherrin, R.A.A., and Wallace, J.H., *Early New Zealand,* pp. 287-8.
14) Barton, R.J., *op. cit.,* pp. 271-2.
15) Elder, J.R., *Letters and Journals, op. cit.,* pp. 360-1.

Chapter 5

1) Sherrin and Wallace, *op. cit.,* pp.. 288-90.
2) *Ibid,* p. 290.
3) *Ibid,* p. 291.
4) Ramsden, E., *Busby of Waitangi,* p. 314.
5) Polack, J.S., *NZ, Being a Narrative of Travels and Adventures,* Vol. 2, p. 192.
6) Bell, F.D., *AJHR,* 1863, D-No. 14, Schedule No. 327. These are also OLC File Nos.
7) *Ibid,* Nos. 312-17.
8) *Auckland Star,* 31 Dec 1881—25 Mar 1882.
9) Wards, I., *The Shadow of the Land,* p. 212.
10) Old Land Claim File No. 1032.
11) Sherrin and Wallace, *op. cit.,* p. 365.
12) Earle, A., *Narrative of a Residence in New Zealand,* p. 66.
13) *Ibid,* p. 191.
14) OLC Files Nos. 27 and 1032-4.
15) Polack, *op. cit.,* Vol. 2, p. 195.
    Rogers, L.M., *The Early Journals of Henry Williams,* p. 127.
16) Earle, *op. cit.,* pp. 59-63.
17) Barton, *op. cit.,* p. 431.
18) Earle, *op. cit.,* pp. 66-8.

Chapter 6

1) Bell, F.D., *op. cit.,* No. 939.
2) Laurenson, G.I., *Te Hahi Weteriana,* pp. 20-24 and *passim.*
3) Bell, *op. cit.,* No. 940.
4) Lee, J., *op. cit.,* pp. 52-5.
5) Sherrin and Wallace *op. cit.,* p. 355.
6) *Ibid,* pp. 366-9, 432.
7) Bell, *op. cit.,* No. 539.
8) *Ibid,* No. 352.
9) *Ibid,* No. 1032.
10) McDonnell, Thomas, Petition of to the House of Representatives, 1856.
11) Ross, R., *Notes on European occupation at Hokianga,* pp. 8-10.
12) Bell, *op. cit.,* No. 401.
13) Sherrin and Wallace, *op. cit.,* p. 368.
14) Petrie, H., Dennis Browne Cochrane, *NZ Genealogist,* Sep. 1984, Vol. 15, No. 148.
15) Stephenson, B., *Samuel Stephenson, 1804-1885.*
16) Davis, C.O., *Life and Times of Patuone,* pp. 34-7.

17) Sherrin and Wallace, *op. cit.,* p. 370.
18) *Ibid,* p. 371.
19) Lee, *op. cit.,* pp. 171 *et seq.*
20) Ramsden, *op. cit.,* p. 86.

Chapter 7

1) Markham, E., *New Zealand, or Recollections of it,* pp. 29 and *passim.*
2) *Ibid,* pp. 23 and 30.
3) Bell, *op. cit.,* No. 541.
4) *Ibid,* No. 326.
5) *Ibid,* No. 327.
6) Markham, *op. cit.,* pp. 38-46 and 58.
7) Davidson, W.S., 'The Settlement of Hokianga, 1820-1920', Thesis, AUC, 1948.
8) Markham, *op. cit.,* p. 47.
9) Bell, *op. cit.,* No. 12.
10) *Ibid,* Nos. 378-9.
11) Markham, *op. cit.,* pp. 56, 60.
12) Bell, *op. cit.,* No. 339.
13) *Ibid,* Nos. 1032-5, 1038.
14) McDonnell, Thomas, Petition to House of Representatives, 28 Ap. 1856.
15) Bell, *op. cit.,* No. 242.
16) Markham, *op. cit.,* p. 57.
    Davis, *op. cit.,* pp. 33-4.
17) Sherrin and Wallace, *op. cit.,* p. 363.

Chapter 8

1) Earle, *op. cit.,* p. 165.
   Rogers, L.M., *The Early Journals of Henry Williams,* pp. 110 *et seq.*
2) Earle, *op. cit.,* p. 160.
3) Smith, *Peopling of North,* p. 19.
4) Wilson, O., 'Papahurihia, First Maori Prophet', *JPS,* Vol. 74, No. 4.
5) Raeside, J.D., *Sovereign Chief, A Biography of Baron de Thierry, passim.*
   Lee, J.R., Reports on location of de Thierry's house, Historic Places Trust.
6) Ramsden, *op. cit.,* p. 88 and *passim.*
7) *Ibid,* pp. 88 *et seq.*
8) *Ibid,* p. 94.
10) Sherrin and Wallace, *op. cit.,* pp. 373-4.
    Gittos, M.B., *Mana at Mangungu,* pp. 83-4.
    Ramsden, *op. cit.,* pp. 117-20.
11) *Ibid,* p. 156.

Chapter 9

1) Gittos, M.B., *op. cit.,* p. 43.
2) Ramsden, E., *op. cit.,* pp. 123-4.
3) Gittos, *op. cit.,* p. 82.
4) Ramsden, *op. cit.,* pp. 134-6.
5) Bell, *op. cit.,* No. 1036.
6) Ross, R.M., *op. cit.,* p. 28.
7) Hocken, T.M. *Bibliography of New Zealand Literature,* p. 489.
8) Gittos, *op. cit.,* p. 89.
9) Bell, *op. cit.,* No. 513.
10) Gittos, *op. cit.,* pp. 91-3.
11) Ramsden, *op. cit.,* pp. 37-8.
12) Davis, *op. cit.,* 35-7.
    Sherrin and Wallace, *op. cit.,* p. 373.
    Gittos, *op. cit.,* p. 97.
13) Bell, *op. cit.,* No. 194.
14) Gittos, *op. cit.,* p. 98.
15) Davis, *op. cit.,* pp. 29-30.
16) *Ibid,* pp. 27-8
    Ramsden, *op. cit.,* p. 166.
17) Gittos, *op. cit.,* p. 99.
18) Bell, *op. cit.,* No. 401.
19) Markham, *op. cit.,* p. 38.
20) Bell, *op. cit.,* No. 512.
21) Gittos, *op. cit.,* p. 63.

Chapter 10

1) Gittos, *op. cit.,* pp. 128-31.
2) Bell, *op. cit.,* Nos. 512-19.
3) *Ibid, passim.*
4) Ross, *op. cit.,* p. 35.
5) Bell, *op. cit.,* Nos. 194 and 968.
6) *Ibid,* Nos. 277 and 311.
7) Bell, F.D., Appendices to the Journals of the House of Representatives, 1862, D-No. 10.
8) Gittos, *op. cit.,* p. 105.
9) Elder, J.R., *Letters and Journals of Samuel Marsden,* pp. 521-2.
10) Polack, *op. cit.,* Vol. 2, p. 40 *et seq.*
11) Adams, P., 'Herd's Point, Rawene', Notes for Historic Places Trust.
    Buller, J., *Forty Years in New Zealand,* pp. 49-50.
12) Thomson, A.S., *The Story of New Zealand,* Vol. 1, p. 285.
13) Gittos, *op. cit.,* p. 108 *et seq.*
14) Parliamentary Paper 1838, Select Committee of the House of Lords, Report on the present state of the Islands of New Zealand.

15) Ramsden, *op. cit.,* pp. 185-6.
Davis, *op. cit.,* pp. 30-1.
Auckland Star, 25 February 1882.
16) Raeside, J.D., *op. cit.,* pp. 102-139.
Hyde, R., *Check to your King,* p. 131.
Thierry, de, C.P.H., *Historical Narrative of an Attempt to Form a Settlement in New Zealand.*
17) Old Land Claim No. 453., File No. 1043.
18) Lee, *op. cit.,* pp. 205-6.
19) Raeside, J.D., *op. cit.,* p. 183.
20) Bell, *op. cit.,* No. 952.
21) Monfat, Le P.A., *Les Origines de la Foi Catholique dans Nouvelle-Zelande,* pp. 104-111.
22) Bell, *op. cit.,* No. 952.
23) Sherrin and Wallace, *op. cit.,* pp. 423-4.
24) Raeside, J.D., *op. cit.,* pp. 265-8.
25) Wade, W.R., *Journey in the Northern Island of New Zealand,* pp.47-8.
26) Simmons, E.R., *Pompallier, Prince of Bishops,* p. 42.

Chapter 11

1) Raeside, *op. cit.,* p. 338.
2) *Ibid,* pp. 256-289.
3) *Ibid,* p. 345.
4) Gittos, *op. cit.,* p. 111.
5) *Ibid,* p. 108-9.
6) *Ibid,* pp. 107-8.
7) Irvine, J., *From Whiti Bedggood of Kaikohe.*
8) Cruise, *op. cit.,* p. 23.
9) Gittos, *op. cit.,* p. 96.
10) Old Land Claim File No. 12. H.R. Oakes.
11) Bell, Nos. 12, 277, 311, 326-7, 339, 539-42, 706, 967.
12) Bell, F.D., Appendix to the Report of the Old Land Claim Commissioner, Appendices to the Journals of the House of Representatives, 1863, D-No. 14, *passim.*
13) Bell, *Ibid.*
14) Old Land Claim File 401, G.F. Russell.
15) Ramsden, *op. cit.,* p. 140.
16) Buick, L., *The Treaty of Waitangi,* pp. 1, 36-59.

Chapter 12

1) Sherrin and Wallace, *op. cit.,* p. 374.
2) Lee, *op. cit.,* p. 211.
3) Bell, F.D., *Report,* 1862.
4) *New Zealand Year-book,* 1969.

5) Bell, F.D., Schedule, 1863. Nos. 482-7.
6) *Ibid,* Nos. 488-96.
7) *Ibid,* Nos. 497-509.
8) Sweetman, E., *The Unsigned New Zealand Treaty,* p. 105.
9) *Ibid,* p. 49.
10) *Ibid,* p. 50.
11) *Ibid,* p. 50.
12) Bell, Schedule, 1863. Nos. 714-726.
13) *New Zealand Encyclopaedia,* 1966, and Sweetman, *op. cit.,* pp. 49-53.
14) Bell, Schedule, 1963, *passim.*
15) *N.Z. Encyclopaedia.*
16) Lee, *op. cit.,* pp. 218-9.
17) Buick, L., *The Treaty of Waitangi,* p. 135.
18) *Ibid,* p. 137 *et seq.*
19) Sweetman, *op. cit.,* pp. 57-9.
20) Healy, E.T., 'Old Land Claims', pp. 198-204, *N.Z. Survey Draughtsmen's Journal,* March 1951.
21) Healy, *op. cit.,* p. 203.
22) Fitz Roy, R., *Remarks on New Zealand,* pp. 11-12.
23) Lee, *op. cit.,* p. 228.
24) De Thierry, C.P.H., *Historical Narrative of an Attempt to Form a Settlement in New Zealand.*

Chapter 13

1) Simmons, *op. cit.,* pp. 40-2.
2) Gittos, *op. cit.,* pp. 112-14.
3) Robinson, H.A., *A History of the Post Office in New Zealand,* pp. 20-2.
4) Startup, R.M., The Postal History Society of New Zealand. Personal communication to the author.
5) Stevens, P.D., 'Pub Architecture', Northland. B.Arch. thesis, University of Auckland, 1952.
6) Gittos, *op. cit.,* p. 126.
7) Webster, J., *Reminiscences of an Old Settler in Australia and New Zealand,* pp. 232 *et seq.*
8) *New Zealand Encyclopaedia,* 1966.
9) Old Land Claim File No. 401.
10) Heaphy, C., Drawing in Alexander Turnbull Library.
11) Jolliffe, J., Journal of, in Mitchell Library, Sydney.
12) Davidson, W.S., 'The Settlement of Hokianga', 1820-1920. Thesis, University of Auckland, 1948.
13) Smith, S.P., *Maori Wars of the 19th. Century,* pp. 52-5.
14) Lee, *op. cit.,* pp. 253-9.
15) Buick, L., *New Zealand's First War, passim.*

16) Pakeha Maori, (F.E. Maning) *Old New Zealand,* p. 200-3.
17) Wards, I., *The Shadow of the Land,* p. 194.

Chapter 14

1) Buick, Cowan, Wards, Sherrin & Wallace, Lee, *op. cit.*
2) Webster, *op. cit.,* p. 280.
3) Raeside, *op. cit.,* p. 193 *et seq.*
4) Mair Papers, Auckland.
5) Gittos, *op. cit.,* pp. 123-4.
6) Buick, *op. cit.,* pp. 103-4.
7) Sherrin & Wallace, *op. cit.,* p. 699.
8) Buick, *op. cit.,* p. 96.
9) White, J., *Recollections of Okaihau fight.*
10) Buick, *op. cit.,* pp. 122 *et seq.*
11) Pakeha Maori (Maning), *op. cit.,* pp. 218-225.
12) Pakeha Maori, *ibid* pp. 232-3.
13) Wards, *op. cit.,* pp. 168-9, 179.
14) *Ibid,* p. 168.
15) Cowan, J., *The New Zealand Wars,* Vol 1, pp. 87, 465.
16) Buick, *op. cit.,* pp. 270-2.
17) Gittos, *op. cit.,* p. 124.
18) A.T.L., personal communication, from Alington, W.H.
19) Irvine, J., *Township of Rawene,* p. 75.
20) Clendon Papers.

Chapter 15

1) Gittos, *op. cit.,* p. 124.
2) Laurenson, *op. cit.,* p. 121.
3) Bell, *op. cit.,* Nos. 270-2.
4) Davidson, *op. cit.,* pp. 25-7.
5) *N.Z. Encyclopaedia,* Russell, G.F.
6) Ingram, C.W.N., *New Zealand Shipwrecks,* p. 31.
7) Irvine, *op. cit.,* p. 65.
8) Davidson, *op. cit.,* p. 38. Lee, *op. cit.,* p. 162.
9) Gittos, *op. cit.,* pp. 125-6.
10) Bell, *op. cit.,* Nos. 1032-8.
11) *NZ Encyclopaedia,* McDonnell, T.
12) Yarborough, A.C., *JPS,* Vol. 15.
13) Gudgeon, T.W., *The Defenders of New Zealand,* pp. 588-94.
14) OLC File No. 316.
15) Bell, *op. cit.,* No. 401.
16) *Pandora* Navy Chart of Hokianga, 1851.
Webster Maori Journal, Jan. 11, 1847.
17) Startup, R.M., Quill and Wax, *op. cit.,* p. 78.

18) *Ibid, passim.*
19) Davidson, *op. cit.,* p. 25.
20) Webster, *Maori Journal,* Jan., Feb., Mar.
21) *Ibid,* 4 June.
22) *Ibid,* 13 June.

Chapter 16

1) Webster, J., *Maori Journal, op. cit.*
2) O.L.C. File No. 971.
3) Webster, *Maori Journal, op. cit.*
4) *Ibid.*
5) Ross, R.M., *Clendon House, Rawene.*
6) *Ibid.*
7) Webster, *Maori Journal, op. cit.*
8) *Ibid.*
9) *Ibid.*
10) Jolliffe, J., Journal of, 12 November 1851-5 December 1851.
11) Webster, J., *Reminiscences of an Old Settler,* pp. iv-vi.
12) Startup, R.M., (Editor) The Postal History Society of New Zealand, Personal comm.
13) Morton-Jones, Hokianga Journal of, Mitchell Library, Sydney.
14) Webster, *Maori Journal, op. cit.*
15) Jolliffe, Journal, *op. cit.*

Chapter 17

1) Hamlin, J. *JPS,* Vol. 24.
2) Yarborough, A.C. *JPS,* Vol. 18.
3) Dieffenbach, E., *Travels in New Zealand,* p. 241.
4) Census 1878.
5) Davidson, W.S., *op. cit.,* p. 26.
6) Taylor, P.H., 'The History of the Kauri Industry', AUC Thesis, Oct. 1950.
7) Lands and Survey Dept. (Auck) File on Motukaraka Claim.
8) Davidson, *op. cit.,* pp. 26-7.
9) *Ibid,* p. 27.
10) *Ibid,* p. 26.
11) Turnbull Library, Personal communication to author.
12) Ross, R.M., *Clendon House, Rawene,* p. 6.
13) Petrie, H., *New Zealand Genealogist,* Sept. 1984, Vol. 15, No. 148, p. 717.
14) Wakefield, E.J., *Adventure in New Zealand,* p. 150.
15) Adams, P. Notes on Herd's Point, Rawene. (Historic Places Trust) White, J. Report, Proceedings at Hokianga (L&S Department, Auckland)

16) Petrie, *op. cit.,* p. 718.
17) Buller, J., *Forty Years in New Zealand,* p. 147.

Chapter 18

1) Buller, *op. cit.,* p. 144.
2) Morton-Jones, *Hokianga Journal,* 1851, *op. cit.*
3) *New Zealand Encyclopaedia,* Maning.
4) *Ibid.*
5) Maning to Carleton, Turnbull Library Mss. Papers 1178, Folder 1.
6) Maning to Webster, Auckland Public Library.
7) Maning to his brother at Hobart, 1864-6.
8) Report on default in payment for work done on a Hokianga-Whangape road. Clendon papers.
9) Yarborough, A.C., *JPS,* Vol. 18, A Hokianga Incident.
10) Morton-Jones, *op. cit.,* p. 52.
11) *Ibid,* p. 55.
12) Ross, *op. cit.*
13) Dalton, B.J., *War and Politics in New Zealand,* pp. 78, 146-50.
14) Minute-book of the Runanga at Waimate.
15) Buller, *op. cit.,* pp. 140-7.
16) Davidson, W.S., *op. cit.,* p. 29.
17) *Ibid,* p. 38.
AJHR 1873, H-24, p. 12.
18) *Ibid,* 1862?, C-1. p. 17.
19) *Ibid,* 1877, C-8, p. 2.

Chapter 19

1) Gazette 1867 p. 491; Gaz. 1868 p. 105; Gaz. 1870 p. 109.
2) Ward, A., *A Show of Justice,* pp. 139-40.
3) *Ibid,* p. 140.
4) *AJHR* 1870, A-No. 7, p. 4 *et seq.*
5) *AJHR* 1862, E-No. 7, p. 16 *et seq.*
6) Ward, *op. cit.,* p. 219.
7) Clendon, J.R., Mss. 478, Folder No. 2, A.P.L.
8) Irvine, J., *Township of Rawene.*
9) Bell, No. 967.
Masters, A., (Rotorua) Personal communication.
10) Ward, *op. cit.,* p. 212.
11) Maning — Webster letters, N.Z. Mss 4/22, A.P.L.
12) Copy of Lease.
13) Bell, *op. cit.,* No. 541.
14) *N.Z. Encyclopaedia,* pp. 615-16., 1902.
15) Harrison, E., *Kohukohu,* pp. 23-4.
16) *N.Z. Encyclopaedia, 1902, op. cit.*
17) *Auckland Weekly News,* 16/4/1892.

18) Census figures.
19) Taylor, P.H., 'History of the Kauri Timber Industry', A.U.C. Thesis, 1950.
20) Maning — Webster letters, *op. cit.*
21) *Ibid.*

Chapter 20

1) Folder No. 2, NZ Mss. 478, APL.
2) Census 1878.
3) Irvine, J., *Township of Rawene,* p. 84.
Brett, H., *White Wings,* pp. 62-4.
4) Personal communication, ATL, (from Alington, W.H., thesis, AUC.)
5) Auckland Provincial Govt. Gazettes, 1870-6.
Stevens, P.D., Pubs. Architecture, Northland. Thesis. U. of A, 1982.
6) Gazette 1876, p. 813.
7) *Ibid,* pp. 829-30.
8) *Ibid,* p. 853.
9) *Ibid,* p. 933.
10) Startup, R.M., (Editor) The Postal History Society of N.Z., pers. comm.
11) Davidson, *op. cit.,* p. 30.
12) Lands & Survey Dept., Motukaraka file, also Bell, F.D., No. 1034.
13) Davidson, *op. cit.,* p. 30.
14) Webster, J., Letter to McLean, Mss. Papers 32: 627, McLean Papers, ATL.
15) *AJHR,* 1907, C No. 4, p. 8.
16) *Ibid,* 1877, C No. 8, pp. 1-2.
17) *Ibid,* 1880, C No. 2, p. 6.
18) Maning, F.E., Letter to Webster, 16/12/76, NZ Mss 4/22 (20), APL.
19) Von Sturmer, S., Letters to Webster, also Hokianga County Council papers.
20) Webster to McLean, *op. cit.*
21) Webster to Maning, McLean Papers, ATL, *op. cit.,* 10/8/1868.
22) *Auckland Weekly News,* 10/2/1899.
23) Proceedings, Auckland Provincial Council, 13 and 26/5/1874.
24) Von Sturmer, *op. cit., passim.*
25) *AJHR,* 1879, G No. 1.
26) O'Hara, R., (NZ Police) Pers. comm.
27) Boese, K., *Tides of History,* p. 194 *et seq.*

Chapter 21

1) Von Sturmer, *op. cit.,* 7/9/75.
2) *Ibid,* 12/12/81, 22/3/82, 31/5/81, 15/12/80.
3) *Ibid,* 23/8/81, 20/9/81.
4) *Ibid,* 31/5/81.
5) *Auckland Weekly News,* Feb. 10 1899, J. Lundon Obituary.

6) Von Sturmer, *op. cit.,* 28/10/84, 7/9/85, 15/6/85.
7) Scott, Dick, *Winemakers of New Zealand,* pp. 33-4.
8) *AJHR,* 1880, H-No. 25.
9) Davidson, *op. cit.,* p. 30.
10) Von Sturmer, *op. cit.,* 15/10/82.
11) Davidson *op. cit.,* p. 31.
12) Taylor, P.H., 'The History of the Kauri Timber Industry', AUC Thesis 1950.
13) Yarborough, A.C., *A New Field for Emigration,* pp. 27 *et seq.*
14) Von Sturmer, *op. cit.,* 20/3/85.
15) *AJHR,* 1889, C-No. 5.
16) *Ibid,* C-No. 1A.
17) *Encyclopaedia of New Zealand,* 1966, Maning, F.E.
18) Maning, F.E., Letters (APL) NZ Ms 4/22.
19) Von Sturmer, *op. cit.,* 6/11/83.
20) Personal Communication to the Author from APL.
21) Yarborough, A.C., *op. cit.,* p. 11.
22) Von Sturmer, *op. cit.,* 13/6/85, 31/5/86, 6/7/86: New Zealand Encyclopaedia.
23) Von Sturmer, *op. cit.,* 7/9/86.

Chapter 22

1) *AJHR,* 1893, H-No. 24.
2) *N.Z. Encyclopaedia,* 1966, Vol. 2, p. 207.
3) Von Sturmer, *op. cit.,* 29 May 1883, and Davidson, *op. cit.,* p. 41.
4) Davidson, *op. cit.,* pp. 40-1.
5) Von Sturmer, *op. cit.,* 10 August 1886.
6) White, G. and Monro, A., *History of Waimamaku,* p. 210.
7) Von Sturmer, *op. cit.,* 7 September, 1886.
8) *AJHR,* 1889, C-No. 5.
9) White and Monro, *op. cit.,* p. 22.
10) *AJHR,* 1889, C-1a, p. 19: 1896, C-1, p. 49.
11) *Ibid,* 1896, H-13, p. 2.
12) Stevens, P.D., 'Pubs Architecture Northland', A.U. Thesis 1982, *op. cit.*
13) *AJHR,* 1892, I-3A.
14) *Auckland Weekly News,* 10 February 1899.
15) *Northern Luminary,* 4 September 1880.

Chapter 23

1) *AJHR,* 1893, H-24, p. 11.
2) *Ibid,* 1907, C-4, p. 7.
3) Survey Office Plan (Auckland) No. 2186.
4) Document in possession of the Hokianga County Council.
5) *Ibid.*

6) A North Auckland Committee, *North Auckland, New Zealand,* p. 23, 1913.
7) Hokianga County Council, *op. cit.*
8) *N.Z. Graphic,* 1898, May 14, p. 606: May 21, p. 641: June 4, p. 697. *Auckland Weekly News,* May 7, pp. 10, 21: May 14, pp. 10, 37 and illus. pp. 3-4: May 21, pp. 2-4 illus.
9) *Auckland Weekly News,* 14 May, 1898.
10) *Ibid.*
11) Hokianga County Council, *op. cit.*
12) *Ibid.*

Chapter 24

1) *AJHR,* 1907, C-4.
2) Lee, J.R., 'The Township of Kohukohu', Essay for the Historic Places Trust, Wellington.
3) Davidson, *op. cit.,* p. 55.
4) Document in possession of the Hokianga County Council.
5) *Ibid.*
6) Ingram, C.W.N., *New Zealand Shipwrecks, 1795-1970,* pp. 278-9.
7) *Ibid,* pp. 352-3.

Chapter 25

1) *AJHR,* 1880, G-8, p. 15. *See also* Grey, Sir G., *Nga Mahi a nga Tupuna,* p. 90, and *Polynesian Mythology,* p. 158.
2) Simmons, D.R., *The Great New Zealand Myth,* pp. 15-59.
3) *AJHR, op. cit., See also* Taonui, Aperahama, *He pukapuka whakapapa mo nga Tupuna Maori,* pp. 1 and 2, and Simmons, D.R., *The Taonui Manuscript,* p. 59.

Bibliography

Manuscript

Adams, P., Herd's Point, (Rawene) Notes at the New Zealand Historic Places Trust, Wellington.

Clendon Papers. APL.

Davidson, W.S., 'The Settlement of Hokianga', Thesis, AUC, 1948, APL.

Hokianga County Council, Early document collection.

Irvine, J., Notes on Rawene in the author's possession.

Jolliffe, J., Hokianga Journal of, (1851). Mitchell Library, Sydney.

McLean Papers, ATL.

Mair Papers, Consulted in 1944 by the author when in the possession of Mr G. Mair, but present whereabouts not known.

Maning Letters, ATL, Papers 1178, Folder 1. *Also* APL, NZ MSS.

Morton-Jones, Hokianga Journal of, (1851). Mitchell Library, Sydney.

Ngapuhi, Te Rarawa, Te Aupouri, and Ngatikahu, Minutes of a meeting of at Whakarapa (Panguru) in June 1924. Copy in the possession of the author, from Mr Graham Alexander, Okaihau.

Ross, R.M., Notes on European occupation at Hokianga. AIL.

Runanga at Waimate, Minute-book of the, Kaikohe Pioneer Village.

Stevens, P.D., 'Pub Architecture, Northland', Thesis, U of A. 1982, APL.

Sturmer, von, S., Letters to Webster, APL.

Taylor, P.H., 'The History of the Kauri Industry', Thesis, AUC, 1950.

Te Rawhiti Block Committee, Minutes of the. AIL, Mss. No. 895.

Thierry, de, C.P.H., *Historical Narrative of an Attempt to Form a Settlement in New Zealand.* APL.

Webster, J., Letters of, ATL.

Webster, J., *Maori Journal* (1847), APL.

White, J., *Lease of land at Ngawha (Kaikohe) in 1873,* APL.

White, J., *Recollections of the Okaihau Fight,* ATL.

Official Records

Appendices to the Journals of the House of Representatives. Particularly F.D. Bell's Report and Schedules, AJHR D No. 10, 1862, and D No. 14, 1863.

Auckland Provincial Council Gazettes.

Auckland Provincial Council Proceedings.

McDonnell, T., Petition to the House of Representatives, 1856. APL.

Maori Land Court Minute-books, Tai Tokerau (Whangarei)
Motukaraka Claim File, and J. White Report on Hokianga (Rawene) L&S Dept. Auckland.
New Zealand Government Gazettes.
Old Land Claim Files, at Archives, Wellington. Some incomplete copies at L. & S. Dept. Auckland.
Parliamentary Debates, Vol. XXXVI (1880).
Parliamentary Paper, 1838, Select Committee of the House of Lords, Report on the present state of the Islands of New Zealand.
Survey Office Plans, Auckland.

Published Works

Barton, R.J., *Earliest New Zealand.* (1927)
Boese, K., *Tides of History.* (1977)
Buick, L., *New Zealand's First War.* (1926)
Buick, L., *The Treaty of Waitangi.* (1914)
Buller, J., *Forty Years in New Zealand.* (1878)
Cowan, J., *The New Zealand Wars,* 2 Vols. (1955 and 1956)
Cruise, A., *Journal of a Ten Months Residence in New Zealand,* London. (1824)
Dalton, E.J., *War and Politics in New Zealand.* (1967)
Davis, C.O., *Life and Times of Patuone.* (1876)
Dieffenbach, E., *Travels in New Zealand,* London. (1843)
Earle, A., *A Narrative of a Residence in New Zealand,* London. (1966). Reprint, London. (1832)
Elder, J.R., *Letters and Journals of Samuel Marsden.* (1932)
Elder, J.R., *Marsden's Lieutenants.* (1934)
Fitz Roy, R., *Remarks on New Zealand,* London. (1846)
Gittos, W.B., *Mana at Mangungu.* (1982)
Graham, G., *JPS,* Vol. 49.
Graham, G., *JPS,* Vol. 48.
Gudgeon, T.W., *The Defenders of New Zealand.* (1887)
Hamlin, J., *JPS,* Vol. 24.
Harrison, E., *Kohukohu.* (1983)
Healy, E.T., 'Old Land Claims', *N.Z. Draughtsmen's Journal,* Vol. 1, No. 6, (1961)
Hocken, T.M., *Bibliography of New Zealand Literature.* (1909)
Hyde, R., *Check to your King.* (1975)
Ingram, C.W.N., *New Zealand Shipwrecks, 1795-1970.* (1974)
Irvine, J., *The Township of Rawene.* (N.D.)
Kamira, Himiona, *JPS,* Vol. 66.
Kawiti, W.B., *Waiomio Limestone Caves.*
Laurenson, G.I., *Te Hahi Weteriana.* (1972)
Lee, Jack. *'I have named it the Bay of Islands ...'* (1983)

McCrae, A., 'A Journal kept in New Zealand in 1820', *ATL Bulletin* No. 3.
Markham, E., *New Zealand, or Recollections of it.* (E.H. McCormick, ed.) 1963
Maxwell, C.F., *JPS,* Vol. 4.
Monfat, Le P., A., *Les Origines de la Foi Catholique dans Nouvelle Zelande,* Lyon. (1896)
New Zealand Encyclopaedia. (1902 and 1966)
New Zealand Yearbook. (1969)
Pakeha Maori, (F.E. Maning), *Old New Zealand,* London. (1884)
Petrie, H., Dennis Browne Cochrane, *The New Zealand Genealogist,* Vol. 15, No. 148. (1984)
Piripi, Morore Kaupeke, *Ko te Timatanga mai o Ngatiwai,* Auckland University Library.
Polack, J.S., *New Zealand, being a Narrative of Travels and Adventures,* 2 Vols, London. (1838)
Raeside, J.D., *Sovereign Chief, A Biography of Baron de Thierry.* (1977)
Ramsden, E., *Busby of Waitangi.* (1942)
Robinson, H.A., *A History of the Post Office in New Zealand.* (1964)
Rogers, L.M., *The Early Journals of Henry Williams.* (1961)
Ross, R.M., *Clendon House, Rawene.* (1978)
Ross, R.M., *Notes on Hokianga Land Claims.* AIL
Scott, Dick, *Winemakers of New Zealand.* (1964)
Sherrin, R.A. and Wallace, J.H., *Early New Zealand.* (1890)
Simmons, D.R., *The Great New Zealand Myth.* (1976)
Simmons, D.R., *The Taonui Manuscript.* (1975) AIL.
Simmons, E.R., *Pompallier, Prince of Bishops.* (1984)
Smith, S.P., *Maori Wars of the Nineteenth Century.* (1910)
Smith, S.P., *The Peopling of the North,* Supplement to the *JPS,* Vol. 5.
Startup, R.M., *Quill and Wax.*
Stephenson, B., *Samuel Stephenson, 1804-1885.* (1984)
Sweetman, E., *The Unsigned New Zealand Treaty,* Melbourne. (1939)
Takaanui, Tarakawa, *JPS,* Vol. 3.
Thomson, A.S., *The Story of New Zealand,* 2 Vols., Vol. 1, London, (1859)
Tregear, E., *The Maori Comparative Dictionary.* (1891)
Wade, W.R., *Journey in the Northern Island of New Zealand.* (1842)
Wakefield, E.J., *Adventure in New Zealand.* (1845)
Ward, A., *A Show of Justice.* (1973)
Wards, I., *The Shadow of the Land.* (1968)
Webster, J., *Reminiscences of an old Settler in Australia and New Zealand.* (1908)
Whetu, T., *JPS,* Vol. 2.
White and Monro, *History of Waimamaku.* (1941)
Wilson, O., *JPS,* Vol. 74.
Yarborough, A.C., *A New Field for Emigration,* London. (1885)

Yarborough, A.C., *JPS,* Vol. 15.
Yarborough, A.C., *JPS,* Vol. 18.

Note: In the book list, the place of publication is shown only against those not produced in New Zealand.

Newspapers

Auckland Weekly News, 16 April 1892, 7, 14 and 21 May 1898, 10 February 1899.
Auckland Star, 31 December 1881, 25 February 1882, 25 March 1882.
New Zealand Graphic, 14 and 21 May, and 4 June 1898.
Northern Luminary, 4 September 1880.

Personal Communications

Alexander Turnbull Library (from Alington, W.H., thesis, AUC) to the author.
Alexander Turnbull Library (from Wise's PO Directories, 1887-90) to the author.
Edmonds, H., of Kaikohe, to the author.
Masters, A., of Rotorua, to the author.
Startup, R.M., (Editor, The Postal History Society of New Zealand) to the author.

Miscellaneous

Heaphy, C., Drawing of Kohukohu, 1839. ATL.
Jolliffe, J., Drawing of Kohukohu, 1851, Mitchell Library, Sydney.
Lee, J.R., *The Township of Kohukohu,* Essay for the NZHPT, Wellington.
Navy Chart of Hokianga, 1851, HMS *Pandora.*
North Auckland, Handbook by a North Auckland Committee, 1913.

Abbreviations

AIL	Auckland Institute Library.
AJHR	Appendices to the Journals of the House of Representatives.
APL	Auckland Public Library.
ATL	Alexander Turnbull Library.
AUC	Auckland University College.
JPS	Journals of the Polynesian Society.
L&S Dept.	Lands and Survey Department, Auckland.
NZHPT	New Zealand Historic Places Trust.
U of A	University of Auckland

Appendix 1
The Old Land Claims

The Old Land Claims were claims made by settlers, speculators and others to the purchase of land from the Maori people in New Zealand prior to the assumption of sovereignty and government here by the British Crown in 1840. The validity of these claims was investigated after that date by Commissioners appointed by the Crown for that purpose. These, on the evidence submitted to them by the claimants, allowed or disallowed their claims, and where they were allowed they recommended to the Governor that a Crown Grant be made of an area proportionate to the value of the goods or money the claimant had paid to the Maori vendor. Or, alternatively, the successful claimant could elect to relinquish the granted land to the Government in return for scrip, which entitled him to purchase Crown Land elsewhere to the same value. Scrip payments were often at the rate of £1 per acre granted, but were generally less.

This procedure was based on the English constitution, the effect of which in New Zealand was that no subject of the Crown could hold a title to land other than that originating in a Crown Grant. And since the sovereignty of the land had been ceded by the Maori people to the Crown, it therefore did not recognise as valid any purchases made before that event.

In the early 1840s the first Land Claim Commissioners, Messrs Godfrey and Richmond, recommended many grants and scrip payments on evidence that was faulty as to the area claimed, few claimants having produced reliable plans of the land in question. This and changes in government policy led to disputes and anomolies which were not resolved until the claims were re-investigated by Commissioner F.D. Bell, who was appointed under the provisions of an Act of 1856, and reported in 1862. He called in most of the grants made consequent on the recommendations of the early commissioners, and required surveys to be made of them. The plans produced from these surveys are now known as the Old Land Claim Plans. Having thus determined the area of land contained in each grant, and also the effect of recent legislation thereon, he produced a general report, and a schedule in which was set out relevant information on the original purchases. In this the revised grants were recommended. Some details of the Hokianga claims so dealt with are given in the table below. The numbers which Bell gave to the claims in his schedule, are not, however, those used by Godfrey and Richmond, but they are the numbers of the surviving files of the individual claims. As to the scrip issued fifteen or more years earlier, obviously no effective action could be taken by Bell to recover excessive payments.

Old Land Claims at Hokianga

The high incidence of scrip payments at Hokianga, in comparison with those in other parts of New Zealand, was apparently due to the view of many claimants that the value of Hokianga land was simply that of the kauri on it. This could only be extracted slowly and with much labour, and the claimants were clearly interested in getting land at Auckland, the new capital, where more attractive business and employment opportunities were believed to be offering.

GRANTS OR SCRIP ISSUED

O.L.C. PLAN NO.	BELL SCHEDULE NO.	CLAIMANT	AREA CLAIMED AND LOCATION	SCRIP OR LAND GRANTED AND REMARKS
270	12	Oakes, H.R.	300 ac. at Pa Punui, Pakanae	Exchanged for land at Auckland
	27	Deloitte and Stewart	2000 ac. at Horeke	Void for uncertainty
	40	Anderson, J.	1000 ac. at WariWari (or Kauri, or Kanui)	Exchanged for £1000 scrip
	41	Angus, R.	1000 ac. at Wari (or Opua)	Exchanged for £50 scrip
	48		3200 ac. (no location)	Exchanged for £722 scrip
	49 50	Baker, J.	Documents missing	
271	82	Cassidy, T.	1500 ac. at Mangataipa (or Waru)	Exchanged for £1053 scrip
	83		1000 ac. at Te Roorungha on the Waima River	Exchanged for £1000 scrip
255	87	Nicholas and Chadwick	1000 ac. at Rangiwhakataka, on the Waima River	Exchanged for £457 scrip
	89	Chambers, C.H.	1300 ac. at Herd's Point (Rawene)	Grant to JJ Montefiore, 416 ac.
436	90			
276	94	Chapman, A.	300 ac. at Te Tio, on the Mangamuka River	Exchanged for £54 scrip
258	95		900 ac. at Papawhakahota, on the Waima River	Exchanged for £136.5 scrip
142	122	Cochrane, D.B.	1000 ac. at Raurau	Exchanged for £800 scrip and grant to Jane Clendon of 200 ac.
	123		1000 ac. at Rukahau on the Mangamuka River	Exchanged for £828 scrip
	124		500 ac. No description	

	140	Cooper, G.	301 ½ ac. at or near Whirinaki	Claim lapsed
	176 177	Egert, S.	350 ac. at Warau, on or near the Orira River —	Scrip £107.25 to J. Wright Disallowed
	190 191 192 193 194	Fishwick, E.	1881 ac. total, all on the Waima River, at Matakaraka, Te Rara and Kote Kototai 600 ac. No location	Exchanged for £1280 scrip Claim lapsed
	208 209	Gundry, W.	500 ac. at Kohi, on the Waima River at Matakaraka 500 ac. at Otarihau, on the Mangamuka River	Exchanged for £525 scrip Exchanged for £500 scrip
267	242	Hunt, R.	3000 ac. on the Mangamuka River. Includes an island.	Scrip £2260 to Hunt and £300 to Bellingham
96	247 248	Jellicoe, H.	1600 ac. at Taka and Te Ngaio	Grant to J.L. Campbell and J Webster, executors of GF Russell, 837 ac.
266 273	272	Kelly, Nicholson and others	2000 ac. at Pakahikatoa, on the Waima River	Scrip £979 to Kelly Scrip £489.5 to Lloyd Scrip £244.75 to Hollingsworth Scrip £244.75 to Baker
259	274 275	Lacourt, J.B. and G.	25,000 ac. No location	Disallowed
186	277	Leef, J.	200 ac. on east head of Whirinaki River	Grant 58 ½ ac. to Leef
122	311	Maning, F.E.	200 ac. at Onoke, west head of Whirinaki River	Grant 99 ¾ ac. to Maning
 123	312 313 315 316-317 314	Marmon, J.	1400 ac. at Hohi, Pukeaitanga (Rangiahua) and Kapakapa, at junction of Huatoia Creek and Hokianga River Rawhia	Scrip £650 exchanged for Pukeaitanga and Kapakapa Grant 523 ac. to Marmon
269	318	Mariner and Bowyer	1500 ac. at Pukuaitangi (Pukeaitanga?) on the Waihou River	Exchanged for £1500 scrip
127	326 327	Martin, J.	45 ac. at Amau Puni (Omapere) 50 ac. at South Head, Hokianga, (Araiteuru)	Grant of 10 ¼ ac. Grant of 50 ac.
350	339	Monro, P.	600 ac. at Mata (Waireia)	Grant of 600 ac. to H Hopkins

274	348-9	Murray, J.	1500 ac. No location	Grant of 540 ac. to Murray
262	352	Nimmo, G.	200 ac. at Motu Kauri	Exchanged for £200 scrip and grant for land at Kohi pending (circa 1864)
	356 357 358	Odeland, J.S.	300 ac. at Pipiro 300 ac. at Te Kauri 500 ac. at Makana Nui, Huatau Creek	Grant of 300 ac., Grant of 300 ac. and Grant of 500 ac., all to T. Lyne (England) Odeland having been drowned
271	369	Pearson, J.	1000 ac. No location	Disallowed
	377	Honan, T.	30 ac. No location	Grant of 30 ac.
264 256	378-9	Pearson, H. (or Doubleday)	80 ac. at Taikatabooa, 2000 ac. at Korappu and Taurouakukupa, all on the Mangamuka River	Exchanged for £1674 scrip
274	386-91	Poynton, T. and Hunt	4800 ac. at Pukahou, Mangamuka River, Papakawau, on the west head of the Omanaia River, Te Ahu and Takaroa, on the Hokianga River, and Pengue, on the Omanaia River	Exchanged for £2560 scrip
277 65 66	399-402	Russell, G.F.	750 ac. at Hui Tohia, on the Waiiti Stream, at Kohukohu, and at Take Tai	Grant of 117 ac. at Hui Tohia and 53 ac. at Kohukohu to Webster and Campbell as executors of Russell, and scrip £251 to Russell for Take Tai
	447	Strout and Harrison	600 ac. at Bukahoe or Kowekatahi, on the Waima River	Exchanged for £340 scrip
	461	Thomas, A.	1800 ac. at Puparahaka, on the Orira River	Scrip to Thomas £1600, to Nesbit for £125, and to Dudly for £100
	464	Thurlow and McDonald	No location	Disallowed
	467	Trusted, W.	500 ac. at Te Kohoro, on the Waima River	Exchanged for £68-13-0 scrip
273	468	Tuite, P.G.	500 ac. at Pakaikatoa, on the Waima River	Exchanged for £174 scrip
	479	Walsh, P.	350 ac. at Pukohu	Exchanged for £280 scrip, and a grant of 70 ac. at Tamaki (Auckland)

87	512	White, W. (Missionary)	1 ac. Motiti Island	Grant of 8 ¾ ac.
85	513		150 ac. at Mata (Te Karae?)	Grant to Wm. Russell of 462 ac.
272	514		2 ac. Ruapapaku Island	Disallowed
265	515		1000 ac. at Rotoponga, on the Waihou River	Exchanged for £1000 scrip
	517	White and Russell	250 ac. at Mangaraupo, on the Mangamuka River	Scrip £250 granted to G. Russell
	518		470 ac. No location	No grant made
254	519		10,000 ac. on the Orira River	Scrip £6099 to W. White Grant of 1280 ac. to MA Burdekin Scrip £160 to F. White
312	539	Kent, R. (by W. Young)	640 ac. at Koutu, Mungero, or One Tree Hill	Grant to G. Nimmo (area not surveyed)
	540	Young, W.	640 ac. at Te Rawana	Exchanged for £640 scrip
	541		100 ac. at Opunune, or Panoni	Grant of 41 ac.. New grant of 41 ac. to J. Webster, 1862
	542		400 ac. Records missing. Note on entry — "Whanui, I believe"	No grant
263 278	624-5	Wright, J.W.	1100 ac. on the Mangamuka River	Exchanged for £1600 scrip
257	706	Honey and Parker	200 ac. at Whang-anamu (Waireia?)	Exchanged for £200 scrip
	748	Burnard, J.	No area or location	Disallowed
	761	Stewart and Deloitte		See No. 27
	810	Annoyle, R.	2000 ac. No location	Disallowed.
	811		1500 ac. at Makuku, on the Waima River	Grant of 359 ac., subsequently cancelled
437	836	Wright, J.	25 ac. at Otonago, on the Mangamuka River	Grant to J.J. Montefiore of 10 ac.
	939	Wesleyan Mission	50 ac. at Tarawaua, on Waihou River	Grant of 76 ¾ ac. Waihou River
78, 79	940 & 943		1500 ac. at Mangungu	Grant of 483 ac.
77	941		200 ac. at Newark (Pakanae)	Grant of 124 ac. 1r. 6p.
80	944		100 ac. at Poinga, on the Waima River	Grant of 36 ½ ac.
197	951 952	Catholic Mission	150 ac. at Purakau	Grant of 104 ac.
	965	Stewart, W.	200 ac. at Horeke	See No. 27.
260	966	Mitchell, T.	1500 ac. No location	No grant
174	967	Hardiman, R.	50 ac. at Ohopa (Waireia)	Grant of 37 ac.

	968	Farden, A.	No location	Claim lapsed
130	969	Birch, A. & W.	300 ac: at Motu Kiore	Grant of 75 ac.
	970	Campbell, B.	300 ac. No location	Disallowed
	971	Mariner, M.	1000 ac. at Kohukohu	Exchanged for £950 scrip
	972 973	Grant, J.	600 ac. at Paieke, on the Orira River 50 ac. at Tarawaua, on the Waihou River	No grant Grant of 50 ac.
	1015	Wing, F.	200 ac. at Waiti	Fanny Wing was a half-Maori child, killed accidentally at Kororareka in the war of 1845 No grant
	1016	Harris, J.	5000 ac. No location	Disallowed
	1020	Cousins, W.	500 ac. No location	Disallowed
	1031	Baker, E.	60 ac. No location	Withdrawn
102 268	1032-38	McDonnell, T. (See also Survey Office Plan No. 4196)	68,300 ac. at Mataka, Horeke and at Motukaraka	Grants to McDonnell and his assignees of 3321 ac.
275 150	1043 1045	de Thierry, C.	4540 ac. 1) On the Waihou River 2) At the mouth of the Waima River 3) At Toutoka, on the Waima River	1) and 2) exchanged for £1610 scrip, and a grant of 109 ac. for 3)

TOTALS

Land claimed	172,515.5 acres
Scrip awarded	£35,362.5
Land granted	10,927.5 acres

(In terms of the FD Bell schedules of 1863)

Additional claims for early purchases, first investigated by F.D. Bell under the 1856 Act, not having been dealt with by the early commissioners.

63	1327	White, F.	588 ac. at Hokianga	588 ac.
86	1328	White, F.	55 ac. at Hokianga	55 ac.
438	1328	White, W.		

Appendix 2

Report to the Government by F.E. Maning on Hirini Taiwhanga and Maori Grievances

This report submitted by F.E. Maning, a former judge of the Maori Land Court, at the request of the Prime Minister, Frederick Whitaker, testifies to the bitterness and disillusionment that beset him in his later life. Apparently happy with his Maori wife, family and friends during his early years at Hokianga, his mood soured during his association with the prominent and successful Pakeha settlers there — the upper social stratum on the River. The purpose of his report, produced in 1882, was to advise the Government on the character and credibility of a Maori deputation that had lately visited London. Organised by Taiwhanga, its object had been to petition Queen Victoria on Maori grievances arising from breaches of the Treaty of Waitangi and other matters. Taiwhanga was the son of Rawiri, one of the Anglican mission's first Maori converts of any distinction. Later the Member of Parliament for Northern Maori, Hirini was a passionate activist in the cause of Maori disabilities, and despite the ambitious Maning's intemperate and virulent attack on him, was a notable personality of very considerable standing and accomplishments.

The petitioners saw the Secretary of State for the Colonies, Lord Kimberly, in July 1882, but he chided them for failing to submit the petition through the New Zealand Government, and sent it back to Sir Arthur Gordon, the Governor in New Zealand. This led to Maning's report, which he apparently made shortly before he left the country in search of relief from the illness that caused his death. The deputation's journey, then, was in vain, since it neither saw the Queen nor received any satisfaction from the British Government.

After a subsequent protracted correspondence between Wellington and London, in which Maning was quoted at great length, the complaints embodied in the petition were categorically, and predictably, refuted. But the Queen did see it — momentarily, it seems — since the Secretary for the Colonies advised the New Zealand Government blandly that she 'was pleased to receive it very graciously', but that 'I have been unable to advise Her Majesty to give any directions for a compliance with the prayer of the memorialists.' So ended that foray into the impenetrable jungle of Imperial politics.*

It is a sad commentary on Maning's life that it ended in this way, with such a vindictive assault on the people who gave him his wife and his family.

* Buick, T.L., *The Treaty of Waitangi* (1914), p. 297.
A.P.L. New Zealand Mss. No. 68.

181, Grey Street, Auckland.

T.W. Lewis, Esq,
Wellington.

Dear Sir,

In compliance with the request of Mr Whitaker conveyed in your telegram, I have to state as follows:—

As a member of the Ngapuhi tribe, Taiwhanga is not a person of any particular standing or importance; he is a free man of the tribe, of no very good character amongst his own people, and would no doubt describe himself as a "Rangatira".

I have known him for many years, and am sorry to be obliged to say that I have only known him as a scheming unprincipled Native and notorious mischief maker; having failed in the chief object of his ambition, which was to obtain some easy place under the Government, he has of late years turned political agitator, and has taken up the Treaty of Waitanga [sic] as his standing text — and he tells the Natives the Treaty has been purposely violated by the European Government in various ways to their great injury. He has had, I believe, by the benevolent intervention of the late Bishop Selwyn, a much better education than most Natives, he speaks English well, has been taught surveying, and has a considerable amount of general, though superficial, information, and is not without some ability.

These advantages he has made use of to convince his more ignorant countrymen that he knows a great deal more than he really does, and that if they will support him in reinstating and vindicating the violated treaty he will accomplish very great things in their favor.

As the more ignorant class of natives have but a very vague and loose idea of what the "Tiriti" really is, or what benefits it confers on them, and as they think Hirini must know a great deal more than they do, and seeing that the battery is directed against the Europeans exclusively, many of them do, notwithstanding his not very reliable character, believe in his statements.

There is also a considerable number of natives not having quite so much faith, and who would not trust Taiwhanga with five shillings of their money, who nevertheless pretend to believe in him entirely and who are quite willing and desirous that he should go to England with the Petition on the chance of his being able to effect something, they scarcely know what, and they are ready to give him every countenance and support here in backing any statements, false or true, that he may make in England, and as Hiriri [sic] has succeeded in cajoling an old native chief, who is in his dotage, out of a sum of money sufficient to take him to England, he has departed on his mission.

Hirini would have been under ordinary circumstances, a very insignificant person, but I think it right to state, that during the last few years I have observed amongst the Northern Natives a growing dissatisfaction with their present position and prospects, which may possibly play into Hirini's hands and assist his natural propensity for mischief, and give him more influence than he could have otherwise obtained.

I trace this disposition in the natives to the following causes:

The Northern Natives have for the last thirty years and upwards been accustomed to procure almost at any time they chose, and with a very small amount of labor, very large sums of money by the produce of their Gum fields, the Kauri forests, and by the sale of land; as long as the Gum was near or on the surface of the land, and to be got with little labor, the natives worked their fields at an enormous profit, and wasted the money in their usual extravagant manner, but when the surface Gum was exhausted, and more labor in digging it necessary than the natives chose to undergo, the Gum fields were mostly sold, and in consequence this source of revenue came to an end.

In like manner as long as the Kauri trees stood so near the water that with a small amount of labor large quantities of logs could be got afloat and rafted to the stations of the timber merchants, the natives got very large sums of money at any time they chose, but when the timber near the water was cut and the labor in getting logs afloat increased, then most, indeed nearly all, of the very valuable Kaurii [sic] Forests were sold to the Europeans, the price paid squandered with the usual Maori improvidence, and the source of wealth from the forests cut off.

The last remaining source from which to procure money easily was the land, much had been sold already in the early days of the Colony, of the remainder they have of late years, after reserving some choice spots for themselves, sold nearly all that was worth anything to the Government, and to settlers, besides much that was scarcely worth anything; they have spent the money with their usual and incurable improvidence. They have still their extravagant habits, their tastes for many luxuries, their desire to have money to spend wastefully in vulgar ostentation, which, since boyhood, they have been accustomed to obtain so easily.

They see now all their accustomed supplies falling off, and the fact beginning to appear that in the not distant future they must, to obtain a comfortable and respectable position, adopt a system of industry, economy, and labor; to them most distasteful, and contrary to all their ideas of what a desirable life should be. They do not accuse their own improvidence or want of foresight, they look only to the fact that the Pakeha has got the land, the forests, and the gum fields, that the Europeans are getting rich while the Maoris are getting poor, and losing their former position and consequence in the country, and they are consequently just in that disconted [sic — discontented?] state of mind in which to catch at any chimera set up by any impudent agitator who promises to improve their condition; And as some of the doctrines regarding the (broken) Treaty of Waitangi are as follows, it is no wonder if they are at present a good deal exercised on the subject, and that Hirini Taiwhanga has some support:

1 — By the provisions of the Treaty of Waitangi the natives have a right to take back most of the lands sold to the early settlers beause the natives were not paid nearly so much for the said lands as they are worth now, after the labor of thirty, forty, or fifty years, has been expended upon them. This is Hirini's gloss upon what he has heard of something called the "unearned increment".
2 — All the foreshores in New Zealand belong to the natives, This meets with general credence and approval, and already certain chiefs in the North have threatened to prevent the Europeans from even letting their boats lie on the beach, the construction of whares [sic — wharves] has been opposed, and valuable whares [sic — wharves] have been threatened with destruction in more than one instance by a chief who was at the time, and is now a member of parliament.
3 — The Natives have a right to establish Native parliaments to control and over-rule the European parliament in all matters relating to the interests or desires of the Maori — This is a much favored idea.
4 — The Natives have a right to establish Courts of Justice and to enact laws independent of the Queen's Courts and laws. This is much in favor with the chiefs who would be judges, and who would pocket all fines, fees, &c, for their own use.
5 — The Natives have a right to levy harbour dues from ships coming into Northern ports, to prevent Europeans from fishing anywhere, and endless other "rights" most of which would be direct breaches of the Treaty of Waitangi, the violation of which they pretend so much to deplore.

The above notions have certainly an acceptance more than is desirable amongst the Northern Natives, and as we know — they are very subject to be led away by any imposter who is sufficiently impudent and will believe in any absurdity which promises them advantage.

I have sometimes thought that Hirini's agitation might possibly in some shape or other eventually prove troublesome; his own personal character is in some degree against him, and the Ngaputi [sic] tribe are less susceptible to those mental hallucinations than most natives, but taking into consideration the uneasy state of mind I have observed them to be in, I cannot help thinking that the circumstances are favorable to the plans of any unscrupulous agitator who wishes for notoriety and to "vex" the Pakeha, which is a very common ambition amongst the Maories.

Hakena Parore: Is the son of Parore, a rather respectable and quiet Ngapuhi Chief who lives in the Kaipara country, and is also connected with the Kaipara natives who are not Ngapuhi.

Parore is on good terms with the settlers, and has some considerable property; he does not take much interest in politics, and has never taken a leading part in the affairs of the Ngapuhi tribe; he is now a very old man, and gave Taiwhanga, it is said, £300, to enable him to go to England, his son Hakena, who accompanies Taiwhanga, has not been heard of much in any way, Puhi, the other companion of Taiwhanga, is a young man of no particular mark hitherto; they are both of respectable standing in the tribe and seem to have been sent to watch the proceedings of Taiwhanga, in whom the natives have not, I think, sufficient confidence to trust altogether in his report on his return, if he had gone alone.

I do not think at present that the "mission" can be said to represent seriously any well defined party having serious or determinately defined views; the expedition to England would probably be described by Taiwhanga himself as "trying it on", and it remains to be seen, if his hopes are disappointed, what shape the agitation may take on his return. I have noticed however that since the Parihaka affair the natives have been a little less pronounced in their declamation, although they make the capture of Te Whiti one of the complaints of the Petition.

Abraham Taonui is just dead; he was a principal agitator and supporter of the Petition; he was a man of considerable influence and would have been of much more had he not been a little too crazy; he was the head of a high family in the Ngapuhi tribe, which is now extinct in the direct line, and is represented by a half caste, by name John Anderson, who is a low and bad character, but of inferior influence.

The Petition.

As to the Petition itself, the principal remark I have to make is that I am perfectly certain that Taiwhanga, himself does not believe one word of the allegations made in it from beginning to end, though no doubt many of the natives do, and others pretend to. Taiwhanga knows well that the open falshoods [sic] of which the complaint consists would be scouted in this country, and he trusts therefore entirely for credence to the ignorance of the people of England of the true state of affairs here, an ignorance which he thinks greater than it is, though no doubt he will meet many in England as ill informed on these matters as he can possibly desire.

The complaint of the Petition affirms that the Europeans have repeatedly and deliberately broken the Treaty of Waitangi by making war against the Natives for the sole purpose of confiscating their lands.

That when the Waikatos were overpowered "armies of soldiers were sent forth to engender strife" against the Maories of Tauranga, and various other places, the motive being to "engender strife" and make it a pretext for seizing the land.

And that in 1881 "a new plan" was "devised by the Government to enkindle strife in respect to the Maories; armies were sent to Parihaka to capture innocent men that they might be sent to prison, &c, &c,"

We know in this country that when "the armies of soldiers went forth to Tauranga to engender strife with the purpose of confiscating the Native Lands" they in fact went forth to subdue rebels then in active rebellion, who were murdering barbarously every European they could lay their hands upon, and that we actually in self defence had no choice left but either to subjugate those rebels or evacuate the Country.

As to "the new plan devised by the Government in 1881" — this alludes to the proceedings taken against Te Whiti whose persistent and increasing aggressions against Europeans were of such a nature (he all the time refusing contemptuously to bring any grievance he might have or be supposed to have into the Queen's Courts of Justice) that we were compelled either to put him down or to evacuate our settlements in that part of the Country also; The former operation was effected by our much abused "armies" without the shedding of one drop of blood, and with less destruction of property than could have at all been expected under the circumstances —. But the theory set up in the Petition evidently is, that for the Natives to commit outrages against the Europeans, even open war and murder, is not a breach of the Treaty of Waitangi, but for the Europeans to resist them is.

But the statement that the Europeans deliberately violated the Treaty of Waitangi and made war for the purpose of confiscating the Natives' land, seems extraordinarily out of place in a Petition from the Ngapuhi tribe, who it is a matter of unquestionable history did, at the very first moment that they perceived the intention of the Government to establish the laws of England in this Country in accordance with the Treaty, at once throw off their allegiance, sacked and burnt the town of Russell, the then seat of Government, [sic] cut down the flag-staff at Kororareka, which they understood to be the symbol of the Queen's authority, maintained active warfare against the Queen's troops for about two years, and when obliged to submit, were pardoned and not one acre of their land confiscated from that day to this.

It is true that the Treaty has often been repudiated by the Natives, but the first to set the example were the Ngapuhi who now petition the Queen, falsely stating that the Colonial Government has made war against the Natives for the purpose of confiscating their lands.

It is quite apparent from the style of the Petition that the historical fact I have mentioned was a source of uneasiness to the writers, they saw that it was an unpleasant circumstance which might at any time be brought against them to shew that it was in reality the Natives who in the first instance had broken the Treaty, thrown away their shield and safe defence, and rendered themselves liable to confiscation and all the rigours of war; they therefore tried quietly to pass over this unpleasant fact with a slight allusion, and a stupid Maori quibble by merely saying "There was no blood in the flag staff" which expression they thought the people in England would take to mean that nothing had been done but the cutting down of the flag staff, and that no blood had been shed.

Certainly there was no blood in the flag staff, but there was blood in the soldiers who guarded it, one of whom they killed before they could get at it. — There was blood in the sleeping infant who they tomahawked on her bed in the block house at the foot of the flag staff —. There was blood in the fifty men killed or wounded at Mawhe, blood in plenty in 110 men or thereabouts who I saw killed or wounded in another place in the course of a few minutes, blood flowed freely from hundreds at Te Ruapekapeka and other places by the hands of the Ngapuhi; the North was filled with blood and ashes by the tribe, and the persons who now send a Petition to the Queen "wafted on the soft airs of affection" to falsely accuse her really loyal and peacable European subjects of violence and robbery.

The people of England in their ignorance of the daring effrontery, hypocrisy, and falshood [sic] which the natives can have recourse to when they have any end to gain may well find it hard to believe that the whole of the allegations of the Petition are false, or that the Petitioners are not an amiable and interesting race of ill used innocents.

I have the honor to be,
Sir,
Yours faithfully,
(sgd) F.E. Maning.

(Author's Note: In copying this report an attempt had to be made to untangle several incomprehensible jumbles of quote marks, since as they were written they did not make sense.)

Appendix 3

The Genealogies *(Whakapapa)*

The genealogies of Maori chiefs are properly the concern of their descendants, who, if they wish to do so, and if, indeed, they have the opportunity, will learn of them from their elders. The author does not, therefore, presume to inform them on these matters. The intention here is to interest Pakeha readers in the relationships between the chiefs involved in the story of Hokianga, and in the pride they took in their ancestry. For indeed, these pedigrees clearly defined their social status and confirmed their rights to dwell unchallenged on their own land.

A number of friends among Maori people have advised the author on these genealogies, and have supplied information, but the primary sources are those given below:

Minutes of *wananga,* or schools of learning, held at Whakarapa (Panguru), Waitangi and Rangiawhia, June to September, 1924. Kindly lent by Mr Graham Alexander, of Waihou Valley, Hokianga.

Family genealogies supplied by Mr Graham Rankin, of Kaikohe, a descendant of Tuhirangi, a brother of Hone Heke.

Genealogies incorporated in a map of Hokianga and the Bay of Islands by John White, to illustrate his lectures on Maori customs. *AJHR,* E No. 7, 1861 (APL).

The Taonui manuscript, January 3, 1849. *He pukapuka whakapapa konga tupuna Maori* (AIL).

Minutes of the Tai Tokerau Maori Land Court, Whangarei.

Should my Maori readers come across matters in these *tatai* with which they disagree, I should appreciate their advice. I have done my best with them from the sources available to me, and I trust that I have succeeded in producing a good result.

1. Hone Heke Pokai (Northern war-leader) and Hone Heke Rankin.

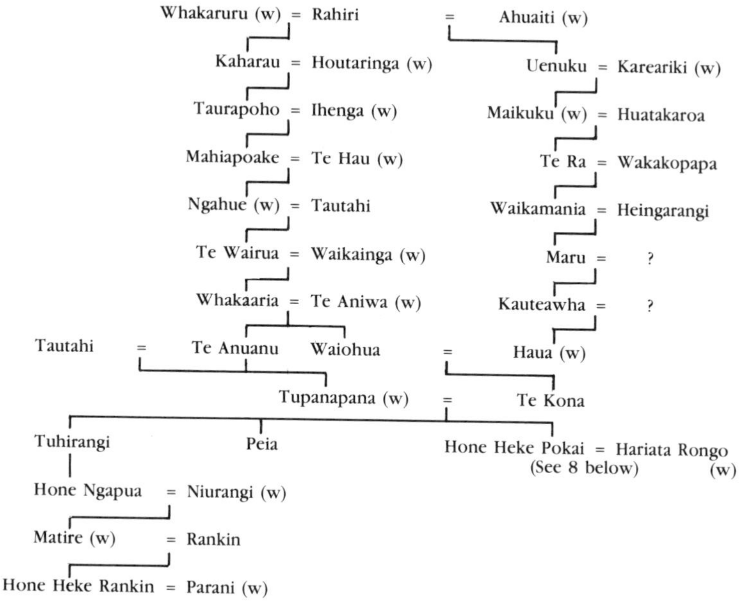

2. Hone Toia, of the Dog-tax 'Rebellion'.

Ahuaiti = Rahiri
Uenuku = Keareariki (w)
Uewhati = ?
Uematengerengere = ?
Te Rangitauwawaro = ?
Te Taonga = Te Kura
Irakau = Rehia
Kakiroa = Tangiao
Rangihinga = Tangiao
Kerekere = Wahine
Kaua = Piungahau
Ngatitaha = ?
Pitawhango = ?
Maraea = Toia
Hone Toia

(See 1. above)

Mahiapoake
Ngahue (w)
Iritoka
Nukuraerae
Kohunga
Mokowahine
Te Ahi
Rena

3. Pi (Pihangu), Chief of Waima, and his son Arama Karaka Pi.

Rahiri = Whakaruru (w)
Kaharau = Houtaringa (w)
Taurapoho = Ruakiwhiria (w)
Mahiapoake = Hau (w)
Ngahue (w) = Tautahi
Te Wairua = Waikainga (w)
Auha = Pehirangi (w)
Te Hotete = Waitohirangi (w)
Moka = Punga (w)
Te Wheoki (w) = Pihangu
Arama Karaka Pi

4. Moetara and Rangatira, Chiefs of Pakanae.

Rahiri = Whakaruru (w)
Kaharau = Houtaringa (w)
Taurapoho = Ruakiwhiria (w)
Tupoto = Kauae (w)
Korokoro = Wahineiti (w)
Whitiki = Whakaturangi
Tangaroa = Hinetapu (w)
Te Haunui = Mihinga
Te Hunga
Aitu
Moetara and Rangatira

5. Papahia, chief of North Hokianga.

Rahiri = Whakaruru (w)
Kaharau = Houtaringa (w)
Taurapoho = Ihenga (w)
Tupoto = Tawakeiti (w)
Kairewa = Waimirirangi
Tamatea = Tiari
Takateauahi = Takiwa
Taotawhana = Toretawhara
Numanga = Te Pihe
Ngono = Te Wairoro
Kaimanu = Kahi

Te Rua Pounamu — Papahia — Whakarongouru

Te Rua Pounamu
Papahia Te Tai
Re Te Tai

Whakarongouru
Rikihana

6. Papahurihia, or Te Atua Wera.

Ueoneone = Reitu
Kauae = Tupoto
Miruiti = Kaumoana
Kapehuanutu = Rurunga
Tikawe = ?
Weherua = Wharenui
Hinaki = Taimania
Tai = Nga Ngo
Urumatariki = Kuri
Tu Hoehoe = Uhareti ?
Papahurihia = Eme (w)
Whakarongohau (w) = Wiremu Titore

Taurapoho = Ihenga (w) See 5 above
Tupoto = Kauae (w)
Tuiti = Marohawhea (w)
Rangihana = Mahuri
Te Karehu = Taonui
Pouahi = ?
Pera = ?
Haumataotao = ?
Hereora = Karakia
Waha = Whakamoe

7. Nene (Tamati Waaka) and Patuone (Maihi Eruera)

Rahiri = Ahuaiti (w)
Uenukukuare = Keareariki (w)
Maikuku (w) = Huatakaroa
Tera = Whakakopapa
Kamama = Papatu
Papaora = ?
Ripia = Takare
Tapua = Kawehau (w)

Rahiri = Whakaruru (w) Second wife
Kaharau = Houtaringa (w)
Taurapoho = Ruakiwhiria (w)
Mahiapoake = Te Hau (w)
Nga Hue (w) = Tautahi
Te Wairua = Wharetoru (w)
Te Ngawa = Kuta (w)
Te Patu
Tua

Patuone (Eruera Maihi) | Nene (Tamati Waaka) | Tari (w)

8. Hongi Hika (war-chief of Bay of Islands)

Te Paraakahuteanui
Mamangai
Tukanikani
Hatupu
Haiti
Tokahaupapa
Te Puta
Te Tahapango = Taingariu (w)

(See 7 above)

Nga Hue (w) = Tautahi
Te Wairua = Waikainga (w)
Auha = Pehirangi (w)

Te Hotete = Tuhikura (w) of Whangaroa
Hongi Hika = Turikatuku (w)
Hariata Rongo (w) = Hone Heke (See 1 above)

9. Muriwai, Hone Kingi, Makoare Taonui, Aperahama Taonui and John Marmon.

(See 7 above)

Te Wairua = Wharetoru (w)
Te Kuta (w) = Nga Peka
Kaikinikini = Rena (w)
Tiakiwhenua = Waiotara (w)

Rangaunu = Waitari
Hone Kingi = Taringauru
Hauauru = John Marmon
Mere (w) = Hemi (a Pakeha)
Hariata (w) = Heperi

Te Ahuriri = Hautai
Makoare Taonui
Aperahama Taonui

Muriwai

10. Hirini Taiwhanga, the subject of F.E. Maning's Report.

Tamakitera = Uranga
Hira = Ngaone
Puni (w) = Mirupokaiape
Te Hauaraki = Moerangaranga
Te Huatahi
Taupure
Te Rea
Tuata = Te Araroa
Tawatawa = Wahi
Taiwhanga = Maata Raawa (w)
Hirini Taiwhanga

11. Pangari (Matu), chief of Orira.

Rahiri = Whakaruru (w)
Kaharau = Houtaringa (w)
Taurapoho = Ihenga (w)
Tupoto = Kauae (w)
Tuiti = Marohawhea (w)
Rangimimiti = Tiraha (w)
Maungawheki
Ruairo
Reo = Turu (w)
Pari
Rau
Tokai
Pangari (Matu)

12. Wharepapa (Tohu Kakahi) Chief of Kohukohu (Ihutai hapu — descended from Ngatirangi of Ohaeawai)

```
Te Tuiti (see 11 above)                     Tama  = Rangiteuia
|                                                  |
Riutaia                                         Horomanga
|                                                  |
Tike                                            Te Taiwhinga (w)
|                                                  |
Turu                                            Te Kerekere
|                                                  |
Te Pari = Taukohi (w)                           Hui (w)
        |                                          |
        |          ┌───────────────────────────────┘
     Haka  =  Punga (w)
  ┌─────────┘
Wharepapa   =   Rewatu (w)
(or Tohukakahi)
┌───────────┴─────────────────────┐
Parehuia (w)              Hori Karaka Tawiti
```

Appendix 4

The Hokianga *Hapu* of Ngapuhi

HAPU	LOCATION
North and north-west Hokianga	
Waiariki	Whakarapa (Panguru)
Ngatimanawa	Whakarapa (Panguru)
Ngaitupoto	Motiti
Ngatihere	Motukaraka
Ngatihau	Motukaraka
Urikopura	Rangiora
Ngatihua	Moturuna
Mahurehure	Tutekehua
Te Uri Mahoe	Mangamuka
Urikopura	Mangamuka
Ihutai	Mangamuka
Te Uri o te Ahu	Omahuta
Ngatiwharara	Kokohuia (?)
Kohatutaka	?
Pehikauri	Te Tio
Ihutai	Raukapara (Orira)
Te Popoto	Rangiahua
Ngatihao	Waihou (Upper)
Patupo	Waihou (Upper)
Te Ngahengahe	Waihou (Upper)
Matapungarehu	Puketi
South Hokianga	
Te Popoto	Utakura
Whanaupani	Horeke — Utakura
Ngatihao	Horeke — Utakura
Ngatitoro	Motukiore
Te Ngahengahe	Motukiore
Te Honihoni	?
Ngatirauawa	Lower Waima
Mahurehure	Waima
Urikopura	Omanaia
Ngatihau	Omanaia
Ngaitupoto	Omanaia
Ngatihere	Oue
Ngatihurihanga	Manawakaiaia
Te Hikutu	Whirinaki

Ngatikorokoro	Pakanae
Ngatiwharara	Pakanae
Pouka	Pakanae
Ngatipou	Omapere
Ngatikorokoro	Waimamaku
Te Roroa) Border-line — Ngatiwhatua?	Waimamaku
Te Roroa)	Waipoua

South Inland Hokianga

Ngatiterahape	Waima
Ngatikaihoro	Waima
Ngatiterouowe	Waima
Kohatutaka	Waima
Te Uri Kaiwhare	Waima
Pokare	Taheke
Ngatipakau	Taheke
Ngai Tu	Taheke
Ngatikaihoro	Punakitere
Ngatimoe	Punakitere
Ngatiue	Punakitere
Ngatitautahi	Punakitere
Ngatuteauru	Otaua
Ngatitera	Otaua
Ngatiwaihengehenge	Otaua

These are derived from the Appendices to the Journals of the House of Representatives of 1862, 1870 and 1878, the last of which is unreliable both as to spelling and the location of the hapu. Other sources were the Maori Land Court Minute-books, a map by John White in the White collection in the Auckland Public Library, and personal communications to the author. The hapu are generally those in existence in the latter part of the nineteenth century, so that those which may have been recognised since are not included. There will also be named whanau, or families, which are not included. The political organisation of the old Maori comprised the iwi, or tribe, and the hapu, which would have originated from a notable ancestor, and had since grown to a sizable and influential group. Some hapu had, at the time of which we write, grown almost to the size and status of iwi, and could perhaps be more correctly called sub-tribes, but the whanau was a very small group within a hapu. Throughout this book, Ngapuhi is the iwi.

Appendix 5

The *Pihe* for Nukutawhiti
by his Daughter Moerewarewa

The *pihe,* or lament, is of such antiquity that it presents its translators with problems of interpretation, on which they do not always agree. But as the most ancient chant relative to Hokianga which has been preserved in its entirety, it is recorded here, with a translation by George Graham. This version appears in *JPS,* Volume 49, 1940.

1. Papa te whatatiri i runga nei Ko ana kauapu he aitu Tu ka riri, Rongomai ka heke.	1. The thunder crashes here above Its flashing an ill omen is Tu now rages; Rongomai descends.
2. Tatara te Waipunaatea Ko Uru, ko Ngangana Ko Aparangi, ko kapiti hono.	2. Recite the incantation at Waipunaatea To Uru, to Ngangana To Aparangi, the joinings close.
3. Ko kapiti hono te ata a te taua, Te hikihiki, te ramuramu Te wheti, te wheta, Te to toroiai, whano.	3. Closing in around is the shadow of strife, Raise up the ramuramu fronds Raise up with precision Thrust (them) out: arouse in chorus.
4. Whano! Whano! Whanowhano mai te pi,	4. Arouse! arouse ye! Dilate your eyes!
5. Ka riri Tu! Ka Ngiha Tu! Ka wewehi Tu! Ka wawana Tu-e!	5. For Tu now rages: Tu now burns: Tu now terrifies Tu inspires dread.
6. Ka taka i Hokianganui, ai e! Ka taka te waro-o Pipiraueru, koia a!	6. He has fallen at Hokianganui, alas! He has fallen into the chasm Pipiraueru, indeed, ah!

7. Ka taka Wawauatea nei
Ka taka te waro o
Pipiraueru, koia a!

8. Kia kotikotia
Te uru o te ariki
Pipiraueru, koia e!

9. E tapu
E tapu Tumatatangaroa.

10. Tangaroa
E ngaro Tu
Ki tona heiwa.

11. Heiwa, heiwa,
Tukua ki te marae!

12. Werowero! werowero
Te tara homaira!
Werohia ki tai o whakarewa
Whakarongo te taraki a tai,

Me ko tai manawareka
Te manawa ki a Tu.

13. Uaeae a! Uaeae a!

14. Hikihiki
Hikihikiwarawara

15. Koia Tangaroa i taua

Homai ra, he kino e Tu!

16. Whangainga
Kia ta ai.

17. Koropana ia
Te kawe ki te marae

7. He has fallen unto Wawauatea
Fallen unto the pit of death.
Of Pipiraueru indeed, ah!

8. Severed be
The head of the Ariki
At Pipiraueru e!

9. Oh sacred
Sacred is Tumatatangaroa!

10. Oh Tangaroa
Unavenged is Tu
Of his Heiwa.

11. The heiwa, the heiwa
Present it unto the marae!

12. In defiance now give challenge!
The spear-point hither point
In challenge to the drifting sea
Harken unto the gannet on
the sea
On the self-elated sea
'Tis a welcome to Tu!

13. Strike deep! Aha! Strike deep!
Aha!

14. Uplift the chorus chant
Uplift in thundering tones e!

15. For now indeed is Tangaroa
in combat,
With him severely deal, O Tu!

16. That subject to the spells
He may be overcome.

17. There he lies prone
As carried unto the marae!

18. Whitirua	18. To and fro, twice was he drifted
Te Ikatere ki paenga Kia uru	Like a stranded fish. At last cast up ashore:
19. Ae ae a! Kia uru! ae ae a!	19. Aha! Aha!
20. Ae ae a! Kia uru! ae ae a Pi (Ka mutu i konei)	20. At last cast up ashore, aha! (It is ended here)

Should the reader be interested, a full explanation of the pihe, according to the author, George Graham, is contained in the *JPS* paper quoted above. For the Nukutawhiti story in this book, see Chapters 1 and 2.

Appendix 6

The Lament of Hone Heke

Tera te puia ki Kaikohe i raro
Kia tangi atu au
He mea katawhe [ka tau wehe?] te aroha i roto ra
Homai me riringi ki te hua roi mata e mapu noa nei
Kei [ki?] te aha te tapu e wakawehia nei [whakawehe ana?] he ingoa irikau
Ki te muri e raranga
Ho ake [hoaki?] rawa nei te rangi o te mahara
Ka eke i te ngaro
Ka noho taute au.

There on the volcanic hill, with Kaikohe below me
I weep
Separated from those I love
My tears pour out like a flood
Where is the tapu gone whose fearful name was heard carried on the wind
The memories of the departed ones overwhelm me
I sit here mourning.

At the final battle of the War in the North at Ruapekapeka (see Chapter 14), at least twelve chiefs were killed according to a British Army estimate, while in the whole war, Heke and Kawiti, by their own account, lost sixty killed and eighty wounded. Hone Heke, angered by British domination and by his lost faith in the Treaty of Waitangi, had precipitated this conflict. So, in the lament we find him, after Ruapekapeka, sad and disillusioned on Kaikohe Hill, mourning his friends who had died in vain. And why, he asks, did the powerful tapu of his tohunga, Te Atua Wera, fail to save these lives?

The lament has been preserved in Sir George Grey's collection in the Auckland Public Library, and in John Webster's Maori diary of 1847, also in the Library. Webster's version is used here, with corrections where believed necessary. The English version is by the author, with the assistance of Graham Rankin, a descendant of Hone Heke's brother.

Index

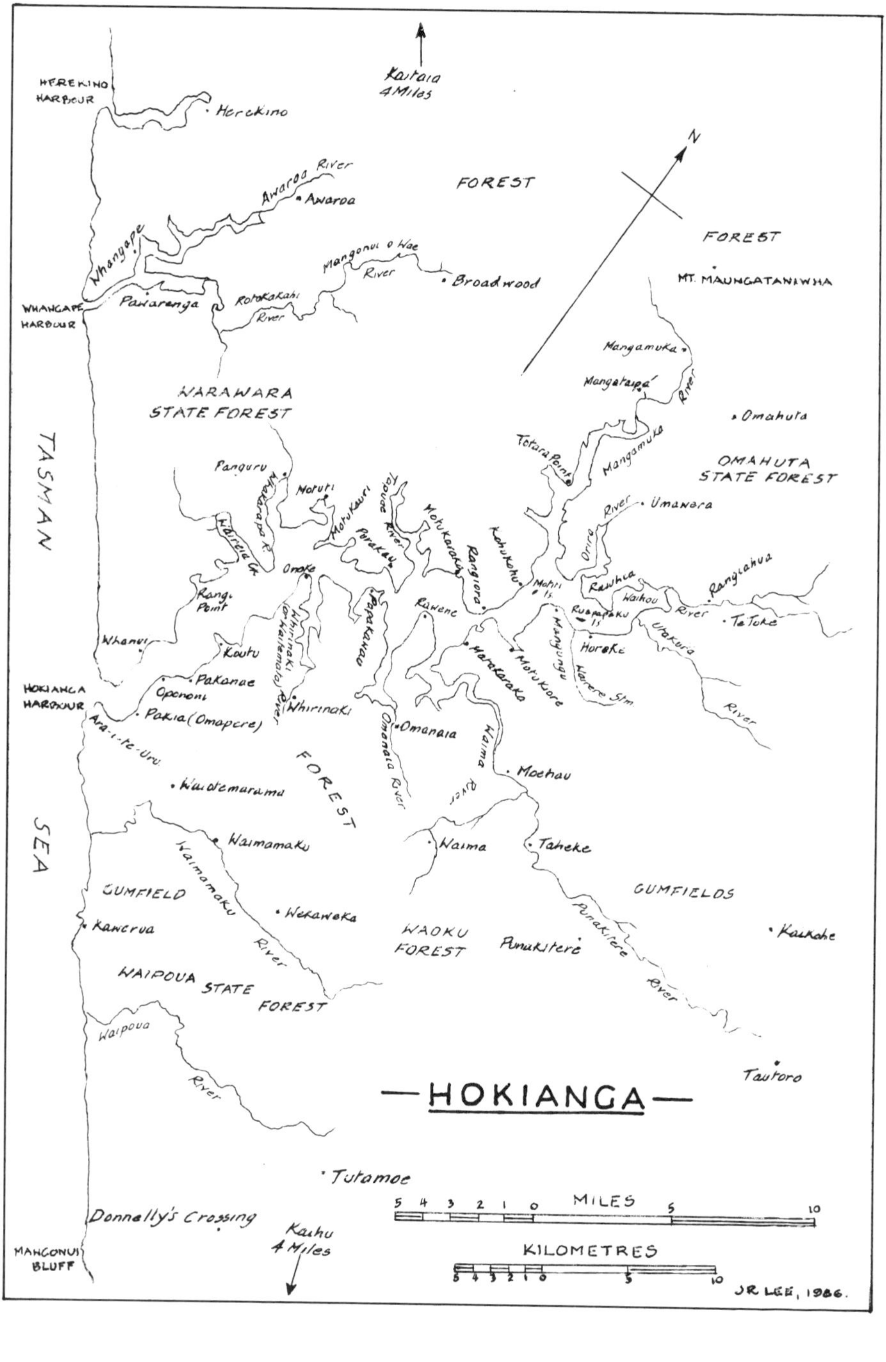
Kaitaia 4 Miles
HEREKINO HARBOUR
Herekino
Awaroa River
Awaroa
FOREST
N
FOREST
Whangape
Mangonui o Wae River
Broadwood
MT. MAUNGATANIWHA
WHANGAPE HARBOUR
Pawarenga
Rotokakahi River
Mangamuka
Mangataipa
River
WARAWARA STATE FOREST
Omahuta
Totara Point
Mangamuka
OMAHUTA STATE FOREST
TASMAN
Panguru
Whakarapa R.
Motuti
Motukauri
Orira River
Umawera
Rangiora
Omake
Rangi Point
Rawene
Rawhia
Rangiahua
Waihou River
Te Tuke
Horeke
Whanui
Koutu
Pakanae
Opononi
HOKIANGA HARBOUR
Pakia (Omapere)
Whirinaki
Omanaia
Omanaia River
Motukiore
Utakura River
Arai-te-Uru
FOREST
Moehau
Waima River
SEA
Waimamaku
Waima
Taheke
GUMFIELD
Waimamaku River
Wekaweka
GUMFIELDS
Kawerua
WAOKU FOREST
Punakitere
Punakitere River
Kaikohe
WAIPOUA STATE FOREST
Waipoua River
Tautoro
HOKIANGA
Tutamoe
MILES
5 4 3 2 1 0 5 10
KILOMETRES
5 4 3 2 1 0 5 10
Donnelly's Crossing
Kaihu 4 Miles
MANGONUI BLUFF
JR LEE, 1986.